The Public Interest Institute
to The Heartland Institute
2016

MEDIA VOICES

"As iron sharpens iron, so man sharpens his fellow man."
Proverbs, 27, 17.

To Frank, after thirty years.

MEDIA VOICES
Debating Critical Issues in Mass Media

George McKenna
City College of New York

Dushkin Publishing Group
Guilford, Connecticut 06437
ISBN: 0-87967-245-5

STAFF

Jeremy Brenner — Managing Editor
Brenda Filley — Production Manager
Charles Vitelli — Designer
Libra VonOgden — Typesetting Coordinator

Copyright ©1982 by the Dushkin Publishing Group, Inc., Guilford, Connecticut. All Rights Reserved. No part of this book may be reproduced, stored, or otherwise transmitted by any means—mechanical, electronic, or otherwise—without permission from the Publisher.

Library of Congress Catalogue Card Number: 81-70655

Manufactured in the United States of America

First Edition; Second Printing

PREFACE

In LITTLE DORRIT, a novel by Charles Dickens, there is a character named Mrs. General. This highly refined, genteel person was a professional matron and chaperon to young ladies, and her chief task was to "form" their minds. Dickens describes the way she went about her task:

> Mrs. General had no opinions. Her way of forming a mind was to prevent it from forming opinions. She had a little circular set of mental grooves or rails on which she started little trains of other people's opinions, which never overtook one another, and never got anywhere. Even her propriety could not dispute that there was impropriety in the world; but Mrs. General's way of getting rid of it was to put it out of sight, and make believe that there was no such thing. That was another of her ways of forming a mind—to cram all articles of difficulty into cupboards, lock them up, and say they had no existence. It was the easiest way, and, beyond all comparison, the properest.

Dickens says that Mrs. General's way of dealing with clashes and contradictions was to "varnish" them. She "dipped the smallest of brushes into the largest of pots, and varnished the surface of every object that came under consideration. The more cracked it was, the more Mrs. General varnished it."

The accepted pieties and proprieties have changed radically since Dickens's time, but there are still plenty of Mrs. Generals around to form the minds of the young. Their style, of course, has changed with the times. A century ago they tended to be stuffy Victorian types, while today most of them have learned how to "hang loose." Modern Mrs. Generals may invite their listeners to call them by their first names and sit with them in a circle; they may urge young people to "get in touch with yourselves," get rid of hangups, and, in general, "get with it." What they do not tell them, or at any rate do not equip them to understand, is that there are competing points of view on most subjects and that these points of view must be given a fair hearing before being accepted or rejected. What the Mrs. Generals do instead, when confronted with a clash of opinions, is to varnish over them. Contention is held to be a sign of bad manners.

With apologies to every Mrs. General, past and present, this book is dedicated to the proposition that healthy, free-swinging public debate is a blessing. An attempt has been made to find advocates of the most varied and competing points of view concerning the mass media, to put them together in one volume, and let them fight it out.

This does not mean that all the arguments are equal, so that when the fighting is over and the dust has settled they will have cancelled out each other. That attitude sounds suspiciously like Mrs. General's brand of respectable nihilism, her "little circular set of grooves or rails" on which opinions "never overtook one another, and never got anywhere." The conviction underlying this book is that there are indeed right and wrong opinions, but that the best means of understanding them is to examine vigorously-expressed opposing views. Robust, uninhibited debate is a blessing not because it makes noise but because it offers the surest means of breaking out of Mrs. General's circular track.

ACKNOWLEDGEMENTS

I am grateful to some leading authorities on the mass media for their advice, some participants in the media for their opinions, and some reference experts for helping me locate materials for this book. Professor Charles Winick of City College of New York and Professor Michael Robinson of George Washington University offered valuable advice concerning leading issues. Dr. Joseph T. Klapper of CBS's Office of Social Research provided pertinent background and bibliographical information. James B. Poteat, Chief Librarian of the Television Information Office, allowed me to make use of T.I.O.'s library, and supplied me with some hard-to-find materials. Jack C. Landau, Director of the Reporters Committee for Freedom of the Press, offered his perspectives on issues which increased my understanding. Reporter Myron Farber of the *New York Times* and Susan Veatch, Editorial Director of WCBS Radio, granted me interviews which have formed part of this book.

This book would never have appeared were it not for the encouragement and support of Rick Connelly, Vice-President and General Manager of the Dushkin Publishing Group. I am also grateful to Jeremy Brenner of the Dushkin Publishing Group for his very able editorial supervision.

Finally, I thank my dear wife, Sylvia, for everything; for holding me together.

George McKenna
New York City
August, 1981

Contents

Preface

Chapter 1. THE MEDIA AROUND US ... 11

Chapter 2. WHO CONTROLS THE MEDIA? FEW OR MANY? ... 21
    Fewer and Fewer Controlling More and More, BEN BAGDIKIAN ... 22
    A Plethora of Media Voices, LEE LOEVINGER ... 31
    Irrelevance, Not Monopoly Is the Problem, GEORGE REEDY ... 38

Chapter 3. DO THE MEDIA HAVE TOO MUCH POWER; OR NOT ENOUGH? ... 43
    The Story of the Pentagon Papers ... 43
    Justice BLACK's Opinion ... 45
    Justice BURGER's Dissent ... 47
    Justice HARLAN's Dissent ... 48
    We're Governed by the Media, TOM BETHELL ... 49
    The Power of the Press—Far From Absolute, TOM WICKER ... 53

Chapter 4. ARE THE MEDIA BIASED? ... 65
    A Handful of Men, SPIRO AGNEW ... 67
    A Debate on CBS's Coverage of Defense Issues, ERNEST LEFEVER and WILLIAM SMALL ... 75
    The Organization, Not Ideology Shapes the News, EDWARD JAY EPSTEIN ... 84

Chapter 5. ARE WE MANIPULATED BY THE MEDIA? ... 88
    The "Selling" of the President, JOE MCGINNIS ... 89
    Image-Making Doesn't Work, PATTERSON and MCCLURE ... 98
    The Case of RONNEY ZAMORA ... 104
    MRS. ZAMORA's Testimony ... 104
    Summation for the Defense ... 108
    Summation for the Prosecution ... 110
    Don't Blame TV for Violence, STEPHAN ROHDE ... 111

Chapter 6.	WHAT ARE THE MEDIA'S RIGHTS AND RESPONSIBILITIES?	113
	The Tornillo Case: Newspapers Need Not Print Replies, Chief Justice BURGER's Opinion	114
	Newspapers Must Serve the People, LEWIS WOLFSON	117
	The *Red Lion* Case	121
	Red Lion Discriminates Against Broadcasters, EDWIN DIAMOND	123
	Don't Shoot the Messenger, WCBS Editorial	126
	The Need for Competing Views, Editorial Reply	127
	An Interview with SUSAN VEATCH	128
	The Case of the *New York Times* vs. Sullivan	134
	The Press's State of Mind, *Herbert* vs. *Lando*	140
	A Chilling Decision, TOM WICKER	145
	The Press Doesn't Own the First Amendment, MICHAEL KINSLEY	147
	The Duty of a Citizen, *Branzburg* vs. *Hayes*	154
	The Right to Gather News, Justice STEWART's Dissent	163
	Newspapers Need Blanket Protection, Justice DOUGLAS's Dissent	167
	Epilogues to the *Branzburg* Case: "Dr. X" and MYRON FARBER	169
	A Conversation with MYRON FARBER	171
	Epilogue Two: Police Raids on Newsrooms	172
	Epilogue Three: The Lie that Won the Pulitzer Prize	174
	First Amendment Hubris, ANTHONY LEWIS	175
	Protecting Sources is No Special Privilege, FLOYD ABRAMS	177
	Does the Press Deserve Special Protection?	178
	The First Amendment Does Not Give Greater Protection to the Press than to Speech, ROBERT BORK	178
	Protection for Confidential Sources is Essential for Good Journalism, FLOYD ABRAMS	185
Chapter 7.	THE MEDIA AND PUBLIC POLICY: WHAT SHOULD BE DONE?	189
	The Case for More Regulation, KEVIN PHILLIPS	190
	We Must Fight Government Incursion, WILLIAM PALEY	199
	The Need for Self-Criticism, JOSEPH KRAFT	204
Afterword		220
Index		222

Credits

Chapter Two

Page 22. From, "Conglomeration, Concentration, and the Flow of Information", statement to The Federal Trade Commission; proceedings of the Symposium on Media Concentration, by Ben Bagdikian. December 14 and 15, 1978.

Page 31. From, statement to the Federal Trade Commission, Bureau of Competition; proceedings of the Symposium on Media Concentration, by Lee Loevinger. December 14 and 15, 1978.

Page 38. From, statement to the Federal Trade Commission; proceedings of the Symposium on Media Concentration, Bureau of Competition, by George Reedy. December 14 and 15, 1978.

Chapter Three

Page 45. From, New York Times Company v. United States, 403 U.S. 713 (1971), opinion by Justice Black.

Page 47. From, New York Times Company v. U.S., 713, (1971). Dissent by Chief Justice Burger.

Page 48. From, New York Times Company v. U.S., 403, 713, (1971). Dissent by Justice Harlan.

Page 49. Excerpts of "The Myth of an Adversary Press", by Tom Bethell. Copyright ©1976 by Harper's Magazine. All Rights Reserved. Reprinted from the January, 1977 issue by special permission.

Page 53. "Who Elected the Press", from ON PRESS, by Tom Wicker. Copyright ©1975, 1977, 1978, by Tom Wicker. Excerpted by permission of Viking Penguin Inc.

Chapter Four

Page 67. From, address before the Midwest Regional Republican Committee Meeting, Des Moines, Iowa, November 13, 1969, by Spiro Agnew.

Page 75. From, debate between William Small and Ernest Lefever, before the National Women's Republican Club, N.Y., January 15, 1975. Reprinted with permission.

Page 84. From, NEWS FROM NOWHERE: TELEVISION AND THE NEWS, by Edward Jay Epstein. Copyright ©1973 by Edward Jay Epstein. Reprinted by permission of Random House, Inc. Most of this material originally appeared in *The New Yorker*.

Chapter Five

Page 89. From, THE SELLING OF THE PRESIDENT 1968, by Joe McGinniss. Reprinted by permission of Simon and Schuster, a division of Gulf & Western Corporation. Copyright ©1969 by Joemac, Inc.

Page 98. From, THE UNSEEING EYE: THE MYTH OF TELEVISION POWER IN NATIONAL ELECTIONS, by Thomas E. Patterson and Robert D. McClure. Copyright ©1976. Reprinted by permission of G.P. Putnam's Sons publishers.

Page 104. From, "Testimony of Mrs. Zamora", from TV ON TRIAL, produced by WPLT-TV, May 23, 1978. Reprinted by permission of WPLT-TV, Miami, Florida.

Page 108. From, "Summation of the Defense", from TV ON TRIAL, produced by WPLT-TV, May 23, 1978. Reprinted by permission of WPLT-TV, Miami Florida.

Page 110. From, "Summation for the Prosecution", from TV ON TRIAL, produced by WPLT-TV, May 23, 1978. Reprinted by permission of WPLT-TV, Miami Florida.

Page 111. From, "Fairy Tales and Game Shows", by Stephan Rohde, The Los Angeles Times, 1978. Copyright ©1978. Reprinted by permission of The Los Angeles Times.

Chapter Six

Page 114. From, Miami Herald Publishing Co. v. Tornillo, 418, U.S. 241 (1974). Opinion by Chief Justice Burger.

Page 117. From, "Whose First Amendment?" by Lewis W. Wolfson. Reprinted by permission from *The Progressive*, 408 West Gorham Street, Madison, Wisconsin 53703. Copyright ©1974, The Progressive, Inc.

Page 121. From, Red Lion Broadcasting Co. v. Federal Trade Commission, 395, U.S. 367, (1969).

Page 123. From, "Media Myths that Limit Free Speech", by Edwin Diamond. Reprinted with permission from *TV Guide®* Magazine. Copyright ©1977 by Triangle Publications, Inc., Radnor, Pennsylvania.

Page 126. From, WCBS Radio Editorial, November 6, 1980. Reprinted by permission of WCBS Radio.

Page 134. From, New York Times Company v. Sullivan, 376, U.S. 254, (1964). Opinion by Justice Brennan.

Page 140. From, Herbert v. Lando, (1979). Opinion by Justice White.

Page 145. From, "A Chilling Court", by Tom Wicker. Copyright ©1979, by The New York Times Company. Reprinted by permission.

Page 147. From, "The Press Doesn't Own the First Amendment." Taken from, "Journalist's Privilege," by Michael Kinsley. Reprinted by permission of *The New Republic*. Copyright ©1979, by The New Republic, Inc.

Page 154. From, Branzburg v. Hayes, 408 U.S., 667 (1972). Majority opinion by Justice White.

Page 163. From, Branzburg v. Hayes, 408, U.S. 667, (1972). Dissent by Justice Stewart.

Page 167. From, Branzburg v. Hayes, 408, U.S. 667, (1972). Dissent by Justice Douglas.

Page 175. From, "First Amendment Hubris", by Anthony Lewis. Copyright ©1981 by The New York Times Company. Reprinted by permission.

Page 177. From, Letter to the Editor, *The New York Times*, April 26, 1981, by Floyd Abrams. Reprinted by permission.

Page 178. From, "The First Amendment Does Not Give Greater Freedom to the Press Than to Speech", by Robert Bork. Reprinted with permission from *The Center Magazine*, a publication of the Hutchins Center for the Study of Democratic Institutions, Santa Barbara, CA.

Page 185. From, "Protection for Confidential Sources Is Essential for Good Journalism", by Floyd Abrams. Reprinted with permission from *The Center Magazine*, a publication of the Hutchins Center for the Study of Democratic Institutions, Santa Barbara, CA.

Chapter Seven

Page 190. From, "Controlling Media Output", by Kevin Phillips, *Society* November/December, 1977. Copyright ©1977 by Transaction, Inc. Reprinted by permission.

Page 199. From, address before Associated Press Broadcasters Convention, Denver, Colorado, June 6, 1980, by William Paley. Reprinted by permission.

Page 204. From, "The Imperial Media", *Commentary*, May, 1981, by Joseph Kraft. Copyright ©1981, by the American Jewish Committee. Reprinted with permission.

CHAPTER 1

The Media Around Us

In his poem *The Dry Salvages* T.S. Eliot wrote that the sea is within us and all around us. Its "many voices" reach far inland: "The salt is on the briar rose/The fog is in the fir trees."

Something like this oceanic ubiquity characterizes the mass media in America today. Americans are surrounded and inundated by media voices. They wake in the morning—many to clock radios—and turn to the media to find out what has been happening in the last eight hours. They ride to school or work listening to radios or reading newspapers. If they stay home they can watch a succession of game or talk shows, soap operas, or cartoons. During evening "prime" hours sixty-six percent of American TV sets are turned on, and by bedtime the number has only slightly declined. Americans, of course, have preferences, but studies have suggested that they will watch almost anything rather than turn off their sets.

All around us are the evidences that we live in an age dominated by mass media: teenagers carrying giant "boom boxes," joggers with headsets, politicians denouncing the *Washington Post*, professors cutting articles from the *New York Times*, the father watching the evening news in one room while his kids watch re-runs in another, a woman listening to a succession of messages on her kitchen radio—news, weather, traffic reports, commercials, and advice on everything from childrearing to selecting the right restaurant.

The Media and Politics

The press has been called "the fourth branch of government." At first glance the statement seems absurd. The press has no official status in our country beyond what is granted to it by the Constitution's First Amendment: "Congress shall make no law. . . abridging the freedom of speech or of the press. . . ." The press has no authority to coerce us. Unlike the three official branches of government (the legislature, the executive, and the judiciary) it may not make laws, or carry them out, or authoritatively interpret them. But the press can do something else that is extremely critical in a democracy: it can influence opinion. All three branches of government need the support, or at least the tolerance, of the public. To affect public opinion, therefore, is to touch the very springs of power in America. This is not a particularly new or original observation. Over a century ago Abraham Lincoln noted the peculiar power of the press: "With public sentiment, nothing can fail; without it, nothing can succeed. Consequently, he who molds public sentiment goes deeper than he who enacts statutes or pronounces decisions."

Today's politicians readily understand Lincoln's words. Congressmen, especially the newer breed, spend much of their time contriving ways to get on the air or to get a few lines in the newspaper. In his book CLEARING THE AIR former

CBS News correspondent Daniel Schorr recounts an incident in which a staff director of a Senate committee urged him to cover a hearing. The director assured Schorr that it would have great "visual appeal," since he had arranged the witnesses to include a black, a poor white, and an Indian in full headdress. Schorr said he wouldn't be able to make it. Well, then, the staff director said, the hearing would have to be postponed. Wait a minute, Schorr said, you're letting a media correspondent dictate your legislative calendar. The staff director replied, Schorr wrote, "that it was not realistic to hold the hearing without cameras—most members of the committee would simply not turn up until informed by their aides that television was present." This sort of exhibitionism has had its counterpart in the executive branch. President Johnson, for example, moved the State of the Union address from its traditional noon hour to the broadcasting industry's "prime time" in the mid-evening, and President Nixon orchestrated his nomination so that his acceptance speech also coincided with prime time.

The pushing and pulling between modern Presidents and the press give us a glimpse of the media's growing political influence.

The most powerful elective office in the land, and probably the world, is the American presidency, but modern Presidents seem to consider their media "image" to be at least as important as their official powers. President Roosevelt made an end run around a generally unfriendly Republican press by communicating directly with the American people through a new medium, radio. President Truman, who was much more of an old fashioned pre-media politician than was his predecessor, tried to dismiss as "red herrings" the media-circulated charges of subversion and corruption in his administration, but that only made the charges seem more plausible. President Eisenhower was coached by a movie actor for his TV appearances, but President Kennedy looked as if he *was* a movie actor—with worshipful young reporters playing supporting roles. After Kennedy's assassination Lyndon Johnson came into office with enormous public support, but press coverage of the Vietnam War and of Johnson's "credibility gaps" deflated his popularity and helped influence his decision not to run again. When Walter Cronkite criticized the war on a special program, Johnson confided to his aides that if he had lost Cronkite then he had lost the country. President Nixon and his lieutenants, notably Vice President Spiro Agnew, conducted a major campaign against the press, denouncing it in public forums, attempting to enjoin the *New York Times* and other newspapers from publishing the Pentagon Papers (see page 43), tapping the phones of reporters, threatening to challenge the licenses of television stations, setting up special bureaus to purge "ideological plugola" from broadcasting, appointing hard-line critics of the media to the Federal Communications Commissions. In spite of these efforts Nixon and Agnew were driven from office in disgrace while the media emerged from the struggle stronger than ever. Watergate had proven to be Nixon's stumbling block, largely because the media relentlessly exposed and publicized the scandal. At first Nixon praised the work of "a vigorous free press" in helping to expose the conspiracy, but as the exposure began to focus on Nixon's own role in the Watergate coverup he complained of the "constant barrage—twelve to fifteen minutes a night on each of the three major networks." As he neared the end of his political career Nixon blamed his loss of support on the "leers and sneers of commentators."

Since Watergate, Presidents and those wishing to become President have generally courted the press instead of fighting it. President Ford treated reporters as buddies rather than adversaries. Jimmy Carter, during his long and uphill climb to the presidency, went out of his way to be accomodating. In a famous memo, Hamilton Jordan, Carter's chief advisor, stressed this point:

> Like it or not, there exists in fact an eastern liberal news establishment which has tremendous influence. The views of this small group of opinion-makers in the papers they represent are noted and imitated by other columnists and newspapers throughout the country and the world. Their recognition and acceptance of your candidacy as a viable force with some chance of success could establish you as a serious contender worthy of financial support of major party contributors.

Jordan wrote that "some people like Tom Wicker [columnist for the *New York Times*] or Mrs. Katherine Graham [then owner and publisher of the *Washington Post*] are significant enough to spend an evening or a leisurely weekend with." Once in office Carter showed that he had not forgotten the spirit of Jordan's memo. He appeared with Walter Cronkite, who served as moderator, in a "call-in" radio show, he submitted himself to numerous televised press conferences, and he revived the Rooseveltian "fireside chat" on TV. Despite these exercises, and despite some occasional recoveries, Carter's popularity plunged during his four years in office. He attributed his defeat by Ronald Reagan to the sudden intensification of the hostage issue in Iran shortly before the election, to Reagan's acting skills during their televised debates, and to unfavorable media coverage of his administration—in short, to "image" problems rather than to anything relating to the substance of his programs. Carter's reaction pointed up the importance which men of action attribute to the work of those who deal in words and pictures. Politicians generally feel that they can be made or broken by their "images."

This awe of the press is shared not just by professional politicians but by all who act in the public arena. Those lucky enough to get their "act" into the media are the ones likely to be taken seriously. TV representatives have not hesitated to take a share of credit for the success of the civil rights movement of the 1960s. They claim that it was because of TV coverage that civil rights demonstrators were able to get their message across, in the most vivid and dramatic forms, to a national audience. If this claim is correct, however, it can have a boomerang effect. It makes more credible the charge that the media were also partly responsible for the violence and kookiness of the 1960s. "I consider Walter Cronkite one of the founders of the yippie movement," said ex-yippie Jerry Rubin in 1978. "Every night he would have his little map with circles showing what was up on the campus front, and pretty soon everyone wanted their campus on the map that night."

Compliments from Jerry Rubin are not the type cherished by media representatives. In the face of such testimonials they usually become modest about their role. All we do, they say, is to report the news. Whether people behave well or ill, whether they act intelligently or mindlessly, if what they do is newsworthy then it is our job to report it. If anything of significance happens—a war, a riot, a demonstration, whatever—the media should not be blamed for reporting it. We mirror reality, media spokesman say, and it makes no sense to curse the mirror for reflecting what it faces.

The "mirror" analogy however, fails to take into account the enormous discretion available to the bearers of the news.

1. To begin with, they can tell us what the news *is*. Philosophers have been known to speculate about whether a tree falling alone in the forest gives off a sound. Can there be a sound without a hearer? There may be some analogy here to the plight of the political activist ignored by the media. "News is what *I* say it is," former NBC anchorman David Brinkley once boasted. "It's something worth knowing by *my* standards." This may sound like a pronouncement from Louis XIV, but it contains a large measure of truth. Is an unreported speech really a speech, especially if few people have heard it? Is a demonstration which is not covered in the media really much of a demonstration? Does it serve the purpose for which a demonstration is intended? Can a political candidate really compete for office if he is ignored by the media?

These are more than hypothetical questions. Citizen's Party candidate Barry Commoner complained of being virtually ignored during the presidential race of 1980 until, desperate for attention, he resorted to a barnyard epithet in a paid commercial. Reporters then descended on him in droves. Right-to-life groups annually complain that they receive little coverage of their Washington marches every January, even though they turn out in numbers exceeding 60,000. Candidates and activists of every viewpoint claim that TV correspondents are not interested in serious, thoughtful speeches but in gaffes, fights, and bizarre stunts. Whether or not these complaints are justified, they remind us that the media have the power—or burden—of judging what news is fit to print and broadcast. When Walter Cronkite used to end his program with "that's the way it is," there were people all over America—from prominent politicians to all sorts of anonymous demonstrators, protestors, crusaders, and would-be reformers—who would have shouted, "but there's more!"

2. The media can decide how they want to "play" the news. The particular angle in which a news item is presented can shape its meaning. Is a war covered from the angle of escalation or de-escalation? In his book *News From Nowhere* Edward Jay Epstein quotes from a Telex sent by an ABC news producer to ABC correspondents and cameramen in Vietnam:

> I think the time has come to shift some of our focus from the battlefield, or more specifically American military involvement with the enemy, to themes and stories under the general heading: We Are On Our Way Out of Vietnam. . . . To be more specific, a series of story ideas suggest themselves.

"Quite predictably," Epstein notes, "a radical change from combat stories to 'We Are On Our Way Out'-type stories followed in ABC's coverage of the Vietnam war."

3. The words, the expressions, the pictures, the intonations given to us by correspondents and cameramen can color the news. The *New York Times* reserves the adjective "strident" for movements whose goals it disagrees with, and it regularly describes right-of-center Democrats as "conservative" or "right-wing", but left-of-center Republicans as "moderate." The pictures in the news can also convey messages vividly, but everything turns on which pictures are selected. Critics have noted instances of pictures being used to make editorial statements.

Epstein recounts an example from the Vietnam period. On one NBC news program David Brinkley played a recording of "Ruby, Don't Take Your Love to Town," a ballad depicting the plight of a disabled veteran whose wife is getting ready to go out philandering; along with it he showed a film depicting a drab room full of mementoes, interspersed with scenes of flamethrowers, helicopters, tanks, and bodies. All of this was presented on a "news" program, though the song was fictional (and was actually about World War II, not Vietnam) and the visual material was carefully selected, as one of the producers told Epstein, "to create an atmosphere of futility and absurdity."

The mass media, then, may not constitute a "fourth branch of government" in any official sense, but they certainly possess political influence. Yet political power is not the only kind of power wielded by the media. It may not even be the most important kind. For most Americans politics is an alien and remote concern. It is the *social* sphere—our manners and mores, our theological beliefs, our tastes in music and art, our methods of raising our children—which touches our lives most directly. In this sphere, Americans tend to believe, coercion should be kept at a minimum and a variety of institutions should play a role: families, schools (private or public, depending on the family's preference), churches, and voluntary associations of all kinds. Today it is in this sphere that the media exert an awesome influence. To compare the relative attraction of the political and social spheres and at the same time to see the influence of the media in the latter sphere, one can try a simple experiment with any group of young people: ask them to identify their congressman, or the Secretary of State, or the Chief Justice of the Supreme Court; then read from a list of leading pop singers and TV celebrities, asking them to name the songs or programs with which they are identified. The chances are that their appalling ignorance about the political system* will be more than matched by abundant, media-derived knowledge of who's who in stardom. With a few exceptions such as CBS's "Sixty Minutes," it is not news or public affairs programs on TV which enjoy the highest

---

*A study conducted by the National Assessment of Educational Programs of thirteen-and seventeen-year olds in 1978 reported: twenty-five percent didn't seem to realize that the President, judges, and generals must obey laws just like anybody else; nearly fifty percent thought that Congress is appointed by the President; most thought it was illegal to start a new political party. In the same year another study of 1000 high school students aged 17 to 18 revealed the following: Only 11% of the students could name their state's two U.S. Senators; 16% did not know when the U.S. declared its independence; 25% did not know where the Declaration of Independence was signed; 32% could identify the Chief Justice of the Supreme Court; 4% could identify the three Presidents who preceded Gerald Ford.

Nielson ratings; it is the various "sit-coms" and dramas, played every weekday night during prime time. These programs, and the commercials which support them, are doing much more than entertaining us. They also help to form values, and in that capacity they usurp part of the territory traditionally occupied by family, church, schools, and other social institutions. Radio, TV, newspapers and magazines hand out advice on everything from etiquette to theology. An issue of *Redbook* magazine featured an article by Dr Spock on "What to Tell Your Child About God." Newspapers commonly feature columns answering readers' queries on personal subjects, which in the past would have been addressed to parents, clergy, or intimate friends. These questions cover areas as personal as: how to raise our children, how to find sexual fulfillment, how to achieve inner peace, how to conquer inferiority complexes, how to shed excess pounds, how to respond to misfortune, or how to look attractive. If ordinary people, our neighbors for instance, were to give us all this advice we would probably tell them to mind their own business. But there is nothing ordinary about the national media in America. The most attractive faces, the most persuasive speakers, the most resonant voices, the most facile writers, the most arresting pictures, all find their way into the media. This, in part accounts for the increasingly blurred distinctions between information, entertainment and prescription. What, for example, are we to make of TV "docu-dramas"? The very name suggests that history will be at least mingled with entertainment if not subordinated to it. Are we really learning the truth about the topic presented—or are we getting distortions, deliberately inserted for their dramatic effect or their acceptability to television viewers? The non-expert has no way of knowing.

On the other side of the coin, programs which are billed as pure entertainment may contain both information and prescription. Underlying many "sitcoms" and dramas presented during evening hours are certain implicit messages. Political scientist Michael Robinson studied a large number of prime-time "entertainment" programs and reached this conclusion:

> With few exceptions, prime time has become a plug for sexual openness and freedom. But the plug doesn't stop there. Entertainment television serves as a soft-core progressive statement about love, marriage, drugs, blacks, women, and gays. Between the news breaks and the commercials, the values on prime-time television are consistently liberal chic.

This does not mean that people can be "brainwashed" by the mass media. No conclusive evidence has been produced showing that people go out and do what they read about, or hear, or see on TV. Though the attorney for Ronney Zamora, a fifteen-year-old charged with the murder of an old woman, argued that his client was mesmerized by all the violence he had watched on TV (see page 104), the argument failed to convince the jury. After all, millions of others watched the same programs without being moved to commit murder. The influence of TV and the other mass media is far more indirect. What they can do is to affect the general climate of popular expectations, and thus help to shape popular culture. The word "culture" derives from a Latin word meaning to till the soil. The mass media prepare the soil out of which grow popular values and expectations. Putting the matter a little differently, the media "mediate" between individuals and the world in which they live.

The world is much too rich and complicated to be grasped entirely by any one person. What we do is to *select* the information that seems important to us, and leave the rest out. But what do we use as a principle of selection? How do we decide what to include and what to leave out? Over half a century ago, in a book called *Public Opinion,* Walter Lippmann wrote about "stereotypes." By a stereotype Lippmann meant a "mental image" of reality based on our expectations of what we think reality *ought* to look like. For example, if we expect that a gathering of political "radicals" will look a certain way, we will tend to focus our eyes on those who do look that way, ignoring those whose appearance contradicts our stereotype.

> There is, of course, some connection between the scene outside and the mind through which we watch it, just as there are some long-haired men and short-haired women in radical gatherings. But to the hurried observer a slight connection is enough. If there are two bobbed heads and four bearded in the audience, it will be a bobbed and bearded audience to the reporter who knows beforehand that such gatherings are composed of people with these tastes in the management of their hair.

What is remarkable about Lippmann's words, which appeared in 1922, is how they match the complaints voiced by many peace activists during the '60s. What bothered them was the tendency of reporters to focus on the most bizarre and extreme individuals as "typical" demonstrators. When CBS reporter Dan Rather and his film crew covered the 1967 "march on the Pentagon," they ignored all the members of the clergy, professors and parents with children in strollers, focusing instead on four very weird-looking demonstrators carrying a Vietcong flag—an unrepresentative group, but one which may have fit preconceptions of what "Vietniks" should look like.

All of us carry stereotypes, "pictures in our heads," around with us; we use them to catagorize and classify the world outside of us. The ultimate power of the media is the power to create a whole repertory of stereotypes for our use. Here is what a good cop looks like. Here is how an agitator acts. Here is a right-winger. Here is a typical teenager. Here is the way black people shake hands. Here's a really sexy girl. Here's how a truly virile man acts. What Lippmann called "the subtlest and most pervasive of all influences" over our lives is this power to structure our expectations. The way we act depends greatly on the way we see the world. And what we see is based in large part on what we expect to see. To be in the business of creating expectations, then, is to occupy a very strategic position in American life.

This does not mean that the mass media are the only cultural influence in America. Churches, schools, families and voluntary associations also play their roles. However, American life has changed dramatically since Lippmann published his book in 1922, and these changes have reinforced the powers of the media—powers to which, even then, he was calling to our attention.

First, the media have become far more vivid. A 1922 newspaper, even a "sensational" one, looks sedate compared to a modern tabloid. Layouts have become more eye-catching, print is cleaner, prose is punchier, and we have more and better graphics. Nor does this even begin to spell out the difference. We have radio, TV, stereophonic music, movies full of color and sound. If stereotypes are "pictures in our heads," we now have apparatus for painting the pictures right into the head, without the intermediary of print. What is more, we have people who have adapted their own styles to this mode of "instantaneous" communication. We have disk jockeys who talk very much like the music they play, writers who can hold the attention of an imbecile, advertising people who can squeeze so much into so little time, and cameramen and directors who know all the tricks. Our media today are more sensational, more adapted to the tastes of mass audiences, and more sophisticated than they were in the past.

Second, just at the time when the media have become more sensational, other social institutions seem to be losing some of their power. Schools, churches, and families once projected their own unique views of the world which to some extent countered the images of the media. Schools reminded children that not everything was easy, churches gave their congregations some vision of a transcendent reality, and families countered the media's image of the family with the real experience of mothers, fathers, and other relatives. But for every ten marriages in 1976 there were five divorces. (In 1920, when Lippmann was writing *Public Opinion,* for every twelve marriages there were 1.6 divorces.) Illegitimacy and homes with both parents working have also increased sharply. Television, it seems, has stepped into the void. One study, involving interviews with a number of children selected at random, showed that forty-four percent of them preferred TV to their fathers! As for school, children spend less time there than they spend in front of their TV sets. More importantly, the schools themselves have become increasingly media-oriented. There is an increasing use of filmstrips, videotapes, teaching machines, magazine-type workbooks, and other paraphernalia derived from modern media. Some teachers assign TV programs as homework, and others complain that they can't hold the class's attention because they can't compete with "Sesame Street." Churches seem to be experiencing a similar identity crisis. Instead of counter balancing the world of the media, they find themselves being pulled into its orbit. Church historian Martin E. Marty wonders whether "religious" broadcasting may not do more harm than good to authentic religion. After watching "the ruffled-shirted, pink-tuxedoed men and the high-coif-ferred, low-necklined celebrity women who talk about themselves under the guise of Born Again autobiographies," will viewers be able to switch off their sets and go down the block "to a congregation of real believers, sinners, off-key choirs, sweaty and homely people who need them?" Dr. Marty answers: "Never. Well, hardly ever."

Not only family, church and school, but almost every other social institution once prominent in America has fallen on hard times. Political parties, which once commanded an almost religious loyalty, have lost not only many of their members (those who call themselves "independents" have grown in number to such an extent that they now outnumber Republicans and have almost caught up with Democrats), but have also lost their old mystique. People get their news and entertainment from the media and their welfare from the government; they don't need the ward-heelers and the torchlight parades which parties once provided. People also used to be deeply attached to labor unions, which provided not only economic benefits but also a kind of social and psychological "home" for people who might otherwise be rootless. Today labor leaders are scarcely distinguishable from Chamber of Commerce officials, and their followers may be happy or angry with them but have little sense of belonging to a family. Neighborhoods once defined certain cultures peculiar to their "turf." In some inner-city areas this may still be true, but for the most part suburbia and the freeway have obliterated the traditional meaning of "neighborhood."

At the very time that the voices of the media have become so alluring, then, the old cultural institutions, which once checked and balanced the media, have lost influence. If "culture" derives from a word meaning to till the soil, then a great stretch of American soil is being tilled by radio, television, newspapers and magazines. The traditional institutions of American culture are almost in the position of the family farmer, watching in awe as huge combines take over the land.

It is hard to say just how much the media affect our ways of thinking and acting, or how we would act without them. We have no conclusive way of testing such questions, for the simple reason that we have no perfect control group. All of us are exposed in some degree or another to the mass media, even though some of us may be more immersed than others. What we can do is to become more conscious of the media in our lives, to learn more about them and about the people who run them. Broadly speaking, this is the aim of this book.

Here are the questions to be raised and discussed:

1. Who controls the media? Is there a small, monolithic, elite or a diversity of competing interests?

2. How much power is in the hands of the media? Do they constitute a government in themselves, or is there actually too little power in their hands?

3. Are the media biased, or do they provide a balanced and objective view of reality? If there is any bias, does it come from the ideology of those who control the media?

4. Do the media—television in particular—manipulate us? Can we be "sold" political candidates the way we are sold commercial products? Can TV violence move people to commit violent acts?

5. What are the rights and responsibilities of the media? Should there be a government-mandated "right to reply" to charges and arguments made in the media? How much immunity should the media have from slander suits? Are there circumstances when Reporters should have to identify their sources?

6. Should the media be regulated? To what extent, and in what manner? Would regulation of any sort threaten the freedoms protected by the First Amendment?

To help the reader formulate answers to these questions this book has provided a variety of materials, ranging from essays to Supreme Court opinions. The materials include speeches, dialogues, magazine articles, newspaper columns, and letters to editors. Most of the readings will take one side or another on the above questions, though some will fall in the middle and others will argue that the question needs to be reformulated. The purpose is to probe these issues thoroughly, to circle around them like a wolf worrying his prey, to let speaker after speaker try to answer them—then to back off and approach them again from another angle. The reason for this method is not simply to be fair to all sides. The philosophy underlying this book is that we do not gain real knowledge of a topic until we have studied it from a variety of perspectives and viewpoints, and that the best way to do that is to allow spokesmen to explore it in their own ways and their own words. The attempt here is to revive the ancient art of the dialectic, a form of discourse in which, as the philosopher Hegel once put it, "one shrewd thought devours another."

It seems particularly just that we subject the mass media to this kind of analysis. Since the voices of the media surround us every day, talking to us, singing to us, supplying so many of "the pictures in our heads," it is essential that we learn to develop the habit of talking back. We need to ask critical questions of the media, and not be satisfied with facile answers. We need to bear in mind that these media voices are not simply "messengers" but major actors in the political and social arena. We need to make certain that the media have their rights protected but also that we have ours protected, including our right to hear a variety of viewpoints, to have our privacy and autonomy respected, and to have a fair degree of access to the very powerful organs of mass communication which technology has given us.

The voices and viewpoints in this book should be useful to anyone contemplating a career in the mass media, but their main purpose is to serve the citizen. A citizen is more than a wage-earner and more than a passive spectator. The essense of citizenship is participation in the life of the community. This book, then, is aimed at those who want to understand the things that influence our environment and behavior so that they in turn can exert some measure of control over them.

It may be, of course, that the best form of control would be to do nothing but to let the laws of competition and self-regulation do their work, and that tampering with the media will pose grave threats of freedom. *Laissez-faire* is an arguable position. But it needs to be argued, not simply asserted. The readings in this book are meant to stimulate that process of reflection so that citizens can make rational choices. Surely this is the spirit behind our tradition of press freedom. Let truth and falsehood grapple, said the poet John Milton in 1644, for, "who ever knew truth put to the worse, in a free and open encounter. . . ?"

CHAPTER 2

Who Controls the Media? Few or Many?

In 1919 Justice Oliver Wendell Holmes said:

> When men have realized that time has upset many fighting faiths, they may come to believe even more than they believe the very foundations of their own conduct that the ultimate good desired is better reached by free trade in ideas—that the best test of truth is the power of the thought to get itself accepted in the competition of the market. . . .

Holmes was defending free speech by comparing it to free trade. When we enter the marketplace we should be able to select what we want from a variety of merchandise. So, too, when we shop for ideas: we can only make wise selections by seeing the full range of competing viewpoints.

So far so good. The problem comes when somebody starts tampering with the free market. There are at least two ways of tampering with it.

COERCION. One way is to hound some of the sellers off the street by intimidation. In the realm of ideas this method has a long history. We all know the stories about the martyrs, heretics, visionaries, dissidents and oddballs of all sorts who have been jailed, tortured or lynched, and we can be reasonably certain that there were many others who *might* have come out into the open with their views but decided that silence was better for the health. Holmes's point, however, is that the real victims of this persecution were not the dissidents themselves but the public at large. They were deprived of the full range of competing viewpoints which alone permits a wise choice.

America has had its periods of official repression, but on the whole Americans have been remarkably free from it. Our First Amendment puts in writing a guarantee of freedom of speech: "Congress shall make no law . . . abridging the freedom of speech, or of the press. . . ."

Because Americans have been relatively free from official coercion, can we automatically assume that they enjoy a "free trade in ideas"? Not quite. It was mentioned above that there are at least two ways of tampering with "free trade." The first is coercion. What is the second?

MONOPOLY. Suppose that, on a certain morning, one of the sellers of goods were to "buy out" all the others. He would then be the sole proprietor.

Competition would have given way to monopoly. And who would be the losers? Probably not the former competitors, for the whole deal might have been concluded with smiles and handshakes. The losers, if we take Holmes' formula seriously, were the consumers. They were the ones deprived of the full range of choice.

Many observers argue that something like this has been happening in the American media over the past century. Gone are the days when practically countless numbers of little printers and editors had more or less equal shares in the market of public opinion. Even the days of the small-town independent newspaper seem to be ending, as newspaper chains gobble them up. The number of competing newspapers has drastically declined, and wire services have standardized reporting. Television, which a majority of Americans now consider the most "credible" of media for disseminating opinion, is divided into three commercial networks. They are owned by giant media conglomerates which also own newspapers, television stations, magazines, books, and records.

For some critics of the media this growing concentration of ownership represents a deadly threat to the "free trade in ideas." They charge that it makes for standardization and uniformity of opinion, that it discriminates against ideas which are unfashionable, that it deprives the public of the full range of opinion—and that it does it all so smoothly that the public is not even aware of being shortchanged.

This is the position of media critic—and former editor and reporter—Ben Bagdikian. The following statement of his was delivered orally before a special "symposium on media concentration" conducted by the Federal Trade Commission at the close of 1978.

FEWER AND FEWER . . . CONTROLLING MORE AND MORE

Ben Bagdikian, statement to the Federal Trade Commission, 1978

Let me give my background briefly as some explanation of the source of my information and opinions. For nineteen years I worked for daily newspapers as a reporter, foreign correspondent, Washington correspondent and an editor. I have been a magazine editor and have written for most national magazines of general circulation. Throughout this period I have done media research and criticism. I was a Guggenheim Fellow researching ownership patterns of the press. For two and a half years I did research at Rand [Corporation, a private "Think Tank"] on the impact of modern technology on the future of American informational media and for the last three years on factors that lead to success or failure of newspapers. For the last two years I have been on the faculty of the Graduate School of Journalism at the University of California at Berkeley.

This symposium is looking at the phenomenon of increasing control of information organizations in the United States by a relatively small number of national and transnational corporations. I understand that some important executives in publishing have expressed concern that people outside the corporate end of their business—that is, journalists, researchers, academics, civic activists and others—will approach the problem with a prejudice against their motives. Let me confirm their worst fears by beginning with a quotation on that subject. I quote:

> "I rather think that the influence of the American press . . . is declining. This, I believe, is because so many newspapers are owned or influenced by reactionary interests and predatory corporations, and are used selfishly to promote the welfare of these reactionary interests, rather than the welfare of the public."

End of quote.

I would not express my own concern in that language and there are portions of that quotation that seem to me to be exaggerated. But I should point out that the quotation is not from a journalist or academic but from one of the trade's pioneers in chains and conglomerates, the original William Randolph Hearst. He uttered those words in 1924, at which time he was among the first to show the power of owning newspapers, magazines, movie companies and other assorted properties that affect the public mind.

Today we are looking at a phenomenon that might have surprised even Mr. Hearst. In 1924 he and other chain operators controlled 31 corporations that owned 153 papers, or 8 per cent of all dailies. Today there are 167 chains that control 1,082 papers, or 61 per cent of all papers. It took the first 60 years of this century for chains to control 27 per cent of all our papers. It has taken only the last 16 years for chains to reach control of 61 per cent of all papers and 75 per cent of all daily circulation.

Newspapers are only one medium that influences our culture and our politics. The phenomenon of fewer and fewer people controlling more and more of our public intelligence affects every mass medium in our country. The concentration of control of our newspapers, magazines, broadcasting, books and movies has reached alarming levels. Fewer than 100 corporate executives have ultimate control of the majority of each medium in the United States. According to the Census of Manufacturers twenty corporations, each with a chief executive officer, control 52 per cent of all daily newspaper sales. Twenty corporations control 50 per cent of all periodical sales. Twenty corporations control 52 per cent of all book sales. Twenty corporations control 76 per cent of all record and tape sales. If one counts the three networks and the ten corporations whose sponsorship dominates prime time, 13 corporations control two-thirds of the audience in television and radio. Seven corporations control 75 per cent of movie distribution.

These 100 men and women constitute a private Ministry of Information and Culture for the United States.

In fact, there are fewer than 100 corporations because some of them are among the top twenty controllers of more than one medium. For example, 27 per cent of all television stations are controlled by newspaper companies. A magazine company, Time, Incorporated, owns magazines, 17 weekly newspapers, five book publishing houses, a film company, and has interests in cable, and records. RCA owns the National Broadcasting Company, a record company, and the book publishing houses of Random House, Ballantine Books, Alfred Knopf, Pantheon, Vintage and Modern Library. The biggest newspaper conglomerate, Times-Mirror, owns the *Los Angeles Times,* the *Dallas Times-Herald, Long Island Newsday* and other papers, four magazines, TV stations, cable systems, 50 per cent of a news service and New American Library. CBS is one of three companies with two-thirds of the prime-time audience, owns 20 magazines, three record companies, and the book publishing houses of Holt, Rinehart and Winston, Popular Library and W.B. Saunders Co.*

This really means that when it comes to the mass media that create a major ingredient of our social and political environment, the men and women who control most of it would fit in this room. If that were the case of a government bureaucracy there would be justified alarm among the public and especially among the entrepreneurs who now control our media environment. And I would share their alarm for two reasons: government has police powers to enforce self-serving propagandistic use of our mass media. And even under the best of conditions it is not safe to repose in a small group of human beings, governmental or not, such closely controlled power over the ideas, information, and values that are propagated by our mass media. The small number of private corporations that are increasingly gaining control over our mass media do not have governmental powers. But they are too small a group of fallible human beings to have such unified control. Even if they should be philosopher-saints in their wisdom, this country was founded on the theory that no small group, even philosopher-saints, should have so much power over public information and discourse.

This pattern of control is compounded by two new developments in media ownership. One is the inclusion of journalism and other media companies in large conglomerate corporations that are also in other industries, industries that regularly are reported—or not reported—by the same corporations' media properties. A company like ITT, deeply involved with foreign governments and domestic policy, that also controls publishing companies is in a position of direct conflict of interest that we would not condone with government officials or agencies. We know that for many years William Randolph Hearst used his newspapers, magazines, wire services and movie production companies to urge the United States to

*[Eds. note] These interrelationships were as of 1978.

declare war on Mexico, not out of a pure instinct for news but because he feared expropriation of his mining properties in Mexico. Today there is greater potential than ever for using journalism as a by-product by large conglomerates who have an explicit desire to influence public opinion and government policy in their favor.

The other new development is a pattern of several traditionally competing media coming under ownership by the same parent corporation. It has always been assumed that a newspaper article might be expanded to a magazine article which could become the basis for a hardcover book which, in turn, could be a paperback, and then, perhaps, a TV series and finally, a movie. At each step of change an author and other enterprises could compete for entry into this array of channels for reaching the public mind and pocketbook. But today several of our media giants own these arrays, not only closing off entry points for competition in different media, but influencing the choice of entry at the start on the basis of how a later treatment by the same company will profit.

Book publishing, for example, used to be satisfied by a conventional profit in the sale of hardcover books. But now that most book sales are controlled by 20 companies, many of which also own other media, increasingly hardcover books, those basic repositories of information and reflection, are selected not because the public will buy them for themselves, at a profit for the book company, but because they will do well in the same company's magazines, in its mass paperback sales or in its television and movie treatment. Not only does this constrict the basis on which book manuscripts are selected, but it has begun to destroy the special quality of presentation that is unique to each medium and that represents a necessary richness of subject matter and approach. We now see book manuscripts assigned and selected so that a television movie can be made from which a mass paperback based on the television movie can be sold, all by a company that had this media incest orchestrated by its marketing computers.

The question inevitably arises whether the media really have any influence. The answer is not always simple. During the administration of Franklin Delano Roosevelt, the majority of newspapers, then the major medium, were hostile to the New Deal in their news columns and in their editorials. But they were dealing with a population whose desperation at finding food and shelter was more persuasive than the slanted news and angry editorials against Roosevelt's programs. But we do not always deal with desperate overwhelming, personal problems. Instead, between crises we accumulate unspectacular information and ideas that shape our values and those values in turn influence how we meet crises when they arise. In this everyday, unspectacular laying down of the national consciousness I think the evidence is clear that our media do have a subtle but profound effect.

In explicit things like the impact of television on violent behavior, the report of the U.S. Surgeon General, when read in the original, shows beyond doubt that the persistent portrayal of violence on television affects every American's attitude toward violence, regardless of social class.

Perception of our whole society, and of particular groups in our society is learned mostly from our mass media. We are increasingly a society of polarized, homogeneous communties—tending to separate by race, by economics and by social class. We no longer live in small communities where there is personal contact across class lines. We are seeing the disappearance of the community, all-class school. Millions of Americans are growing up without personal knowledge of other Americans who are of a different skin color, or ethnic background, or economic class—except for what they see, read and hear in the mass media.

Media operators, when confronted with this, tend to disclaim all influence on human behavior. When they do so, they fly in the face of the overwhelming weight of evidence of the most careful studies and of common experience. They are also ignoring their own appeals to advertisers. When media operators compete for their share of the $27 billion annual advertising expenditures, they insist to the advertisers that their medium can influence human behavior. If our media cannot influence human behavior then they are selling false goods to the commercial entrepreneurs, the politicians, and the special interest groups who buy space and time to advertise their wares and to influence public opinion.

It would mean that some of our most powerful corporations—IBM, Xerox, Proctor & Gamble, General Motors, General Mills, Mobil Oil—are fools because they spend billions of dollars every year advertising to sell their goods and to influence public opinion. They would be fools if they continued to spend this money without some evidence that it does in fact change the way people think and behave. I do not believe that they are fools and I don't think that media operators treat them as fools.

I see no alternative but to assume that our media have a profound effect on our national culture and values and that we should be concerned about control of our media.

My concern over the nature of control over the media is not so much my disagreement with the personal values and politics of many media owners. I do not want homogeneous newspapers, broadcasts, magazines and movies, even if all of them were compatible with my personal beliefs. History forces us to be concerned. History tells us that the only safe source of information is pluralistic. History also tells us that potential power must be regarded as real power. Government laws that permit severe regulation do not make the media operators less worried simply because the government says it doesn't really intend to use these powers. I don't believe government when it says that and media operators are wise not to believe it. Licenses to exercise power will be used. But neither can I look with equanimity when the small number of people who control our media say they are benevolent, and that they do not really intend to use their ultimate power of control over information. We are being careless with history unless we assume that whoever has power, sooner or later will use it to the fullest.

Media operators sometimes argue that the public would not stand for their using their power to control news. I suggest that the public knows what it will stand for and not stand for only when it knows that it has a choice. For important portions of our social and political life, what the media do not tell us, we do not know. If a local newspaper is ordered by its owner to tell only negative stories about a disliked politician—and occasionally that happens—then the people in that community may never know anything positive about that politician. If television tells 90 million Americans every night that anger, aggression, and shooting are the prime-time norm for human relations, millions of children will grow up with a diminished sense of compassion, tenderness and empathy, and with a greater tolerance for aggression and violence.

In many ways, the American media pattern is superior to that in most developed countries. We have more newspapers than most countries. We have more radio and television stations. We make more movies and publish more magazines. Government does not have a monopoly on all mass communications, as it does in many societies, and it does not have a monopoly or near-monopoly on broadcasting as it does in many democratic countries. Instead we have more than 1,700 daily newspapers, none of them under government control. We have 8,600 radio and 700 commercial television stations, all regulated by government but privately owned, and 10,000 periodicals, and so forth. But the units of these that reach the largest audiences are increasingly coming under the control of a small number of corporations.

When we remember that 20 corporations control access to most of the American audience in each of these media, the very large number of units becomes ominous rather than reassuring. It means that today more than half of this enormous machinery for affecting the public mind, despite its size and power, is controlled by fewer than 100 corporations.

There is a peculiarity of American political organization that makes media concentration and monopoly particularly dangerous. This peculiarity further diminishes the advantage we enjoy in a large number of communication outlets.

To a greater extent than any other developed country, the United States is organized at a local level. We vest in cities, towns and counties important governmental functions that in other societies are governed at a national level. Our education, policing, land use, and other vital functions are decided by each community through its local political machinery. This is why we have local papers rather than national ones and this is why our basic Communications Act called for local broadcast stations, not national ones, on the basis that each community has peculiar needs no national medium can fill.

The developing patterns in daily newspapers illustrate what I mean.

In most developed countries there are a number of papers published in the principal city and distributed in every part of the country the same day. All the serious national and international news is in these papers. Local papers are of relatively small importance because the central functions that affect people's lives are exercised at the national level and presumably will be reported by the national papers. The large number of national papers in these other countries means there is commercial competition. But, more important, it means that there can be differences in basic political or social content, from which people may make a choice, each paper concentrating on a slightly different point of view and reporting a different spectrum of information. If a radical paper buries a story embarrassing to its adherents, a conservative rival will happily report it and the information will enter the public arena.

In this country we have only one truly national paper, *The Wall Street Journal,* transmitted overnight by satellite to printing plants all over the country and delivered by newsstand or mail the same day in every part of the country. But it is a specialized financial paper. We have a few papers of unusual influence, like *The New York Times, The Los Angeles Times* and the *Washington Post,* but they are not available in every part of the country the same day of publication. There are a number of subsidiary reasons for the lack of a national press in this country but the major reason is that no national newspaper can tell the people of a particular city or region what they need to know in order to govern themselves. *The New York Times* is of little help to Des Moines when Des Moines elects members of its school board.

This pattern of localism, and the degree to which the health of urban society depends on it, makes disturbing two contemporary developments in the press. First, is the now almost-standard pattern of local monopoly for daily papers throughout the country. And second, the consolidation of these monopolies into dominating metropolitan publications that pre-empt the economic base for new papers in each community but do not provide each community with the news it needs.

Monopoly is an established fact in American daily newspapers. There are 1,760 daily papers in the country in about 1,600 communities, and in ninety-seven and one half per cent of these communities there is only one local newspaper company. Those of you who live in the 34 cities of the country that still have newspapers in face-to-face competition should realize that you are in a two and one half per cent minority.

The other disturbing development is that most of our cities do not have daily papers. We have 7,000 urban places in the country but only 1,760 newspapers, leaving about 75 per cent of our urban communities without their own paper. It was not always this way. In 1890 there were 1,348 urban places and 1,600 daily papers, an excess of 19 per cent of papers over urban communities. The 75 per cent of our urban communities without their own paper often have access to a metropolitan or other paper from another community. And many papers would insist that they try to cover all of the cities where they sell papers. But the fact is that they do not and cannot. It is not unusual for a metropolitan paper to have significant distribution over 40 counties. *The Atlanta Constitution and Journal,* for example, circulates significantly in 55 counties, only 16 of which have their own daily paper. The average county in the United States has 26 local governments, 22 of them with taxing power. A paper that covers 40 counties, in order to do minimal civic reporting, would have to cover over 1,000 governmental bodies. This is just a start of adequate community reporting and no paper comes even close.

These developments put a different light, I think, on the development of chains, conglomerates and other extreme concentrations of control over our mass media. It means that in many media, particularly newspapers and in the uniformity of network programming, large numbers do not mean competition but the opposite.

The most clear example of what I mean is in the case of daily newspapers. There are in the United States 1,759 daily newspapers of general circulation, a figure that has remained almost constant for a generation. These daily papers are owned by 834 companies. If the ownership were distributed evenly this would mean about two papers per company. But of course ownership is not distributed evenly because 167 of these companies, the chains or groups, that own more than one paper in more than one community, own 62 per cent of all daily papers. If ownership of chain papers were distributed evenly among chains it would mean between 5 and 6 papers per chain. But that is not the case. The 25 largest chains own 31 per cent of all dailies and a majority of all chain papers. But chain-owned papers are bigger than the average American daily, so in terms of circulation, the 25 largest newspaper corporations control 52 per cent, or a majority, of all papers sold daily in the United States.

But as we look at the accumulation of media power by the largest companies we see an even tighter concentration. The ten biggest chains control 36 per cent of all circulation and 20 per cent of all newspaper companies.

Put another way this shows that one per cent of all newspaper companies control 36 per cent of all papers sold daily and own 20 per cent of all newspaper companies.

At the start of 1977 there were 1,759 dailies in the country, and 677 remained independently owned. About 250 of these 677 have less than 5,000 circulation and therefore have too small a cash flow to interest a chain. The larger chains are bidding furiously for the remaining 400 and predictably most will be absorbed. In fact 100 of the remaining 400 were bought by chains in the last 20 months.

The rate at which the big chains are swallowing small chains and accumulating control of our daily printed news is seen in just the last ten years. Ten years ago the ten biggest chains controlled 11 per cent of all daily newspaper companies. Today the ten biggest chains control 20 per cent of all daily papers. So not only is the independently owned daily paper predictably going to disappear, but control of all papers is rapidly accumulating disproportionately among the biggest corporations in the news business.

Concentrated control of news is different from control of other commodities. The principal difference, of course, is that this is not control of automobiles, detergents and breakfast cereals but control of public information. But this control of public information becomes even more critical when we look at the pattern of local monopoly in daily newspapers.

We have already noted that of the cities that have their own daily paper, 97 and one half per cent have a local monopoly. This, too, has progressed with frightening speed. From the turn of the century we have gone from almost two-thirds of newspaper cities with competing papers to 2 and one half per cent. And I believe that it is only a matter of time before competing daily papers in the same city will be a peculiarity of a handful of cities either of great size or where publishers compete with each other for reasons other than economic profit.

This means a great deal when we look at what it means to have most of our news controlled, as it is today, by a few national and transnational corporations. Concentration of control in the marketplace is not limited to newspapers and other media companies. It is true of a large segment of our economy. There is similar and frequently even greater concentration in other industries, and with even a greater rate of accumulation of control from an earlier period of hundreds of individual entrepreneurs. In the automobile industry, for example, two generations ago there were more than 200 individual companies making automobiles in the United States and today there are only four.

But because almost all of our papers are local monopolies and because chains particularly try to stay away from competing papers we have a different situation in the newspaper industry.

In the automobile industry, the remaining giant corporations compete with each other and with foreign companies, all of which acts as a restraint against over-pricing and reduction of quality. General Motors, Ford, Chrysler and American Motors compete with each other and they all compete with Volkswagen, Toyota and so forth.

That is not true in the newspaper business. Of the 1,082 papers owned by chains, half of 1 per cent, or 50, have local printed competition. Of these 50 papers, only seven, or seven-tenths of one per cent have face-to-face competition, or competition in the same time of day. Of the 50 chain papers that have any competition at all, whether dividing the market into AM and PM segments between them or in face-to-face competition, 16 are in agency agreements permitted by the special exemption from antitrust laws. This means that among the 50 chain papers that have any kind of local printed competition, 16, or one-third of them can legally fix prices and share profits.

The result is that 97 per cent of all chain papers have no economic competition in their cities. If you eliminate the ones with agreements to fix prices and share profits, you still have 95 per cent of all chain papers with no local competition. It seems to me that this places a different light on the growing control of news by a few corporations. It means that each of these noncompeting corporations has a network of monopoly operations. So the daily newspaper industry is not comparable to other concentrated industries where at least the giants compete with each other. It is more like the telephone or other utility companies that have sanctioned monopolies. In the ultimate test, a real choice available to the consumer, the consumer loses, 95-to-5. . . .

Ben Bagdikian's views are representative of many critics, inside and outside of the broadcasting industry.

What can be said on the other side? A number of things:

*Despite the chains and the mergers, America does have a diversity of voices, and technology has made the diversity even richer.

*We need powerful media to keep their eyes on an increasingly powerful government.

*Some of the critics' "remedies" may actually harm the free trade in ideas.

These were among the points made by Lee Loevinger, a former Federal Trade Commissioner who in recent years has been representing the print and broadcast industries, when he appeared before the FCC's 1978 "symposium." Some of his comments follow.

A PLETHORA OF MEDIA VOICES

Lee Loevinger, statement to the Federal Trade Commission, 1978

The preceding speakers in this FTC symposium on media concentration have, with very few notable exceptions, either asserted or assumed that there is a great and increasing concentration of control of the mass media in this country. I shall undertake to present that diverse and unorthodox viewpoint from antagonistic sources that has been so praised in the abstract but is so often despised in actual confrontation.

Initially, it should be noted that I address only matters related to the mass media of newspapers and broadcasting and am not now concerned with the book industry. My firm and I represent a number of newspaper publishers and broadcasters and I have in the past represented the National Association of Broadcasters, although I do not do so at the present. However, I do not speak for or represent any of my clients, employers, or firm in this forum.

It appears that most of the prior speakers have been perpetual and habitual critics of the media who have presented a litany of cliches and buzzwords. They have recycled much used arguments and data and at least a couple have recycled the contents of briefs in losing cases.

I propose to expound, as fully as time permits, these points:

1. Speakers who have viewed with alarm and called for government action have ignored the real world.

2. Actual concentration of mass media in the United States is not increasing, but decreasing.

3. The United States has a plethora of media voices. To talk of media concentration in the United States is like speaking of press freedom in Russia.

4. The dangers of government power are far greater than the dangers of media power.

5. The FTC is a particularly inappropriate agency to act in this area. It is unsuited structurally, functionally and by experience.

6. Although the media, like all other human institutions, are far from perfect, the United States has the most free, the most diverse, the most competitive, and the best mass communications system that has ever existed in the history of the world in this or any other country.

First let me attempt to suggest the nature of the real world of mass media. None of the speakers in this symposium has addressed the basic newspaper problem of the present time. This is the increasing cost of distribution and delivery caused by demographic dispersion.

A broadcasting station operating according to its FCC specified power and performance characteristics can increase its audience at no cost whatever. The cost of operating a broadcasting station is essentially the same whether the audience is three, three hundred, three thousand or three million. In contrast, the home delivery of newspapers to the suburbs and the bedroom or residential areas of our cities is increasingly difficult and expensive. It involves record-keeping, delivery trucks, human labor, and vast expenditures of energy and other expensive resources. It is subject to the hazards of weather and other impediments and publishers are unable to insure delivery with complete reliability.

Another difference between broadcasting and newspaper publishing is that broadcasting can change and update a news story literally in the middle of its delivery. In contrast, every change in the text of a newspaper requires a new edition to be effective; and each edition multiplies the costs of printing, distribution and delivery.

The economic effect of these aspects of newspaper publishing has been that the greatest increases in newspaper circulation have occurred in small town newspapers rather than large city newspapers. This phenomenon is noted in the *Saturday Review* (February 13, 1971), which reports that:

> The modernization of the small-town newspaper dramatizes a striking difference between the newspaper industry and most others since the Second World War. While other industries have advanced with larger firms swallowing up the smaller and weaker, in the newspaper industry the stability and growth of the small and weak have been at the expense of the strong. . . .
>
> In plain English, the smaller the city the greater the growth. . . . Here is the real explanation of the paradox of an almost zero growth in the number of daily newspapers in the midst of overall industry expansion.

The statistics cited by the *Saturday Review* support the conclusions stated. Without belaboring this point further, let me go on to my second point.

Since World War II, media concentration in the United States has been decreasing, not increasing. From 1922 to 1950 there was some increase in concentration of newspaper ownership and in affiliation between newspapers and broadcasters. From 1950 up to the latest year for which data are available there has been a continuing decrease in media cross-ownership and media concentration of ownership. An analysis of the concentration of control of media outlets in every major market in the United States which was done by expert economists for the NAB and which is a matter of public record in the FCC cross-ownership proceeding shows that there has been a small but steady decrease in the percentage of media cross-ownership and in the concentration ratio of mass media outlets in American metropolitan areas since 1950. By 1974 the concentration ratios and cross-ownership percentages were at the lowest point that they have ever been since the beginning of broadcasting.

Furthermore, since 1922 the total number of media outlets, that is newspapers and broadcasting stations, has increased and has increased much faster than the population. The number of daily newspapers decreased very slightly from 1922 to 1945. That number has, however, remained virtually constant ever since 1945. On the other hand, during that period, broadcast outlets have increased more than one thousand percent, or ten times over. Thus, the total number of media voices, that is the number of media outlets with separate owners, has increased at a very much faster rate than the population.

Even the data used by that veteran media critic, Ben Bagdikian, tend to prove this point. Mr. Bagdikian announces portentiously that in 1924 thirty-one corporations controlled 153 American daily newspapers throughout the country. By 1978, he says, 167 corporations controlled 1,082 daily newspapers throughout the country. It is obvious that these data have relevance only to a national market. But looking at the United

States as a national journalistic market—which is a legitimate viewpoint—these data show that there are 167 competitors in a market in which there were formerly only thirty-one. This is more competitors than there is in any other national market that I can think of. This also means that there are seven times as many newspapers in the country which have resources and facilities for a potential national news bureau. By any analysis, these data show increasing competition and an increasing diversity on a national scale.

Third, a fact of increasing importance is that this country has a plethora of media voices. This is demonstrable in several ways. Mr. Bagdikian is himself living proof of this. He has a long and distinguished career as a newspaper writer during virtually all of which he has been a persistent and outspoken critic of newspapers and publishers. American newspapers are increasingly presenting diverse views from antagonistic sources on different pages of the same edition, and often on the same page. For example, the *Washington Star* presents views ranging from the high priestess of the left, Mary McGrory, to the guru of the right, William Buckley, together with a variety of writers in between, including Ralph Nader, J.J. Kilpatrick, Tom Wicker, and many others.*

In terms of numbers the daily newspaper population of this country has remained constant at slightly more than 1,750 since the end of World War II. However, as anyone can observe, the local news of small towns and suburban communities is not reported exclusively by daily newspapers. The daily newspapers are supplemented by nearly 10,000 weekly and semi-weekly newspapers which have also remained constant in numbers during the last quarter of a century. Other periodicals, such as the local magazines, like the *Washingtonian,* have increased in number from about 7,000 to nearly 10,000 in the same period.

Broadcasting stations have increased from none prior to 1922 and only a few hundred in the late 1920's to 10,000 or more. The country now has approximately 9,000 radio stations and more than 1,000 television stations, plus some 4,000 television translators which extend the range of the television stations to remote and otherwise inaccessible parts of the country.

The numbers of diverse media and media voices naturally differ somewhat depending upon the size of the market. However, there is no significant market in the United States that does not have a substantial number of diverse media in it. The average number of media available in the largest fifty markets is more than two hundred representing more than 170 separate owners, or voices, and with a substantial majority originating in the local market. There are corresponding, although somewhat smaller, numbers for all of the other markets.

The problem that confronts America today is not a concentration of mass

---

Editor's note: In 1981, less than three years after Loevinger's remarks, the *Washington Star* went out of business.

media voices but a confusion arising from the plethora and cacophony of voices. Alan Toffler in FUTURE SHOCK, says this:

> ... The advance of communications technology is quietly and rapidly de-monopolizing communications without a shot being fired. The result is a rich destandardization of cultural output.
> Whether man is prepared to cope with the increased choice of material and cultural wares available to him is, however, a totally different question. For there comes a time when choice, rather than freeing the individual, becomes so complex, difficult and costly, that it turns into its opposite. There comes a time, in short, when choice turns into overchoice and freedom into unfreedom.

Indeed, the plethora of media voices may be largely responsible for the attitudes which have resulted in the falling level of voter participation that has been so much bemoaned by recent observers. James Reston has said that:

> ... many people seem to be stunned by the torrent of contradictory information that hits them every hour of the day from the radio, the television and the newspapers. It isn't that they don't have enough "facts", but that they are drowned in "facts". ...

Leading political analysts and pollsters for both parties have reported that many voters or potential voters are suffering from an information overload, that the undecided voter may have received more information than the die-hard partisan, and that it is the information overload that causes his indecision.

Any literate person can verify for himself the observation of the editor of the *Detroit Free Press* who wrote that:

> The mix and multiplicity of general, suburban and specialized newspapers; general, local and educational television; general and specialty magazines, radio, movies and the paperback industry will overload, many thousands of times, the available minutes which any individual has available.

The situation has been characterized by the respected reporter James Reston who has said:

> Actually with the rise of television and radio broadcasting stations, the sources of information in the United States have dramatically increased in recent decades, breaking the monopoly of the printing press. ...
> Out of this vast network of stations and newspapers now pours out night and day the greatest flow of information and the loudest clash of divergent opinion ever inflicted on a long suffering people in the history of the written and spoken word.

Fourth, it is manifest that the media do not even approach monopoly status in the United States. But there is one, and only one, true monopoly with far-reaching power in this country. The only real monopoly in the United States is the United States Government.

No matter how the media voices are counted, they are far from a monopoly. There are three national television networks, plus *ad hoc* networks. There are four national radio networks, plus innumerable interconnected stations. There is AP and UPI providing the nation's newspapers with reports, plus numerous Washington newspaper bureaus and correspondents. There are thousands of national magazines and tens of thousands national newsletters, all carrying news of interest to a variety of groups.

Every other nation in the world has government controlled broadcasting and some form or degree of press censorship. The history of the world, including recent history and current events, is so full of examples of repression and oppression by governments that it is needless to mention them. But there is not and has not been in modern times a single person imprisoned for dissident views or a single person oppressed or killed by the mass media. It is the power of government that must be restrained to preserve democracy and human liberty, not the power of the media.

Fifth, the point must be made that of all the government agencies, the FTC is the most inappropriate to investigate or act in the area of the mass media. To begin with, it is structurally unsuited to such a role. The combination of investigatory, prosecutory and adjudicative functions not only tempts abuse but is inherently suspect and gives the impression of unfairness. Whether this structure is appropriate for dealing with the commercial issues that the FTC was established to oversee I do not now consider. Certainly such a structure is peculiarly inappropriate for dealing with the sensitive matters involved in investigating or adjudicating media structure. Both the FCC and the Department of Justice are far superior in this respect. The FCC has a greater separation of functions and a truly adjudicatory appellate review board. The Department of Justice is merely investigatory and prosecutory and is subject to the discipline of presenting and proving its cases before a court. . . .

Finally, it must be noted that, no matter what imperfections the theorists or critics may find in the structure or performance of our mass media, the United States today has a mass media communications system that is the most free, most diverse, most competitive, and the best that has ever existed in history in this or any other country in the world. Indeed, no other country comes even close to this country in the freedom, diversity, competitiveness and efficiency of its mass media.

Of course, our communications system is not perfect; and, of course, it never will be. This is for two inescapable reasons. First, our system is constructed and operated by human beings and all human beings have some imperfections. Second, and possibly more important, there is simply no agreement on what perfection in the mass media would be.

The mass media are certainly not static in any sense. They are changing continuously in response to new technology and new demands and needs of the public. There cannot be any serious doubt that the mass media have steadily been improving for many decades. There is every reason to believe that the mass media in this country will continue to improve unless they are subjected to intervention by the monopoly power of government. It is not the power of the media that the American public must fear but the monopoly power of an ever increasing federal government and expanding federal bureaucracy.

The participants in the debate then took questions from the audience.

MR. LEVITCH: My name is Joel Levitch, and I'm from New York. I'm a free-lance broadcast journalist.

Now, if you are asking yourself why you have never heard anyone ever describe himself as that before, don't worry, I'm the only one in the United States, and I have a confession: I can't make a living.

We have been talking a lot in the last couple of days about entry, as that is a primary consideration in the determination of possible antitrust violations. The fact is that the production and distribution of national news and public affairs programming in this country is a 100 percent entry-proof industry.

Those who try to market national news and public affairs programming to the stations cannot do it economically, and those of us who go to the network and attempt to enter the process at that point are turned away as a matter of policy.

You may remember, in 1974, that Frank Manchiewicz had the undaunted gall to decide that he wanted to be a free-lance broadcast journalist, and he went to Cuba and got an exclusive interview with Mr. Castro. And he took that interview to CBS News and said, "Will you buy this?" And they looked at it and they said, "Mr. Manchiewicz, what we like about this is not your interview and not you. We like the fact that you have access to Fidel Castro. So we'll go back and we'll shoot another show, which we will own and which we will produce. And then we'll show it." I don't know why Mr. Manchiewicz said he would do it, but he did. In the final analysis, CBS bought six minutes of the Manchiewicz original interview, and he had to cancel the balance of the numerous interviews which he had set up.

What does all this mean? I think it's obvious, and I am amazed that in two days no one has brought it up.

It means there are three small groups of men who sit within one square mile of one another in New York City, and who determine who is going to do the analysis of national news and public affairs television programming in this country. I wasn't the first to point this out. There was a famous former vice president, I'm afraid who was the first one to make this case. But it's true.

As a result, 25 film producers have filed an antitrust suit against the networks. And it's my understanding (although we don't have their answers back,) that it will be the networks' claim that we are trampling on their First Amendment rights.

I guess I would ask Mr. Loevinger, whether, in analyzing this in his own mind, he sees this as anything other than the abuse of monopoly power.

MR. LOEVINGER: I think you overstate the case slightly, but I'm willing to assume your premise that three TV networks have control of all the TV programming in the country. It's a goddam sight better than having one government agency; that's what I'm against.

People seem to forget what monopoly power—monopoly is one. Two is not twice as much, two is four times as much, and three is nine times as much as one. Because there's always a chance for rivalry and for change, and indeed, this sort of thing does occur—it does occur. As Don Baker pointed out, there was a time when ABC was way down at the bottom, the despised one-half of not quite a three-network economy. It's now up at the top. It's changed. Whether it's a change for the better or for the worse I leave to everyone's personal judgment. But that's another matter. Change does occur. But, believe me, there's a lot of difference between one and three— and I'm against one. . . . ■

One of the commentators at the symposium was George Reedy, a former press secretary to President Lyndon Johnson. In the same unpretentious, down-to-earth way that he wrote his classic TWILIGHT OF THE PRESIDENCY (World Publishing Co. 1970) Reedy develops his argument here. He worries not about the power of the press but its increasingly "gray" and "characterless" quality; he thinks that this follows from the increasing concentration of the press. His conclusion, then, appears to be that the trend toward media concentration will not make the press more influential but less so.

IRRELEVANCE, NOT MONOPOLY, IS THE PROBLEM

George Reedy, from Comments to Federal Trade Commission, 1978

The only thing I'm going to try to do in this brief 10 minutes is to look at this problem from a different standpoint. There is a tendency, which philosophers and psychologists have been commenting on for about 3000 years, for human beings to consider current problems in terms of conditions 10 or 20 years earlier. I have a strong feeling we may be doing that today.

There is also a tendency on the part of human beings when they discuss a problem to discuss it *in vacuo*—in this particular instance, as though the press were "an island, complete unto itself."

Actually for a number of reasons, I think we may be talking about an institution which is no longer what we assume it to be in our descriptions and also an institution that is something of a museum piece.

This thought came to me when I looked at Ben's paper and started to list the evils of monopoly that he outlines. I agree that those evils, the evils of monopoly, definitely exist. But it's very difficult for me to make the assumption which is implicit in his first paragraph, that we live in a society of greater violence today than we did 50 years ago, and that the press to some extent has a responsibility for that violence.

There may have been less violence 50 years ago where Ben grew up but not where I grew up in an area where half of the inscription on the Church of the Holy Name was shot off by a series of bullets that missed their intended victim, a gentleman named Hymie Weiss.

In the next paragraph I see that millions of Americans are growing up without personal knowledge of other Americans, who have a different skin color or ethnic background or economic class. Again, Ben does not think the situation was this bad 50 years ago and he assumes that the press has some responsibility for it.

I grew up in a part of Chicago where I didn't discover until I was 12 years old that I was living in the United States rather than the Republic of Ireland; and that the national anthem was "The Star-Spangled Banner" rather than the "The Wearing of the Green" or "The Shean Bhean Beacht." Other ethnic groups were regarded as "the enemy" and I doubt whether I saw any black man who wasn't shining shoes until I was full grown. But my sons have no consciousness of ethnic identity and went to school with blacks as a matter of course. We have not reached ideals of brotherhood but we are better off than we were 50 years ago.

I come to the next paragraph which says that obviously the press must have tremendous influence on human behavior; otherwise people wouldn't advertise in it. It seems to me it's perfectly obvious that it's the other way around, that in 99 percent of the American press today—and there are some exceptions—the part of the newspaper that moves the people is precisely the advertising. It is often more interesting than the news columns.

Let me give you an example. On Wednesday, when the *Milwaukee Journal* puts out its food paper, which contains the super market advertising, if one wishes to buy a copy at a street sale, it is absolutely essential to make an advance arrangement with the local drug store. Furthermore, it is necessary to be a permanent customer of that drug store in order to have the privilege.

In one respect the American press has gotten back to what it was originally. The early colonial press was really nothing but a collection of editorials, accompanied by little or no news other than advertisements for the sale of slaves, the sale of rum, and the sale of tobacco—the three things in which our ancestors were the most interested.

When I look at the monopolization of the press, I don't like it. There are many things about the press that appall me, as a second generation newspaperman. The two top impressions I get are:

One, it has become dull.

And, two, it has become irrelevant to our daily lives.

I'm not at all concerned about the brainwashing impact of the press, the monopoly press. It seems to me that in the last 10 years I have attended 40 to 50 conferences in which people who believe they have been brainwashed by the press, have been brainwashed into believing that it's great to protest the "brainwashing of the press." I cannot help but wonder what impels them to protest brainwashing when they have been brainwashed already. There is a flaw in that logic somewhere. Such meetings always begin by admonishing the press against oversensitivity.

Second, the meetings admonish the press that they are not exempt from the laws of the land and they cannot hide behind the First Amendment.

And then after that the meetings suggest that it's a very bad situation and we should draw up some antimonopoly legislation.

Personally, I think we ought to be kindlier to the press, because when I see it, to a great extent, I'm reminded of one of Dennis Brogan's lines, "One tips one's hat as when a funeral passes by."

The outstanding factor of the press, and if I were a publisher, this is what I would worry about—is its irrelevance.

Most of the press today—and again I would except some papers, the same ones that Ben did, and a couple of others—should be the same way I go through the card catalog at a public library. It gives me a series of topics. If I am interested in those topics, what I do then is go to other sources of information which are quite readily available, to find out what I regard as that which I need to know.

I think it's very instructive to look at the experience of cities that have been totally deprived of newspapers for a considerable period of time. It's amazing how quickly those cities adjust to life without newspapers. Pittsburgh, Detroit, New York—and one really cannot say that television is an adequate substitute for the press. It doesn't carry the "Dear Abby" column. It doesn't carry the crossword puzzle. It doesn't carry the want ads which are really a form of news.

What is happening today is, however much the press may once have influenced American thought, it certainly does not influence it now. All one has to do is to look at the attitudes of newspapers in any part of the country, and the attitudes of the votes when they go to the polls.

I think that we are developing totally new means of communication which are outside of the press. They rise in all sorts of interesting fashions some of them rather obscure.

As a general rule, I doubt whether large numbers of people ever got most of their information from the press, anyway. It's my belief that the average citizen is informed by other citizens, who in turn are informed by other citizens, who in turn are informed by other citizens and ultimately you do get to somebody that reads the press, reads the newspapers, listens to all the television programs, reads all the magazines. You run into them every day at lunch. They have their pockets stuffed full of clippings, they know more about Outer Mongolia than Cy Vance does and they are better informed on the common market than the Secretary of the Treasury. . . .

I believe what is going to happen to us is that the trend toward concentration is going to continue. That as it continues, there is going to be increasing characterlessness of the press.

What we are talking about as the press now is going to become, by and by, largely the announcement feature of our society, like the old Acta Diurna, that were posted on the walls of the Roman Forum in the times of the Caesars to announce the decisions of the Roman Senate. We are in the business right now, of developing alternative means of communication, strangely enough through institutions we don't even think of in these terms. We are working through all kinds of newsletters, through organizations that keep their members informed of all sorts of things; through college lectures. If you go into any college campus in the United States in the evening, you'll find little groups of earnest citizens, listening to lectures on Tibet, on Germany, or the common market, on any issue that you can think of. The listeners go out the next day and they spread the word.

The one last point that I want to make involves a phenomenon that has really puzzled me. Ben Bagdikian, a few years ago, wrote an article on the tremendous surplus of journalism students in regard to jobs. The facts of life are that most journalism students get jobs and get them fairly quickly when they graduate. They do not get them in newspapers, no. But what is happening in our society is that those journalism students are picking up jobs in other forms of communication, which include public relations, which include advertising, which include newsletters, which include internal communications.

I think that what we have got to do here is to try to reverse something which cannot be reversed, to start examining our society for these alternative forms of communication to see what they are doing; where they are going; and how we can continue to be a free people with a really healthy vigorous dialogue—something that does not exist in today's press. ■

Anyone interested in pursuing the question of media concentration should consult Morton Mintz and Jerry Cohen's AMERICA, INC. (Dell, 1971) for a detailed discussion of how and why the media have become concentrated. Jack Newfield and Jeff Greenfield's A POPULIST MANIFESTO (Praeger, 1972) also discusses the problem and offers solutions. On the other side, former CBS President John D. Backe argued along the same lines as Lee Loevinger in an article in the March/April 1978 issue of *Society* magazine; he suggested that the media are far more diverse than their critics allege. Backe wrote this article before he was fired from CBS by Chairman William Paley.

The arguments about diversity in the media have to be seen in the context of the whole society, including the governing organs of the society. If the media are so powerful as to constitute an unelected, monolithic, and unaccountable form of government, then it can be forcefully argued that there is a need for greater diversity and competition. But if it is the other way around—if the government is so strong as to be able to intimidate the media—then what is really important is that the media be strengthened in order to resist government pressure. Big government, it could then be argued, requires a big media establishment to balance it. But big media are, by definition, concentrated and unified media.

One can see the drift of this argument. It tends toward the conclusion that diversity in media is not necessarily good. Such an argument turns upon the question of how powerful our media actually are, especially when seen in relation to the national government. To some observers, our nation's lawmakers seem so awed by the presence of the media, and cowed by the pressure of the media, that America can almost be said to be governed by the media. To others, however, the trouble is that the media have too little power and the government too much.

As a case study of the relative power of the press and government in America, the Pentagon Papers controversy of 1971 offers students of the media a view of what can happen when the most influential newspapers in the nation embark on a collision course with the executive branch of the federal government.

CHAPTER 3

Do the Media Have Too Much Power; or Not Enough?

"I have seen a senior aide to a President, sitting over an early morning cup of coffee, rise and literally punch the front page of the *New York Times*." Daniel P. Moynihan, United States Senator from New York, recalled this scene in an article he wrote for *Commentary* magazine in 1971. At that time he was serving as an advisor to President Richard Nixon.

The Nixon administration openly fought the press. Today the tension lies more below the surface, but it shows itself in occasional bitter jibes from Presidents and their staff. One of President Carter's aides used to talk about "the imperial press," and President Reagan, while still a candidate in 1980 complained about an "incestuous" relationship between reporters for the various newspapers, implying that a cabal of some sort exists among them.

What seems to annoy politicians most about the press is that it wields power without ever having to face the voters. "Who elected these guys, anyway?," said Patrick Buchanan, one of Nixon's advisors. The question assumes that members of the media are doing more than reporting the news. The assumption is that they are also making news, wielding power without having to account for it to the voters. Is it true that the press has really become a powerful organ of government?

This question became central to critics of the media after the *New York Times* began publishing the Pentagon Papers in 1971.

The Story of the Pentagon Papers

The story of the Pentagon Papers goes back to 1967, when Robert McNamara, President Johnson's Secretary of Defense, began having second thoughts about American involvement in Vietnam. He assembled a special "task force" and asked its members to write a review of U.S. involvement, which stretched back to the late 1940s. He advised them to "let the chips fall where they may." The result was a mammoth study—in forty-seven volumes—which documented the role of American policymakers in deceiving the American public, casually disregarding both national and international law, cynically sending young men off to fight a war which the decision-makers conceded was unwinnable, manipulating both the press and the Congress, and knowingly inflicting terrible losses on the civilian population of Vietnam.

The report was stamped "top secret," but one member of the task force was determined to make it public. His name was Daniel Ellsberg.

Ellsberg, an employee of the RAND corporation (a Defense Department "think tank") had once been a passionate hawk, but shortly after visiting Vietnam he underwent a change of heart. Being one of the compilers of the Pentagon Papers, Ellsberg had easy access to it; he smuggled it out and photocopied all 7,000 pages of it. After some unsuccessful attempts to persuade members of Congress to make it public, he passed a copy to the *New York Times*. Three months later the *Times* began publishing parts of it.

Why the three months delay? During that time the newspaper had a special team sifting through it, deciding which were the best parts to print. It may be that nobody will ever know the bases on which those decisions were made, for the whole operation was kept top secret. A special room was set aside for it, and those who worked on it were sworn to secrecy. In other words, the *Times* behaved very much like the government, and demanded the same loyalty from its staff.

Once the *Times* started publishing the Pentagon Papers the Nixon administration asked a District Court judge to restrain any further publication pending a hearing on the merits. The judge granted the injunction—the first time in American history that a newspaper was restrained in advance by a court from publishing a specific article.

What were the merits of the case? The government argued that the Pentagon Papers were stamped "top secret" for good reason: they contained information which, if made public, could do irreparable harm to the security of the United States. The *Times* countered that none of the material which it published or planned to publish was of such a nature, although a lot of it could be embarrassing to those who got us into Vietnam. Indeed, this was the issue. Had the government been using its "top secret" stamp, not to protect the nation but to save the hides of politicians and bureaucrats? Was it now continuing the coverup at the expense of the First Amendment?

The *Times*' lawyers conceded that, if Ellsberg had given them material whose publication would cause the loss of a war or the death of American soldiers, the newspaper would be duty bound not to publish it. Well, then, how did the *Times* know that some of *this* material was not of such a nature? Because, the *Times* answered, we went through it carefully and decided that it was not. But who is the better judge of what should be kept secret, the government or the *Times*? And if the *Times* can set itself up as a judge of such matters, isn't it acting like a government? Isn't it, in fact, usurping the power of government?

Those were among the questions raised by the dissenting justices in the case of *New York Times Company v. United States*. The case was decided by the Supreme Court, with unusual haste, two weeks after the original restraining order was served on the newspaper. (By this time Ellsberg had also leaked a copy of the Pentagon Papers to the *Washington Post*. The government, after being turned down by a lower court, secured a restraining order from a Court of Appeals after the *Post* began printing excerpts from the Papers. The *Post*, then, appeared with the *Times* in this case.) For the majority of the Court the real issue was whether the First Amendment protected newspapers against prior restraint by the government. By a margin of six to three the Court ruled that it did.

Though the justices divided into a majority and a minority, they all had such different views that each wrote a separate opinion. Below are three of those opinions.

THE PRESS SERVES THE GOVERNED, NOT THE GOVERNORS

Justice Black's opinion, from New York Times Co. v. U.S., 1971

. . . In my view it is unfortunate that some of my Brethren are apparently willing to hold that the publication of news may sometimes be enjoined. Such a holding would make a shambles of the First Amendment.

Our Government was launched in 1789 with the adoption of the Constitution. The Bill of Rights, including the First Amendment, followed in 1791. Now, for the first time in the 182 years since the founding of the Republic, the federal courts are asked to hold that the First Amendment does not mean what it says, but rather means that the Government can halt the publication of current news of vital importance to the people of this country.

In seeking injunctions against these newspapers and in its presentation to the Court, the Executive Branch seems to have forgotten the essential purpose and history of the First Amendment. When the Constitution was adopted, many people strongly opposed it because the document contained no Bill of Rights to safeguard certain basic freedoms. They especially feared that the new powers granted to a central government might be interpreted to permit the government to curtail freedom of religion, press, assembly, and speech. In response to an overwhelming public clamor, James Madison offered a series of amendments to satisfy citizens that these great liberties would remain safe and beyond the power of government to abridge. Madison proposed what later became the First Amendment in three parts, two of which are set out below, and one of which proclaimed:

"The people shall not be deprived or abridged of their right to speak, to write, or to publish their sentiments; *and the freedom of the press, as one of the great bulwarks of liberty, shall be inviolable."* The amendments were offered to *curtail* and *restrict* the general powers granted to the Executive, Legislative, and Judicial Branches two years before in the original Constitution. The Bill of Rights changed the original Constitution into a new charter under which no branch of government could abridge the people's freedoms of press, speech, religion, and assembly. Yet the Solicitor General argues and some members of the Court appear to agree that the general powers of the Government adopted in the original Constitution should be interpreted to limit and restrict the specific and emphatic guarantees of the Bill of Rights adopted later. I can imagine no greater perversion of history. Madison and the other Framers of the First Amendment, able men that they were, wrote in language they earnestly believed could never be misunderstood: "Congress shall make no law . . . abridging the freedom . . . of the press . . ." Both the history and language of the First Amendment support the view that the press must be left free to publish news, whatever the source, without censorship, injunctions, or prior restraints.

In the First Amendment the Founding Fathers gave the free press the protection it must have to fulfill its essential role in our democracy. The press was to serve the governed, not the governors. The Government's power to censor the press was abolished so that the press would remain forever free to censure the Government. The press was protected so that it could bare the secrets of government and inform the people. Only a free and unrestrained press can effectively expose deception in government. And paramount among the responsibilities of a free press is the duty to prevent any part of the government from deceiving the people and sending them off to distant lands to die of foreign fevers and foreign shot and shell. In my view, far from deserving condemnation for their courageous reporting, the New York Times, the Washington Post, and other newspapers should be commended for serving the purpose that the Founding Fathers saw so clearly. In revealing the workings of government that led to the Vietnam war, the newspapers nobly did precisely that which the Founders hoped and trusted they would do. ■

THE DUTY TO RETURN STOLEN PROPERTY

Chief Justice Burger's Dissent

... The newspapers make a derivative claim under the First Amendment; they denominate this right as the public "right to know"; by implication, the Times asserts a sole trusteeship of that right by virtue of its journalistic "scoop." The right is asserted as an absolute. Of course, the First Amendment right itself is not an absolute, as Justice Holmes so long ago pointed out in his aphorism concerning the right to shout "fire" in a crowded theater if there was no fire. There are other exceptions, some of which Chief Justice Hughes mentioned by way of example in Near v. Minnesota ex rel. Olson. There are no doubt other exceptions no one has had occasion to describe or discuss. Conceivably such exceptions may be lurking in these cases and would have been flushed had they been properly considered in the trial courts, free from unwarranted deadlines and frenetic pressures. An issue of this importance should be tried and heard in a judicial atmosphere conducive to thoughtful, reflective deliberation, especially when haste, in terms of hours, is unwarranted in light of the long period the Times, by its own choice, deferred publication.

It is not disputed that the Times has had unauthorized possession of the documents for three to four months, during which it has had its expert analysts studying them, presumably digesting them and preparing the material for publication. During all of this time, the Times, presumably in its capacity as trustee of the public's "right to know," has held up publication for purposes it considered proper and thus public knowledge was delayed. No doubt this was for a good reason; the analysis of 7,000 pages of complex material drawn from a vastly greater volume of material would inevitably take time and the writing of good news stories takes time. But why should the United States Government, from whom this information was illegally acquired by someone, along with all the counsel, trial judges, and appellate judges be placed under needless pressure? After these months of deferral, the alleged "right to know" has somehow and suddenly become a right that must be vindicated instanter.

Would it have been unreasonable, since the newspaper could anticipate the Government's objections to release of secret material, to give the Government an opportunity to review the entire collection and determine whether agreement could be reached on publication? Stolen or not, if security was not in fact jeopardized, much of the material could no doubt have been declassified, since it spans a period ending in 1968. With such an approach—one that great newspapers have in the past practiced and stated editorially to be the duty of an honorable press—the newspapers and Government might well have narrowed the area of disagreement as to what was and was not publishable, leaving the remainder to be resolved in orderly litigation, if necessary. To me it is hardly believable that a newspaper long regarded as a great institution in American life would fail to perform one of the basic and simple duties of every citizen with respect to the discovery or possession of stolen property or secret government documents. That duty, I had thought—perhaps naively—was to report forthwith, to responsible public officers. This duty rests on taxi drivers, Justices, and the New York Times. . . . ■

THE COURT HAS ACTED IRRESPONSIBLY

Justice Harlan's Dissent

. . . With all respect, I consider that the Court has been almost irresponsibly feverish in dealing with these cases.

Both the Court of Appeals for the Second Circuit and the Court of Appeals for the District of Columbia Circuit rendered judgment on June 23. The New York Times' petition for certiorari, its motion for accelerated consideration thereof, and its application for interim relief were filed in this Court on June 24 at about 11 a.m. The application of the United States for interim relief in the *Post* case was also filed here on June 24 at about 7:15 p.m. This Court's order setting a hearing before us on June 26 at 11 a.m., a course which I joined only to avoid the possibility of even more peremptory action by the Court, was issued less than 24 hours before. The record in the *Post* case was filed with the Clerk shortly before 1 p. m. on June 25; the record in the *Times* case did not arrive until 7 or 8 o'clock that same night. The briefs of the parties were received less than two hours before argument on June 26.

This frenzied train of events took place in the name of the presumption against prior restraints created by the First Amendment. Due regard for the extraordinarily important and difficult questions involved in these litigations should have led the Court to shun such a precipitate timetable. . . .

Forced as I am to reach the merits of these cases, I dissent from the opinion and judgments of the Court. Within the severe limitations imposed by the time constraints under which I have been required to operate, I can only state my reasons in telescoped form, even though in different circumstances I would have felt constrained to deal with the cases in the fuller sweep indicated above.

It is a sufficient basis for affirming the Court of Appeals for the Second Circuit in the *Times* litigation to observe that its order must rest on the conclusion that because of the time elements the Government had not been given an adequate opportunity to present its case to the District Court. At the least this conclusion was not an abuse of discretion.

In the *Post* litigation the Government had more time to prepare; this was apparently the basis for the refusal of the Court of Appeals for the District of Columbia Circuit on rehearing to conform its judgment to that of the Second Circuit. But I think there is another and more fundamental reason why this judgment cannot stand—a reason which also furnishes an additional ground for not reinstating the judgment of the District Court in the *Times* litigation, set aside by the Court of Appeals. It is plain to me that the scope of the judicial function in passing upon the activities of the Executive Branch of the Government in the field of foreign affairs is very narrowly restricted. This view is, I think, dictated by the concept of separation of powers upon which our constitutional system rests.

In a speech on the floor of the House of Representatives, Chief Justice John Marshall, then a member of that body, stated:

> "The President is the sole organ of the nation in its external relations, and its sole representative with foreign nations." 10 Annals of Cong. 613.

From that time, shortly after the founding of the Nation, to this, there has been no substantial challenge to this description of the scope of executive power. . . .

Even if there is some room for the judiciary to override the executive determination, it is plain that the scope of review must be exceedingly narrow. I can see no indication in the opinions of either the District Court or the Court of Appeals in the *Post* litigation that the conclusions of the Executive were given even the deference owing to an administrative agency, much less that owing to a co-equal branch of the Government operating within the field of its constitutional prerogative. ■

The issue of the media's exercise—some would say usurpation—of Governmental powers, is a topic of concern for many commentators.

Tom Bethell, a Washington editor of *Harper's* and *The American Spectator*, is convinced that the media, especially the prestigious Eastern newspapers like the *New York Times* and the *Washington Post*, have become "departments of the federal bureaucracy." He outlines this view in the following article.

WE'RE GOVERNED BY THE MEDIA

Tom Bethell from "The Myth of an Adversary Press", *Harper's*, January 1977

. . . The news media have now become a part of the government in all but formal constitutional ratification of the fact. For all intents and purposes, the *New York Times* or CBS News can best be understood as departments of the federal bureaucracy.

I do not wish to adopt an accusatory tone—to speak with the voice of Spiro Agnew. It may well be that the new media-government alliance is a good one, all things considered. It almost certainly is unavoidable, given the technology upon which it relies. It is, however, a new combination—one that could not have been foreseen by the framers of the Constitution—and my concern is simply to try and describe it, not an easy task, given that media and government alternately dance together in close embrace, and break apart to make confusing gestures of mutual defiance. Much of the time what we are witnessing is the equivalent of a marathon dance, in which media and government lean on each other because they need each other to survive and prosper. . . .

The Pentagon Papers case provided the media with an opportunity to preempt government policy. It is worth recalling that the episode began when Daniel Ellsberg, a former Pentagon and RAND corporation employee, handed copies of the Papers to Neil Sheehan, a *Times* reporter. This points up a rather neglected fact—that being an "investigative reporter," in its most essential phase, is purely passive, a matter of being on the receiving end of a phone call, a classified document.

The Pentagon Papers had been classified top secret by the Executive Branch, and since publishing them would be equivalent to declassifying them, the *Times's* editors found themselves immediately faced with a decision normally made by government. In order to make this decision, the paper instituted a proceeding that can only be described as the newsroom Cabinet meeting—one of the most striking developments in the media in recent years. Sanford Ungar, in his book THE PAPERS AND THE PAPERS, provides an interesting account of these meetings, although without fully seeming to realize the extent to which he was describing the usurpation of government function by the media. Ungar notes that the *Times's* foreign editor, James L. Greenfield, "a man with State Department experience during the Kennedy Administration," was given "overall charge of the assignment," which, in accordance with the media's imitation of government, was given the bureaucratic code name "Project X." He quotes Greenfield as follows: "What I tried to do from the very beginning, and what Abe [Rosenthal] wanted me to do . . . was really to revert back *as if I was in the government,* what would I think [of the material] and the consequences of publication.' " (My italics.) In effect, of course, Greenfield *was* once again in the government.

Later on, after a court injunction had temporarily stopped the *Times's* series on the Papers, the *Washington Post* got them and they immediately began *their* newsroom Cabinet meeting, although this time, as Ungar notes, "The *Post's* decision-making processes took place in the living room and an adjoining library in [executive editor Ben] Bradlee's house." He added that "in its own assessment of how to avoid endangering national security, the *Post* made a *policy decision* not to quote any diplomatic or military cables fully and not to name any CIA agents." (My italics.) And as Ben Bagdikian, a press critic who resembles many press critics in often seeming more like a press cheerleader, would later write: "They were competent judges of what was dangerous to the country and what was not; they handled this kind of information every day."

So there it was. Editors, feeling that they had the "competence" to override the government, overrode it. Later on the Supreme Court upheld this new relationship between the press and the government, with only Justice John Harlan taking due note of the new constitutional arrangement. . . .

Harlan noted—and it is surely hard to refute him on "strict" constitutional grounds—that the Executive Branch's determination of what should be considered secret deserves preference over the media's determination. "Even if there is some room for the Judiciary to override the Executive determination," he wrote, "it is plain that the scope of review must be exceedingly narrow. I can see no indication in the opinions of either the District Court or the Court of Appeals in the *Post* litigation that the conclusions of the Executive were given even the deference owing to an administrative agency, much less that owing to a co-equal branch of government operating within the field of its constitutional prerogative."

In practice, however, the problem with this argument is that the Constitution has a way of meaning whatever public opinion wants it to mean, and by the time the Pentagon Papers case had arrived at the Supreme Court, the opposition of the government to the publication of the Papers had had the effect of amplifying the story enormously within the echo chambers of the media, which operate at maximum volume when opposition to media policies exists.

Once again Sanford Ungar was perhaps unconsciously revealing when he wrote about the Pentagon Papers struggle:

> Hand in hand with elation at the *Post* was a sense of anticipation for any government moves against the newspaper. Although legal action would be expensive and potentially threatening, half the excitement of the story had become the *Times's* confrontation with the government over freedom of the press; the case before Judge Gurfein was already a major front-page story in the *Post*. No one at the *Post* was saying it publicly, but the editors—and especially Bradlee, who delights in a good fight—would have been disappointed if the Justice Department had not dragged their newspaper into court too.

Precisely. The opposition of government not merely has the effect of intensifying the story—causing it to resonate in the media echo chamber with melodramatic denials, rebuttals, and injunctions—it also has the effect of changing it to one of government secrecy versus the people's right to know, and in this confrontation the media must always triumph, because they have securely in their grasp the means of forming a public opinion sympathetic to their cause. . . .

It is, surely, simply absurd to claim that the framers of the Constitution intended anything like this to happen, notwithstanding the tendency by newsmen of late to place some such interpretation on the First Amendment. As a counterbalance to this propaganda—there is no other word for it—perhaps we should recall some remarks about the press made by Thomas Jefferson in a letter, written in 1803, to Governor McKean of Pennsylvania. Jefferson was upset at the time because he considered the credibility of the press was being undermined by "its licentiousness and its lying," and that the best solution to the problem might be "a few prosecutions of the most prominent offenders. . . . Not a general prosecution, for that would look like persecution; but a selected one."

The media today, of course, no more resemble the press of Jefferson's day than an atom bomb resembles a platoon of barefoot militia, so the appropriate interpretation of the First Amendment is, as it were, up for grabs; and, because they very largely control public opinion with the same channels of communication that they use to present the news, the news media have done a very effective job of imposing an interpretation that is congenial to them. This interpretation may be briefly summarized as follows: in the media's dealings with government, secrecy is good; but in the government's internal dealings, secrecy is bad.

It is interesting to note that in what is, I believe, the only reference to the press in the Federalist Papers, Alexander Hamilton wrote: "What is liberty of the press? Who can give it any definition which would not leave the utmost latitude for evasion? I hold it to be impracticable; and from this I infer that its security, whatever fine declarations may be inserted in any Constitution respecting it, must altogether depend on public opinion," an opinion which must encourage quiet smiles of satisfaction among those people who own or control the means of producing public opinion. . . .

GOVERNMENT BY THE MEDIA

Although we clearly do now have something very close to a new system of government, in which editors holding the equivalent of oversight cabinet meetings have left the pamphleteers with portable presses ("No Taxation Without Representation!") very far behind, it is not so clear that our present system is thereby a bad one. It is preferable, surely, to the British system, under which, for example, sternly upheld libel laws prohibited publication of damaging information about the drug Thalidomide. There is not even any question that it is better than the press of the totalitarian regimes. By and large it is no doubt true that the "policy decisions" of our prominent editors and media executives are responsibly arrived at, even if not constitutionally foreseen. The *New York Time's* decision to declassify (in effect) the Pentagon Papers was almost certainly more thoughtfully arrived at than the Executive's decision to classify them in the first place. . . .

But what is undeniable, as a result of the recent struggles between media and government, is that the media [have] emerged with vastly more power. This power is not a power greater than government's, but one that is indistinguishable from it. Government and media figures are increasingly interchangeable anyway, just as their roles are symbiotic. Even their pay is comparable. And there is an ever-increasing exchange between the two camps; James Greenfield goes in one direction, Henry Wallich in the other. When Air Force One lands and a cluster of figures emerges from the plane, who is media, who is government? One group gets headlines, the other bylines. Both enjoy the same daily "fix." So a parity between the two has developed, and it is a relatively recent development. Journalists in Washington today play an ex officio policy role that would have been unrecognizable in the bad old days (recalled by some journalists with an understandable shudder of distaste) when their badge of office was a green eyeshade and a whiskey bottle on the desk. Armed, now, with a novel interpretation of the First Amendment that has shifted the locus of acceptable secrecy, they will not easily surrender their new importance. It translates into wealth and social status, after all. Proximity to power in Washington has always conferred status, and today important journalists do not merely have proximity, they have the real thing. . . . ■

Looking back on the case of the Pentagon Papers, *New York Times* columnist Tom Wicker argues that such examples "are exceptions to rather than examples of the rule." He specifically takes issue with Tom Bethell in the course of developing his point that there exist a number of limitations on the power of the press, especially on the power of the press to disclose the secret machinations of government.

POWER OF THE PRESS — FAR FROM ABSOLUTE

Tom Wicker, from ON PRESS (New York, 1978)

. . . In the late fall of 1967 General William C. Westmoreland, the Army Commander in Vietnam, and Ambassador Ellsworth Bunker came home from Saigon to tell the nation that its unpopular Southeast Asian war slowly was being won. In public statements and private sessions with reporters, businessmen, members of Congress, the two officials delivered the message—the corner was being turned, light was visible at the end of the tunnel.

Some time after these couriers had returned to Vietnam, I had a visitor in my corner office at the *New York Times* bureau in Washington; I was then still the bureau chief. He was brought in by Neil Sheehan, the *Times's* Pentagon correspondent in 1967, and I vaguely remembered him—Dan Ellsberg, the militant young ex-Marine I had first met when following Hubert Humphrey around Saigon in 1966. He explained that he was working in the Pentagon as an employee of the Rand Corporation, a "think-tank" heavily involved in defense research.

"You guys have been conned," Ellsberg told me. When I asked him what he meant, he laid out in some detail what I thought was an appalling story.

Westmoreland and Bunker, he said, had come to the United States strictly for propaganda purposes. What's more, the figures they had publicized—villages under control, Viet Cong killed, captured, or defecting, all the then-familiar lists of Vietnam quantifiers—had been hoked up for best effect.

"You should have seen what they *wanted* to tell you," Ellsberg said. The first figures Bunker and Westmoreland had cabled to the Pentagon were so wild, he said, no one in Washington would have believed them for a moment. Whereupon, he went on, Pentagon officials aware of the rising skepticism of the Washington press had cabled back to Saigon that the figures had to be revised downward if they were to have any credibility at all. As Ellsberg told the story, the cables had flown back and forth until agreement had been reached on what the traffic would bear—the level of statistical claims Bunker and Westmoreland could foist off on the American public with plausibility. These, of course, were the figures those of us in the press had been reporting in good faith as representing the factual situation in Vietnam, as described by the commanding general and the ambassador.

I had been skeptical of the Westmoreland-Bunker performance anyway and I could see right away the significance of Ellsberg's story; so could Sheehan. If we could print documentary proof of the deception Ellsberg was alleging, the pretense that the war was being won would be shattered, an administration already lacking basic credibility would be in deep political trouble, and the war might even become insupportable.

"Can you get copies of those cables for us?" I asked Ellsberg.

A slender, intense young man, looking then much as he did when he later became famous, Ellsberg seemed almost to recoil from my suggestion. Of course not, he said; the cables were Top Secret.

"But they'd prove the government's been lying," I argued.

Ellsberg said he could vouch for *that*. He'd seen those cables; from them and from other evidence, he knew what he was talking about.

"Your word's just not enough," I told him. "It wouldn't prove anything by itself. They'd just call you a liar, or too emotionally involved. And the *Times* wouldn't print a story making a charge that serious unless we could document it."

This seemed to surprise Ellsberg, who'd apparently thought a "leak" of this magnitude would produce immediate headlines. Still, he would not agree to procure the cables. He thought he could go to jail if he did—that releasing Top Secret material was against the law.

In fact, releasing the cables probably would not have been against the law, so far as the law is clear; but in that relatively innocent period, neither Ellsberg nor I knew it. We both thought that classification of documents was a serious matter and believed that anyone violating the rules controlling such documents obviously was breaking the law. As a young Navy officer, I'd briefly been in charge of classified materials—code books and the like— at a base in Japan; and I remembered the rigorous logging and checking procedures for which I'd been responsible and the solemn warnings of superiors that I could be court-martialed for mishandling or losing any of those weapons manuals, code books, and other documents. At the least, I believed, Ellsberg could lose his security clearance, hence his job, by producing those cables for us and getting caught at it; at worst, neither he nor I then doubted, he might go to prison.

Nevertheless, and recognizing that it was he who would take the risk, I made him a strenuous argument that if (a) the government was lying and (b) he could produce the cables as irrefutable proof of it, then (c) maybe the war he and I had come to abhor could be greatly affected, even brought to an end. So (d) he had a duty as a concerned citizen to try to put those cables in our hands. For my part—it was *easy to promise*—I could guarantee prominent play in the most prestigious newspaper in the country, plus absolute, unyielding protection of the identity of the source of the documents.

Long afterward, Dan Ellsberg told me this argument had impressed him, perhaps even started him on the road to release of the Pentagon Papers three years later. Looking back on it, in the light of all that's transpired since, I'm not sure I'd argue as strongly as I did then. It's just *too easy* to urge someone else to take such risks as I then thought were involved; and I have a clearer sense now of the lengths to which the government may go in tracking down such leaks and punishing the culprit. In any case, even the Pentagon Papers didn't stop or materially affect the course of a war two administrations were determined to wage. I think I overstated to Ellsberg both the possibilities of publication and his duty to bring it about. Worse, the likelihood is that my zeal for a major story out of our bureau was a greater influence on me at the time than I recognized.

Ellsberg eventually produced one cable, from Saigon to Washington, apparently the first in the series he had told us about; and while it tended to bear out his story, the crucial need was for the whole series of cables showing how the fake figures for publication had been bargained out between the two capitals. Ellsberg couldn't get hold of the rest of the cables, and ultimately the story eluded us—only to be subsumed in the Tet offensive, which soon did more to turn the public against the war than any newspaper story could have.

The story of the cables we couldn't print provides at least one kind of answer to a question that in one form or another is frequently heard nowadays: Who elected the press?

Put another way—if the press can decide for itself what to publish, whether the government wants it published or not, what check *is* there upon the power of the press?

Because of its constitutional sanction in the First Amendment, on one hand, and because of its supposed power to affect public opinion, on the other, many people have come to believe that the press—more often "the media"—is the least checked and controlled of all American institutions. It has been called "the fourth branch of government," which is largely true, and sensible men believe that its power is sufficient to overcome or shake the powers of the other three. Such power, if it existed, would be ominous indeed.

As I have said, my belief instead is that —in my lifetime at least—"despite the freedom conferred by the Constitution, the American press operated under severe limitations, inherent in its nature and that of the country, which effectively restrained the power derived from freedom."

These limitations may not be readily seen—particularly by those who feel their privacy invaded or their policies inhibited by a sometimes bumptious press. They exist, nevertheless. Sometimes, as in the case of the widely accepted "Eastern press conspiracy" popularized first by Goldwater, then by Nixon and Agnew (and more or less credited by Lyndon Johnson), the situation is the reverse of the common view.

The publishers and editors of, say, *The New York Times, The Washington Post, Newsweek, Time,* and *The Boston Globe,* together with the chieftans of the television networks, *may* have generally similar political and social views—although even that is a dubious proposition, considering the range of attitudes among executives like William S. Paley of CBS and Andrew Heiskell of Time, Inc., and editors like John B. Oakes of *The New York Times* (until December 31, 1976) or Osborn Elliott, formerly of *Newsweek.* It's true that Katharine Graham, as head of the Washington Post Company, publishes both the *Post* and *Newsweek,* and that Heiskell is married to the former Marian Sulzberger Dryfoos, a member of the board of directors and the sister of the publisher of *The New York Times.*

To make a "conspiracy" out of such thin stuff is ridiculous; even Agnew usually charged no more than a "fraternity," and that, among other things, slighted Mrs. Graham. But even the idea of a fraternity—a sort of publishers' club—falls of its own weight as soon as the sometimes savage competition between the television networks is realized, or in any analysis of the *Post's* determined drive to equal or replace the *Times* as the nation's leading newspaper. Does Macy's conspire with Gimbels? Neither do Ben Bradlee and Abe Rosenthal. To suppose, as Richard Nixon did, that such hard-charging competitors together "decided that they would have to take that particular line"—to "get Nixon," he meant—is simply paranoid. If the "fraternity" ever made such a decision, why did the rest of the members leave it mostly to Bradlee and the *Post* to try to "get Nixon" for Watergate during the crucial months from June 1972 until the election in November?

But the real point is that the exact opposite of "conspiracy" or "fraternity"—competition—is a major limitation on the power of the press in America. Agnew was not wrong to assert that because of closings and mergers of newspapers over the years, "many, many strong independent voices have been stilled in this country." Obviously, the nation is the poorer for the loss of the New York *Herald Tribune*, *Life*, the *Saturday Evening Post*. The twelve dailies that were being published in New York City before the long newspaper strike of 1963 have been sadly reduced to three. But there is much evidence that the trend toward newspaper failures has been reversed and that newspapers are flourishing in America—at last count 1768 dailies plus any number of weeklies and semi-weeklies. However, 97.5 percent of the dailies have no in-town competition and there are fewer than fifty American cities with competing daily newspapers.

Newspaper independence also has been diminishing in another sense—the growing prevalence of chain ownership. In 1930, only 16 percent of American daily newspapers, with 43 percent of total daily circulation, were chain-operated. By 1960, 30 percent of all dailies, with 46 percent of circulation, had been brought into chains; today, 60 percent of all dailies, with 71 percent of circulation, are controlled by chains. The biggest in number of newspapers—73—is the Gannett chain; the most circulation—3,725,000—is claimed by the 34 papers of the Knight-Ridder chain, itself the product of a merger between two chains.

Worse, 52 percent of national newspaper circulation is supplied by the twenty-five largest chains, and the bigger chains are beginning to swallow the smaller chains—as Samuel I. Newhouse did in 1976 when he added the eight Booth newspapers in Michigan to the twenty-two he already owned, making his chain second in circulation nationally, with 3,530,000 readers.

But Newhouse does not impose editorial unanimity on his newspapers and most chain operators grant their individual newspapers considerable editorial autonomy. Chain formation and expansion seem mostly a financial rather than a journalistic or a political operation. The disappearance of so many weak competitors has made surviving dailies attractive to purchasers, combined operations offer many opportunities for cost reductions, and most mergers and acquisitions turn out to be advantageous stock operations rather than cash transactions aimed at journalistic and political power.

Some chain proprietors may even agree privately with Lord Thomson of Fleet, whose international chain controls fifty-seven American newspapers, mostly small ones, and who once described his operations as follows:

"I buy newspapers to make money to buy more newspapers to make more money. As for editorial content, that's the stuff you separate the ads with."

That attitude surely does little for the quality of newspapers so published. But some other chains—that of *The New York Times* is one I know about—have tended to interfere with local editorial control only to *improve* the quality of some of the newspapers they own. As to newspaper quality, therefore, chain ownership is a mixed bag, and some of the best American newspapers—*Newsday,* for instance, and the *Philadelphia Inquirer*—are chained-owned.

And there are a lot of chains; if 60 percent of dailies are chain-operated, it is not by two or three but by 168 multiple ownerships. Thus, while financial ownership of newspapers certainly is concentrated in fewer hands (although often available publicly in the stock markets), it still is rather widely dispersed; and within the chains considerable diversity of editorial opinion and news coverage usually exists. . . .

It seems to be recognized more by critics on the political left than by others that newspapers, radio, and television are full-fledged participants in the free-enterprise system. They are businesses, in the fullest sense of the word, and somewhere in the office of every publisher and network president the proverbial "bottom line" works its inevitable influence.

In any discussion of the press as business—particularly when it is being argued, as I shall, that the press as business is another limitation on the press as powerhouse—two clichés have to be dealt with. The first is that the press deliberately does unethical and unprincipled things to "sell papers," and the other is that advertisers dictate content. But, like most clichés, these contain enough truth to sustain them far past any real relevance.

The sensational "Son of Sam" coverage by the *New York Post* and the *Daily News* showed that a rousing crime story, expertly "hyped," can still "sell papers." *Advertising Age* reported on August 15, 1977, that *Post* sales—normally somewhat in excess of 600,000 daily—had risen steadily during the "Sam" hysteria, with about 100,000 extra sales the day the paper ran a police sketch of the hunted man.

When David Berkowitz was arrested and charged with the "Son of Sam" murders, *Post* sales for the day approached the 1,020,000 record the paper had set on June 5, 1968, when the report of the shooting of Robert F. Kennedy was featured. The *News,* on the day of Berkowitz's arrest, printed an extra 350,000 copies. Even the *Times,* with coverage that was sober by comparison, ran off an extra 35,000 copies, according to *Advertising Age.*

In general, however, the idea of "selling papers" with spectacular stories is something of a hangover from an earlier pre-TV era. Newspapers like most of those run by Rupert Murdoch still operate largely in the old "yellow" tradition, but they are the exception rather than the rule. The *Daily News,* for example, is an excellent newspaper that rarely stoops to the level of its "Sam" coverage and did so in that case only under the competitive goading of Murdoch's *Post.*

Of course, newspapers, television, and radio try to give their audiences what they think is wanted, and at their worst pander shamelessly to what they perceive as the lowest common denominator of audience taste. That is not much different from the sales practices of any business. And it's true that newspapers engage in intense circulation competition, as the broadcasters do in ratings wars, as all businesses do in sales efforts.

But the phrase "selling papers" conjures up particular tricks of pandering or vulgarity to boost sales—a picture of a woman in the electric chair, for example, or of some brutally murdered person, or a headline proclaiming some horror story—"Killer Bees/Move North" in Murdoch's San Antonio paper is a classic of the genre. That sort of thing *did* "sell papers" in the old days of the penny press and "extra" editions; and it did again in the "Son of Sam" frenzy in New York. But those days are mostly gone; today, street and newsstand sales are a small part of most newspapers' circulation, which now fluctuates less according to news developments than to sales and distribution efforts.

It's often charged, for example, that *The New York Times* published the Pentagon Papers in 1971 just to "sell papers." In the first place, the Papers didn't sell papers; circulation records don't disclose any significant rise at the time. In the second place, the costs of such a massive undertaking— editorial preparation over a period of months, clearing space in the paper that could have gone partially to remunerative advertising, legal defense— were heavier than any conceivable circulation returns could have offset. In the third place, all that was well known to *Times* executives before they decided to publish the Pentagon Papers. (Profits from a later book publication may have put the entire operation modestly into the black.). . .

. . . The press in America is a free-enterprise institution, and that gives it an Establishment character. Its executives are respected, usually affluent figures in any community; its institutions share fundamentally in the economic fortunes, good or ill, of the nation and the locality; its stake *as a free enterprise* in the established economic, political, and social systems is as great as that of any other free enterprise of comparable value (no conceivable revolution, from right or left, would leave the press in America to private ownership and control, or preserve the First Amendment). The growth in recent years of "underground" and "alternative" publications—

most of them leftish—is in itself graphic evidence of the Establishment nature of the conventional press. And that's true no matter what the editorial-page policy of some newspapers or the personal politics of editors and reporters.

In one sense, of course, being part of the Establishment may testify to the power of the press. In a stronger sense, I believe, to be part of the Establishment is to accept certain real limitations, conventions, attitudes; to be part of the Establishment is to play fundamentally on the team, not to strike out for more singular glory and power. That Establishment of which the American press is usually a card-carrying member is therefore one of the most effective checks on the theoretical powers of the media.

What *is* the power of the press, anyway? Patently, it isn't the power, say, to send troops to Vietnam or bring them home, to cut or raise taxes, to appoint high officials or manage the national economy.

Is it the power, then, to *cause* such things to be done, or done in a certain manner? Tom Bethell, a Washington editor of *Harper's,* and a thoughtful press critic, wrote in the January 1977 issue of the magazine that in confrontations between "government secrecy and the people's right to know," the media "must always triumph, because they have securely in their grasp the means of forming a public opinion sympathetic to their cause."

The media, Bethell asserted, "very largely control public opinion with the same channels of communication that they use to present the news." He wrote also of "those people who own or control the means of producing public opinion."

Clearly, if the media can "produce" or "form" or "control" public opinion, then the media—perhaps slowly and tediously, but surely—can cause just about anything to happen that the media want to happen. But is that really the case? And even if it were, doesn't it presuppose that the media are monolithically united on what they want?

Taking these questions in reverse, I see no evidence to support the idea that the media will ever be that united on any important question. Even on the press's rights and privileges under the First Amendment—to which Bethell was specifically addressing his article—there's plenty of dispute *within the press.* Both *The New York Times* and *The Washington Post,* for example, were quite cool editorially to Daniel Schorr's publication of the Pike report on the CIA. CBS made no effort to defend Schorr other than legally, or to retain his services. Numerous journalists questioned his action—as some had questioned publication of the Pentagon Papers.

And as one who has confronted many an audience of nonjournalists on the question of First Amendment interpretation, I can testify flatly that even on a matter of such fundamental importance to the media, those same media have abysmally failed—if they've tried—to "produce" or "form" a public opinion favorable to them. Quite the opposite, I'd say.

Even if the media could be monolithically united—and on what controversial subject has that ever happened, or is it likely to happen?—it's not clear that public opinion could then be easily formed or controlled. Highly organized opinion-forming campaigns to make people stop smoking or start using seat belts in their autos or practice birth control haven't come close to succeeding—granted that these campaigns are not all-pervasive. Even in authoritarian societies like Nazi Germany or the Soviet Union, with absolutely controlled media, unanimous by decree in their opinion-forming efforts, a police-state apparatus, from concentration camps to the midnight knock, has proved necessary to control, even more to "produce" opinion.

Literally hundreds of newspapers have editorialized against cigarette smoking; their headlines warn of its dangers; some of them no longer accept cigarette ads; television carries numerous "public service" ads against smoking, and every pack carries its own health warning. But the cigarette companies keep advertising on television, in magazines, in many newspapers, on billboards—and cigarette sales keep going up, particularly among the young.

It may be argued that it isn't necessary for a monolithic media to produce monolithic opinion, in order for the press to have too much power to affect public attitudes. But "affecting" opinion, even greatly, is by no means producing or controlling it. To take only one example, television news coverage no doubt affected public opinion during the 1976 election—but so did the paid advertising of all candidates, the three debates between the two major party candidates, and such directly broadcast events as Ford's White House news conferences and ceremonies. With so many conflicting forces at work on public opinion—not to mention those in the printed press—how can any single force be said to "produce" or "control" opinion?

In fact, the impact of "the media"—far from being that of deliberately forming public opinion—is diffused even within its own organs, as among news, editorial statements, and advertising. It is Balkanized among literally thousands of news organizations—daily and weekly newspapers, television and radio stations. The consequence, in my judgment, is that Woodrow Wilson had it about right when he wrote—before television and radio—that "the news is the atmosphere of events."

I have already called the media "the arena of politics" today. Both atmosphere and arena are environmental terms and perhaps this is the more useful metaphor—the media provide an environment within which things happen and are perceived. And the way things are perceived—public opinion—undoubtedly produces or at least affects further events.

But the media environment is not everywhere and always the same, any more than the earth's physical environment. Just as cold fronts and high-pressure areas move across the country, rain follows sunshine, and snow falls in Vermont while the weather clears in Connecticut, the media environment changes and conflicts and confounds itself. And that environment does not finally control human behavior and attitude—granted that it has great effect on them, as does the weather—any more than other environmental forces. The experiences and attitudes, even the heredity, of that infinite variety of individuals who perceive what happens within the media environment can't be that easily blotted out or overcome. I doubt seriously if any single media influence was as important in the 1976 election as the basic intention of most Americans either to vote for the conservative, familiar Ford, or to vote for change.

One other point may be relevant here. Reporters, editors, and columnists—all of whom have more to do with the content of newspapers and news broadcasts than publishers and network executives do—are a peculiar breed of cat. Irreverent, skeptical (if not always skeptical enough), broadly albeit dilettantishly informed, competitive, operating in a world somewhat set apart from the ordinary—what is a reporter if not first and foremost a privileged spectator?—the reporter's Mecca is always the story, *not* the more conventional forms of power.

I have never known a reporter who actively sought real political power for himself. Those who may have wanted great economic power surely left the press as soon as they could. Aside from a few television newsmen—former Governor Tom McCall of Oregon, Representative Lionel Van Deerlin of California, and Senator Jesse Helms of North Carolina come to mind—most reporters I've known have made poor politicians when they ventured across the line.

Reporters want *journalistic* power and eminence, all right. Power struggles for important newspaper posts or executive positions within the network news operations are savage and frequent. Beyond that, reporters want to be first with the story, distinguished among their colleagues, well paid, influences or checks upon the mighty, giant-killers perhaps, iconoclasts always. But, basically, they want to catch the scoundrel with his hand in the till—rarely to replace him. Reporters love to be heeded by powerful personages, but most wouldn't know what to do with *actual* power (outside their own news organizations) if they had it; and they hold almost as an article of faith, anyway, that power is dangerous unless closely monitored. By whom? By reporters, of course. The monitoring of power, to a reporter, is more important and exciting by far—and a lot more gratifying—than the exercise of power.

What examples does history offer of a journalist who seized dictatorial power and threw generals and politicians in jail? The breed begins and ends—fortunately and significantly—with Mussolini.

No discussion of the limitations that restrict—however subtly—the power of the American press would be complete if the point were not made that the federal government's "national security" powers profoundly inhibit the national press. This may surprise a nation shocked by publication of the Pentagon Papers and Dan Schorr's release of the Pike report, but these really are exceptions to, rather than examples of, the rule.

Take the case of Daniel Ellsberg and those Pentagon cables with which this chapter begins:

The salient fact is that we didn't print or even write Ellsberg's story, even though I was persuaded of its truth, even though it fitted what was then our emerging knowledge of the government's duplicity concerning Vietnam, and even though Ellsberg actually turned over to us one piece of corroborating evidence. We didn't write or print it because we believed we couldn't.

First, the cables were classified Top Secret. This meant that heavy security protected them physically and psychologically, so that ultimately it was impossible to secure basic documentation. And to have been caught trying, it was then believed, might make a reporter or his source liable to legal action.

Second, without such documentation—the cables themselves—this kind of story has little impact anyway. Perhaps Ellsberg might have produced one or two witnesses to support his story. Ordinarily that would be enough—three person's testimony—to justify a news story. In this case, had we had such witnesses, they would have had to be anonymous, their charges would have been sensational, the government's credibility would have been at stake. Obviously the reader still would demand, and rightly so, the documentary evidence the *Times* could not supply.

Third, the government had a position of assumed probity and knowledge—more so then than now—from which to declare its version of events, as Westmoreland and Bunker had been doing. It did not have the need for documentation that the press had. The government could claim: "What we say is true; but the documents that prove it are Top Secret; and you'll have to take our word for it." No newspaper or broadcaster can take such a position.

Fourth, there's a mystique about government secrets, not much less powerful now than in 1967 and 1968. The government can and does classify old newspaper clippings, and nobody yet has shown, for example, that publication of the Pentagon Papers "blew" a single secret of any value. Nevertheless, if the government—particularly the President!—labels something secret, Top Secret, or even just "national security" the mystique sets in immediately. The label makes all but sacrosanct whatever it covers. To publish a "secret" or a "national security" matter is at once to invite charges of lack of patriotism, culpable irresponsibility, endangering the nation, and in extreme cases even treason or espionage.

Nixon almost whitewashed Watergate with "national security" claims. Time and again it has been shown that government officials from presidents down will cover anything embarrassing or inconvenient or duplicitous or scandalous with the "national security" label. Yet, the myth persists that the government's secrets are vital, and the national security depends on their being kept.

No newspaper or broadcaster, therefore, lightly violates classification rules of "national security"—not least because editors, publishers, network executives, and most reporters share the mystique of government secrets and a horror of disclosing them. National security—aside from the difficulty of penetrating its far-flung screen—thus becomes a major inhibition on the national press and its supposedly unchecked power. . . ■

For a fascinating account of the intrigues and maneuverings which culminated in the Pentagon Papers case, see Sanford J. Ungar, THE PAPERS AND THE PAPERS (Dutton, 1972). Floyd Abrams, who served as co-counsel to the *New York Times* in this case, has written a retrospective on it for the *New York Times Magazine*. See "The Pentagon Papers A Decade Later," June 7, 1981, pp. 22. For a viewpoint opposed to that of Ungar and Abrams (both of whom assume that Ellberg's transference of classified documents to newspaper offices was an act of higher patriotism) see Richard Nixon's account in THE MEMOIRS OF RICHARD NIXON (Grosset & Dunlop, 1978), especially pp. 508-515. "I considered what Ellsberg had done to be despicable and contemptible—he had revealed government foreign policy secrets during wartime." (p. 511)

Amid the clash of opinions on the first two issues of this book two facts remain indisputable: first, the number of competing newspapers has drastically shrunk; second, the media, or at least some of the media, are extremely powerful—wealthy enough to hire the most prestigious lawyers in the nation, confident enough to defy the executive branch of the federal government, certain enough of their own righteousness to print top secret documents with no apparent qualms of conscience, and resourceful enough to set up whole departments for the purpose of editing and processing 7,000 pages of documents.

We are no longer dealing, as were the Founding Fathers, with countless little independent printers, each with a few helpers, turning out two hundred or three hundred newspapers every week on primitive presses. Instead we are confronted with a giant press "establishment," churning out news and opinion in massive profusion around the clock.

Are they biased? A century or more ago the question would not have been worth asking. Newspapers were frankly partisan sheets, often controlled by a leading politician or his supporters. Yet it hardly mattered, for there were so many competing newspapers that one bias could be counterbalanced by an opposite bias; readers could take their pick. Today the opposite situation prevails: journalism has become professionalized, so that reporters take pride in not bowing to any politician.

Everyone agrees that the obvious partisanship of newspapers in the past has, for the most part, given way to a much more objective tone in today's newspaper and broadcasting media. What many critics of the media charge is that press bias has simply become more subtle. The argument, and the replies to it, will be developed in the following chapter.

CHAPTER 4

Are the Media Biased?

Are the media biased? Many Americans think so. The most frequently heard complaint is that the news media are biased in favor of "liberalism."

Liberal Beliefs

The term "liberal" is very hard to pin down, but today it would seem to include these elements:

- The belief that government should spend more money on social welfare and less on military programs.
- The belief that racial justice in America requires the use of such strategies as busing and "affirmative action" or racial "quotas."
- The belief that the government should not forbid abortions (should in fact pay for them when women can't afford them), nor should it ban pornography, prostitution, pot-smoking or other "victimless crimes."
- The belief that those suspected of crime, especially the poor, have been so often abused by the police in the past that they require the protections given them by courts in recent years.
- The belief that there must be a "wall of separation" between church and state: religions must not receive state funds; religious activities have no place in public institutions.
- The belief that America's involvement in Vietnam was not only unwise but shameful and immoral.

The Eastern Press

Most of us, of course, are not "pure" liberal or "pure" anti-liberal. We might agree with some of the above propositions and disagree with others. Nevertheless, surveys show that upper-income, college-educated Americans who live in the big cities of America's northeastern sector are likely to subscribe to more of these items than middle-income Americans with less than a college education who live in the South or Midwest. America's most influential news media—its three commercial television networks and newspapers like the *New York Times* and the *Washington Post*—are Eastern-based. Practically all of its correspondents, editors and producers are college-educated and earn incomes markedly greater than the median level. Are they biased in favor of liberalism? And do they pass along their biases?

Here are three schools of thought.

1. LIBERAL BIAS. The first school of thought answers the questions very forthrightly: yes. The media *are* biased and their bias *does* come out in their presentation of the news. Former Vice President Spiro Agnew used to charge that network news is controlled "by a handful of men" who "wield a free hand in selecting, presenting and interpreting the great issues in our nation." Exercising "broad powers of choice," they often present "a narrow and distorted picture of America." They interview the people who curse America rather than those who love it, they sided with Vietnam doves rather than with hawks, with criminals rather than policemen—and so on, down the list of liberal beliefs. Agnew's own misdeeds may have discredited him, but his charges against the media were supported and echoed by many others.

2. THE MIRROR ANALOGY. The news media and their supporters reply to the charge of ideological bias by protesting that the critics are "blaming the messenger." Just as Czar Peter the Great is said to have cut off the head of the messenger who brought him news of a Russian military defeat, so are the news media being blamed for the nasty and "un-American" events they cover. All we do, they say, is to hold up a mirror to reality. Sometimes the reality is not pretty, but that is no reason to blame us.

The weaknesses of the "mirror analogy" were alluded to in chapter one (page 14). Unlike mirrors, those who run the media decide *what* to reflect. The editors and publishers have a great deal of latitude in determining just which parts of reality are "news." This can result in intentional or unintentional distortion.

Media spokesmen are perhaps on safer grounds when they simply challenge their critics to prove the charge of intentional bias. Every time a critic cites an allegedly "liberal" speech carried by the news media, they say, we can show you that the speech wasn't "liberal," or that we carried a "conservative" speech to balance it—maybe not that night, but sometime later. As for our coverage of riots and demonstrations: what are we supposed to do, ignore them? Aren't they news events? The reply, then, is that the critics are using arbitrary and subjective methods for measuring "liberal" bias. The critics are simply responding emotionally.

3. ORGANIZATIONAL THEORY. A third school of thought, best developed in Edward Jay Epstein's ground-breaking book, NEWS FROM NOWHERE, takes a different approach. Yes, Epstein says, the network news programs are systematically biased, but not in favor of liberalism, conservatism, or any other "ism." They are biased in favor of their own survival as news organizations.

What must a TV news organization do to survive? Well, it must keep a number of people happy. It must keep its affiliate stations happy by not broadcasting news which preempts too many entertainment programs, it must keep its viewers happy by making the news lively and action-packed, it must keep its parent network happy by not spending too much money, and it must keep the FCC happy by avoiding "imbalance" in the presentation of news. Put all these together, Epstein says, and you begin to understand why the news programs show what they do show.

For example, those who think that the TV networks are biased in favor of liberalism sometimes cite the fact that TV news gives more extensive "live" coverage to the East than to the Midwest or the Far West. This is true, says Epstein, but it does not stem from liberal bias. It stems from economics. To do "live" coverage of events in Iowa or Utah the networks must lease special "long lines" from the telephone company—at enormous cost. To live within budgetary constraints, then, the news organizations would rather limit "live" coverage to areas east of the Mississippi river, using filmed "magazine pieces" for the rest of the nation. (For extraordinary events, of course, they break these restraints.)

Another charge made against the news media is that they always seem to give more time to those who bad-mouth America and cause trouble than they give to those who represent "the silent majority." Again, Epstein agrees, but argues that the reason stems not from any perverse "leftist" bias but from the fear of boring viewers. A bored viewer may change channels, and studies suggest that once somebody turns a channel in the early evening he probably won't change back. Thus, the "lead-in" to the prime-time entertainment shows has been spoiled, which could mean big trouble for the network's Nielson ratings. So the viewer of the early evening news shows must be given a lot of "action," and the most active scenes are precisely the ones involving confrontations and violence. The "silent majority" is not very exciting.

In summary, Epstein and others of the "organizational" school account for the "bias" of network news by seeing it as an organization's response to the pressures of government, budget, Nielson ratings, and so on.

Below are some samplings of the various schools of thought on the issue of news bias. The author of the first selection requires little introduction. He was certainly one of the most vocal and unrestrained critics of the liberal bias in the news media. And—what particularly worried the Fourth Estate—he did so while serving as Vice President of the United States.

A HANDFUL OF MEN

Spiro Agnew, from address to Midwest Regional Republican Committee, November 13, 1969

Tonight I want to discuss the importance of the television news medium to the American people. No nation depends more on the intelligent judgment of its citizens. No medium has a more profound influence over public opinion. Nowhere in our system are there fewer checks on vast power. So, nowhere should there be more conscientious responsibility exercised than by the news media. The question is . . . are we demanding enough of our television news presentations? . . . And, are the men of this medium demanding enough of themselves?

Monday night, a week ago, President Nixon delivered the most important address of his Administration, one of the most important of the decade. His subject was Vietnam. His hope was to rally the American people to see the conflict through to a lasting and just peace in the Pacific. For thirty-two minutes, he reasoned with a nation that has suffered almost a third of a million casualties in the longest war in its history.

When the President completed his address—an address that he spent weeks in preparing—his words and policies were subjected to instant analysis and querulous criticism. The audience of seventy million Americans—gathered to hear the President of the United States—was inherited by a small band of network commentators and self-appointed analysts, the *majority* of whom expressed, in one way or another, their hostility to what he had to say.

It was obvious that their minds were made up in advance. Those who recall the fumbling and groping that followed President Johnson's dramatic disclosure of his intention not to seek reelection have seen these men in a genuine state of nonpreparedness. This was not it.

One commentator twice contradicted the President's statement about the exchange of correspondence with Ho Chi Minh. Another challenged the President's abilities as a politician. A third asserted that the President was now "following the Pentagon line." Others, by the expressions on their faces, the tone of their questions, and the sarcasm of their responses, made clear their sharp disapproval.

To guarantee in advance that the President's plea for national unity would be challenged, one network trotted out Averell Harriman for the occasion. Throughout the President's address he waited in the wings. When the President concluded, Mr. Harriman recited perfectly. He attacked the Thieu government as unrepresentative; he criticized the President's speech for various deficiencies; he twice issued a call to the Senate Foreign Relations Committee to debate Vietnam once again; he stated his belief that the Vietcong or North Vietnamese did not really want a military take-over of South Vietnam; he told a little anecdote about a "very, very responsible" fellow he had met in the North Vietnamese delegation.

All in all, Mr. Harriman offered a broad range of gratuitous advice— challenging and contradicting the policies outlined by the President of the United States. Where the President had issued a call for unity, Mr. Harriman was encouraging the country not to listen to him.

A word about Mr. Harriman. For ten months he was America's chief negotiator at the Paris peace talks—a period in which the United States swapped some of the greatest military concessions in the history of warfare for an enemy agreement on the shape of a bargaining table. Like Coleridge's Ancient Mariner, Mr. Harriman seems to be under some heavy compulsion to justify his failures to anyone who will listen. The networks have shown themselves willing to give him all the air time he desires.

Every American has a right to disagree with the President of the United States, and to express publicly that disagreement.

But the President of the United States has a right to communicate directly with the people who elected him, and the people of this country have the right to make up their own minds and form their own opinions about a presidential address without having the President's words and thoughts characterized through the prejudices of hostile critics before they can even be digested.

When Winston Churchill rallied public opinion to stay the course against Hitler's Germany, he did not have to contend with a gaggle of commentators raising doubts about whether he was reading public opinion right, or whether Britain had the stamina to see the war through. When President Kennedy rallied the nation in the Cuban missile crisis, his address to the people was not chewed over by a roundtable of critics who disparaged the course of action he had asked America to follow.

The purpose of my remarks tonight is to focus your attention on this little group of men who not only enjoy a right of instant rebuttal to every presidential address, but more importantly, wield a free hand in selecting, presenting and interpreting the great issues of our nation.

First, let us define that power. At least forty million Americans each night, it is estimated, watch the network news. Seven million of them view ABC; the remainder being divided between NBC and CBS. According to Harris polls and other studies, for millions of Americans the networks are the sole source of national and world news.

In Will Rogers' observation, what you knew was what you read in the newspaper. Today, for growing millions of Americans, it is what they see and hear on their television sets.

How is this network news determined? A small group of men, numbering perhaps no more than a dozen "anchormen," commentators and executive producers, settle upon the 20 minutes or so of film and commentary that is to reach the public. This selection is made from the 90 to 180 minutes that may be available. Their powers of choice are broad. They decide what forty to fifty million Americans will learn of the day's events in the nation and the world.

We cannot measure this power and influence by traditional democratic standards for these men can create national issues overnight. They can make or break—by their coverage and commentary—a moratorium on the war. They can elevate men from local obscurity to national prominence within a week. They can reward some politicians with national exposure and ignore others. For millions of Americans, the network reporter who covers a continuing issue, like ABM or Civil Rights, becomes in effect, the presiding judge in a national trial by jury.

It must be recognized that the networks have made important contributions to the national knowledge. Through news, documentaries and specials, they have often used their power constructively and creatively to awaken the public conscience to critical problems.

The networks made hunger and black lung disease national issues overnight. The TV networks have done what no other medium could have done in terms of dramatizing the horrors of war. The networks have tackled our most difficult social problems with a directness and immediacy that is the gift of their medium. They have focused the nation's attention on its environmental abuses . . . on pollution in the Great Lakes and the threatened ecology of the Everglades.

But it was also the networks that elevated Stokely Carmichael and George Lincoln Rockwell from obscurity to national prominence. Nor is their power confined to the substantive.

A raised eyebrow, an inflection of the voice, a caustic remark dropped in the middle of a broadcast can raise doubts in a million minds about the veracity of a public official or the wisdom of a Government policy.

One Federal Communications Commissioner considers the power of the networks to equal that of local, state and Federal governments combined. Certainly, it represents a concentration of power over American public opinion unknown in history.

What do Americans know of the men who wield this power? Of the men who produce and direct the network news—the nation knows practically nothing. Of the commentators, most Americans know little, other than that they reflect an urbane and assured presence, seemingly well informed on every important matter.

We do know that, to a man, these commentators and producers live and work in the geographical and intellectual confines of Washington, D.C., or New York City—the latter of which James 'Reston terms the "most unrepresentative community in the entire United States." Both communities bask in their own provincialism, their own parochialism. We can deduce that these men thus read the same newspapers, and draw their political and social views from the same sources. Worse, they talk constantly to one another, thereby providing artificial reinforcement to their shared viewpoints.

Do they allow their biases to influence the selection and presentation of the news? David Brinkley states, "objectivity is impossible to normal human behavior." Rather, he says, we should strive for "fairness."

Another anchorman on a network news show contends: "You can't expunge all your private convictions just because you sit in a seat like this and a camera starts to stare at you. . . . I think your program has to reflect what your basic feelings are. I'll plead guilty to that."

Less than a week before the 1968 election, this same commentator charged that President Nixon's campaign commitments were no more durable than campaign balloons. He claimed that, were it not for fear of a hostile reaction, Richard Nixon would be giving into, and I quote the commentator, "his natural instinct to smash the enemy with a club or go after him with a meat ax."

Had this slander been made by one political candidate about another, it would have been dismissed by most commentators as a partisan assault. But this attack emanated from the privileged sanctuary of a network studio and therefore had the apparent dignity of an objective statement.

The American people would rightly not tolerate this kind of concentration of power in Government. Is it not fair and relevant to question its concentration in the hands of a tiny and closed fraternity of privileged men, elected by no one, and enjoying a monopoly sanctioned and licensed by Government?

The views of this fraternity do *not* represent the views of America. That is why such a great gulf existed between how the nation received the President's address—and how the networks reviewed it.

As with other American institutions, perhaps it is time that the networks were made more responsive to the views of the nation and more responsible to the people they serve.

I am not asking for government censorship or any other kind of censorship. I am asking whether a form of censorship already exists when the news that forty million Americans receive each night is determined by a handful of men responsible only to their corporate employers and filtered through a handful of commentators who admit to their own set of biases.

The questions I am raising here tonight should have been raised by others long ago. They should have been raised by those Americans who have traditionally considered the preservation of freedom of speech and freedom of the press their special provinces of responsibility and concern. They should have been raised by those Americans who share the view of the late Justice Learned Hand that "right conclusions are more likely to be gathered out of a multitude of tongues than through any kind of authoritative selection."

Advocates for the networks have claimed a first amendment right to the same unlimited freedoms held by the great newspapers of America.

The situations are not identical. Where the New York *Times* reaches 800,000 people, NBC reaches twenty times that number with its evening news. Nor can the tremendous impact of seeing television film and hearing commentary be compared with reading the printed page.

A decade ago, before the network news acquired such dominance over public opinion, Walter Lippmann spoke to the issue:

> There is an essential and radical difference [he stated] between television and printing . . . the three or four competing television stations control virtually all that can be received over the air by ordinary television sets. But, besides the mass circulation dailies, there are the weeklies, the monthlies, the out-of-town newspapers, and books. If a man does not like his newspaper, he can read another from out of town, or wait for a weekly news magazine. It is not ideal.

But it is infinitely better than the situation in television. There, if a man does not like what the networks offer him, all he can do is turn them off, and listen to a phonograph.

"Networks," he stated, "which are few in number, have a virtual monopoly of a whole medium of communication." The newspapers of mass circulation have no monopoly of the medium of print.

"A virtual monopoly of a whole medium of communication" is not something a democratic people should blithely ignore.

And we are not going to cut off our television sets and listen to the phonograph because the air waves do not belong to the networks; they belong to the people.

As Justice Byron White wrote in his landmark opinion six months ago, "It is the right of the viewers and listeners, not the right of the broadcasters, which is paramount."

It is argued that this power presents no danger in the hands of those who have used it responsibly.

But as to whether or not the networks have abused the power they enjoy, let us call as our first witnesses, former Vice President Humphrey and the city of Chicago.

According to Theodore H. White, television's intercutting of the film from the streets of Chicago with the "current proceedings on the floor of the convention created the most striking and *false* political picture of 1968—the nomination of a man for the American presidency by the brutality and violence of merciless police."

If we are to believe a recent report of the House Commerce Committee, then television's presentation of the violence in the streets worked an injustice on the reputation of the Chicago police.

According to the Committee findings, one network in particular presented "a one-sided picture which in large measure exonerates the demonstrators and protesters." Film of provocations of police that was available never saw the light of day, while the film of the police response which the protesters provoked was shown to millions.

Another network showed virtually the same scene of violence—from three separate angles—without making clear it was the same scene.

While the full report is reticent in drawing conclusions, it is not a document to inspire confidence in the fairness of the network news.

Our knowledge of the impact of network news on the national mind is far from complete. But some early returns are available. Again, we have enough information to raise serious questions about its effect on a democratic society.

Several years ago, Fred Friendly, one of the pioneers of network news, wrote that its missing ingredients were "conviction, controversy and a point of view." The networks have compensated with a vengeance.

And in the networks' endless pursuit of controversy, we should ask what is the end value . . . to enlighten or to profit? What is the end result . . . to inform or to confuse? How does the on-going exploration for more action, more excitement, more drama, serve our national search for internal peace and stability?

Gresham's law seems to be operating in the network news.

Bad news drives out good news. The irrational is more controversial than the rational. Concurrence can no longer compete with dissent. One minute of Eldridge Cleaver is worth ten minutes of Roy Wilkins. The labor crisis settled at the negotiating table is nothing compared to the confrontation that results in a strike—or, better yet, violence along the picket line. Normality has become the nemesis of the evening news.

The upshot of all this controversy is that a narrow and distorted picture of America often emerges from the televised news. A single dramatic piece of the mosaic becomes, in the minds of millions, the whole picture. The American who relies upon television for his news might conclude that the majority of American students are embittered radicals, that the majority of black Americans feel no regard for their country; that violence and lawlessness are the rule rather than the exception, on the American campus. None of these conclusions is true.

Television may have destroyed the old stereotypes—but has it not created new ones in their place?

What has this passionate pursuit of "controversy" done to the politics of progress through logical compromise, essential to the functioning of a democratic society?

The members of Congress or the Senate who follow their principles and philosophy quietly in a spirit of compromise are unknown to many Americans—while the loudest and most extreme dissenters on every issue are known to every man in the street.

How many marches and demonstrations would we have if the marchers did not know that the ever-faithful TV cameras would be there to record their antics for the next news show?

We have heard demands that senators and congressmen and judges make known all their financial connections—so that the public will know who and what influences their decisions or votes. Strong arguments can be made for that view. But when a single commentator or producer, night after night, determines for millions of people how much of each side of a great issue they are going to see and hear; should he not first disclose his personal views on the issue as well?

In this search for excitement and controversy, has more than equal time gone to that minority of Americans who specialize in attacking the United States, its institutions and its citizens?

Tonight, I have raised questions. I have made no attempts to suggest answers. These answers must come from the media men. They are challenged to turn their critical powers on themselves. They are challenged to direct their energy, talent and conviction toward improving the quality and objectivity of news presentation. They are challenged to structure their own civic ethics to relate their great freedom with their great responsibility.

And the people of America are challenged too . . . challenged to press for responsible news presentations. The people can let the networks know that they want their news straight and objective. The people can register their complaints on bias through mail to the networks and phone calls to local stations. This is one case where the people must defend themselves . . . where the citizen—not Government—must be the reformer . . . where the consumer can be the most effective crusader.

By way of conclusion, let me say that every elected leader in the United States depends on these men of the media. Whether what I have said to you tonight will be heard and seen at all by the nation is not *my* decision; it is not *your* decision; it is *their* decision.

In tomorrow's edition of the Des Moines *Register* you will be able to read a news story detailing what I said tonight; editorial comment will be reserved for the editorial page, where it belongs. Should not the same wall of separation exist between news and comment on the nation's network?

We would never trust such power over public opinion in the hands of an elected government—it is time we questioned it in the hands of a small and unelected elite. The great networks have dominated America's airwaves for decades; the people are entitled to a full accounting of their stewardship.

■

If Ernest Lefever's name is remembered today it is most likely as the subject of a bitter and well-publicized controversy in late May and early June of 1981, when the Senate Foreign Relations Committee held hearings to consider his confirmation as President Reagan's Assistant Secretary of State for Human Rights. Students of the mass media, however, might remember Dr. Lefever's name from seven years earlier, when he published a controversial book on political bias in the media. It may be that the two controversies are connected.

The 1981 controversy was generated in large part by the publicity given to Lefever's human rights strategy. He stated his belief that America should openly criticize only Soviet-bloc countries for human rights violations. For any countries allied or friendly to the United States which violate human rights, the appropriate remedy, Lefever said, was "quiet diplomacy."

The stormy confirmation hearings were given extensive coverage in the news media, and in the heat of the controversy, Lefever's support withered. In the end, the committee voted by a large margin, 13 to 4, to recommend against Senate confirmation, whereupon Lefever withdrew his name from consideration.

Was it hostile media coverage which doomed his candidacy? Lefever seemed to think so. To Lefever it may have seemed to be an example of the same kind of media bias which his 1974 book found in one network's coverage of foreign affairs.

The book, TV AND NATIONAL DEFENSE, studied CBS News for 1972 and 1973, and concluded that the network tilted toward a "dovish" position on foreign affairs. The study was published by the Institute for American Strategy, and Lefever was forthright in admitting that the Institutes bias was on the hawkish side. Nevertheless, Lefever believed that he and his associates at the Institute had worked out a rigorous methodology for evaluating media objectivity which would not be influenced by the testers' own bias.

Vanderbilt University keeps a library of tapes and tape transcripts of TV news, together with an index to them. Using these materials Lefever and a large staff counted and timed CBS's coverage to see how the network balanced hawkish and dovish statements by those whom it presented on the air.

At the National Republican Women's Club in January of 1975, Lefever presented his conclusions in a debate with William Small, who at that time was CBS's Director of News. (Small is now Director of News at NBC.) The central issue was the one raised by Lefever's book: Was CBS, at a critical period in our history, providing TV viewers with news coverage which was slanted in favor of reducing American military strength?

The following are excerpts from the debate and the subsequent question-and-answer period.

"DOES CBS FAVOR DOVES?" A DEBATE

Ernest Lefever and William Small, from Debate before the National Women's Republican Club, January 15, 1975

DR. ERNEST LEFEVER: Mrs. Wittison, ladies and gentlemen, it's a great pleasure for me to be here.

I don't always welcome a debate format. As a scholar I'm interested in discussing pros and cons, I believe, more than in scoring points. And I've asked myself why am I here.

First of all, I am here as a scholar and a citizen interested in vigorous national debate on defense and foreign policy issues—the subject of my book. I believe, as I think all of us believe, in the full and fair coverage in the mass media—particularly in network TV, which has a kind of "triopoly" on the evening news shows. I believe in full and fair coverage of all important issues. . . .

Today I do not represent any organization, institution or agency. I represent only myself. The study which I authored was sponsored by the Institute for American Strategy, with which I have no present contact, financial or otherwise. I served as a temporary consultant. Nor do I represent the Brookings Institution, which, like the Institute, is a non-profit, nonpartisan educational organization and is tax-exempt accordingly.

In contrast, my debating partner—or shall I say adversary? (we'll see how it works out)—does represent CBS News, a very large corporation, influential and known for the excellence of its work. You'll forgive me if I feel a little like a David confronting a billion-dollar Goliath. . . .

Let me first, then, summarize very briefly some of the principal findings of this study, which took two years and involved a team of about 16 scholars.

The yardstick we used was the Fairness Doctrine of the Federal Communication Commission, and the principle of fairness which really says three things: first, that there should be a fair balance in reporting the intelligence of the day; second, the viewpoints toward daily events should be fairly covered, giving opposing viewpoints on controversial issues reasonable opportunity to be heard. This, of course, should be done in a meaningful perspective. Furthermore, . . . network TV news has a right to editorialize and advocate, as long as it gives an opportunity for other viewpoints to be heard over that network.

Now, down to the study.

When we went about this exhaustive study, we decided to deal only with the CBS News flagship operation, the evening Cronkite show, which has 13.8 million listeners. We covered the years 1972 by transcripts, and 1973 largely by summaries provided by the Vanderbilt TV archives. We did not evaluate the TV evening news as a newspaper. It is not *The New York Times* or a university. We evaluated it as a program of 22.5 minutes, which had many things to say, and we're not at all critical because it gave only 25% foreign and defense policy.

Our central question was this: Did *CBS Evening News* present a fair, accurate and balanced account of national defense issues within the limited time and format, including the need to entertain to hold its vast audience? Our short conclusion is this: a steady and conscientious viewer who relied only on *CBS Evening News* during these two years would have received a sketchy and lopsided picture of most of the major issues of security and survival confronting the United States.

First, he would have received a distorted view of Soviet military might, which during these two years was growing at a galloping rate. During those two years, only one minute out of a hundred and ninety-six hours was explicitly devoted to a direct comparison of Soviet and American military might. In contrast, one minute and forty seconds was devoted to missing tableware in Pentagon restaurants. The evening news carried almost no information about growing Soviet military might. There was no direct reference to the new 4,500-mile submarine missile, the annual production of five to nine nuclear submarines, a new generation of giant ICBM missiles capable of destroying our Minuteman missiles and their silos, and of carrying nuclear warheads. You'll notice, [then] Secretary of State Schlesinger's statement yesterday, noting that the first of these giant missiles has now come into place. There was no reference to the Soviet reconnaissance satellite capability of knocking down our own spy-in-the-sky satellites.

There was no reference to the fact that the Soviet military budget was $90-billion larger than ours and four times as great as admitted by Moscow.

There was an overwhelmingly negative portrayal of the U.S. Armed Services. Certainly every institution in a free society needs scrutiny, including the military, and there's plenty to criticize. But the overwhelmingly negative reporting on the military in 1972 — 62% of the military stories were portrayed in a negative light, 30% neutral and only 8% favorable. There was rarely a story on heroism or compassion on the part of the military in Vietnam or elsewhere. In '73 the percentages were 69% unfavorable, 13 neutral and 18 favorable. The composite picture of the military that emerged from these two years of reporting was a military establishment that fought a bloody and unjust war in Vietnam, where U.S. forces committed atrocities and engaged in illegal bombing; and, at home, an enormous and growing Pentagon budget that was upheld by a military-industrial complex which kept draining the taxpayer by waste, cost overruns and design faults.

But perhaps more serious than this was the failure of CBS News to give the American people a fair and full picture of the different viewpoints Americans held, millions of Americans, toward national security questions. We identified three viewpoints: the one, you might call a hawkish viewpoint, viewpoint A, which said in effect the American Government should do more than it is now doing, or that the threat to national security was greater than perceived by the Government. Position B was the Government position itself; and position C would be called the dovish position, stating that the Government overestimated the threat from abroad and was doing too much to deal with it.

CBS News, during these two years, gave the distinct impression, by balancing the A and the C viewpoints, the hawk and the dove viewpoints, in such a lopsided way that it gave the impression that the debate in America was between the B position and the C position — the Administration position and the position of the people who wanted to do less than the Administration.

In 1972, for example, the evening news gave 3.5% to the A view, 34.6% to the B view, and 61.8% to the C view. These percentages are based upon counting of sentences. Actually, these percentages are for 1972, not for the two years . . .in which explicit viewpoints were expressed. At one point we tried to count narrative sentences, but dismissed that and restricted our viewpoint count to sentences in which views were explicitly stated.

On the United States-Soviet military calculus, CBS gave 16 times more space to C views than to A views, which amounted to a virtual exclusion of a viewpoint held by millions of Americans, and according to some of the best public opinion polls, excluding some majority-held views. For example, our study did not find a single reference to any of these views, which are held by millions and millions of Americans:

(1) the view that the Soviet Union is militarily more powerful than the United States;

(2) the United States should seek to achieve and maintain superiority over the Soviet Union; and

(3) the U.S. Defense budget should be substantially increased.

None of those views was represented in the evening news program. On the contrary, CBS frequently reported the views of persons who advocated substantial defense cuts and who insisted that the Soviet threat had greatly diminished.

In our 1972 theme tabulations, CBS News reported only one item calling for increased military spending, and 13 for reduced spending. It reported 91 items asserting that detente with the Soviet Union was desirable, and only four that it was risky.

The reporting on Vietnam was, of course, the most lopsided of all, as any viewer would soon ascertain. The C views to the A views were 48-to-1. For every hawkish viewpoint carried, they carried a dovish viewpoint 48 times, according to the sentence tabulation in 1972. This led us to four principal conclusions:

— CBS violated the Fairness Doctrine, the industry codes and its own standards;
— it failed to provide many of the facts essential to understanding the complex problems of national security;
— it failed to give a reasonable opportunity for the expression of certain widely held security views;
— it actively advocated the C position without adequately reporting opposing views.

Furthermore, it advocated the C position in the guise of giving straight news.

On Vietnam, for example, only 30% of the C views that were expressed by CBS newsmen themselves came from commentator Eric Sevareid. The bulk came from men who were presumably presenting straight news. Thus, CBS EVENING NEWS had the effect of narrowing the nature of public debate and therefore public decision (because any President, any Congress needs the public support in order to take certain positions) in terms that there was only a debate between the Administration and those who wished to do less.

Let me hasten to say a few words about the response of CBS to the study. Perhaps I'm a naive scholar. I actually harbored the hope that CBS would welcome the study — that some people had gone to the effort . . . to try to make a survey that might help CBS do its job better. But I fear that the study has not met with a thoughtful dialogue between CBS and those who are interested in the findings of the study, although I hope that will still happen. Perhaps the CBS response was predictable. Last November, Walter Cronkite told a newsman in an open interview which was published that he disagreed with the conclusion of the study that said CBS tended to neglect a certain viewpoint, and then he added: "There are always groups in Washington expressing views of alarm over the state of our defenses. We don't carry those stories. The story is there are those who want to cut defense spending" — end of quote.

Apparently Walter Cronkite does not believe people who want to increase defense spending. . . .

I'm very sorry about this response, and I hope the dialogue today may be a little bit more constructive.

MODERATOR: Thank you, Dr. Lefever.

William J. Small has been CBS News Senior Vice President, Director of News, since February 1974. Mr. Small is responsible for executive supervision of all hard news coverage and news gathering, as well as hard news broadcasts, including the *CBS Morning News, Evening News, CBS Saturday News* and the *CBS Sunday News*, and hard news specials.

He has produced for CBS News virtually all Presidential News conferences, live hearings, including several on Vietnam, the 1963 Martin Luther King march on Washington . . . and march on the Pentagon in 1967, and the coverage of the four days following the assassination of President John F. Kennedy.

We welcome you, Mr. Small.

WILLIAM SMALL: Good Afternoon. I'm the billion-dollar Goliath.

I suspect Dr. Lefever calls me that because he knows how David and Goliath ended up.

I'm delighted to be here, and I come with a few apologies. My boss, Dick Salant, would have been here but he is in Australia and didn't want to cancel that trip, and I'm sure you understand. . . .

If [in] the remarks that follow . . . my evaluation of the IAS study seems harsh, it's because this study is an attack on the integrity of those of us who work at CBS News. My colleagues and I are a team of hundreds of highly professional journalists dedicated to coverage of news as complete, as objective as we can make it. We are not, as Dr. Lefever's writings put it, engaged in partial, slanted reporting, nor are we active advocates of any particular national defense positions, nor are we — despite over 200 pages of IAS rhetoric to the contrary — guilty of bias.

We make errors. And so do historians. And so do Brookings fellows. So do advocates of harder defense positions and so do most journalists. And we try to correct our errors on the air. You see, our work product, unlike some, is out in the open. What we do is seen each evening on television. It's susceptible to criticism from the left (and we've heard from the *New Republic* and the *Rolling Stone* and others) as well as from the right. And we take criticism seriously. But as CBS President Arthur Taylor put it in a public memorandum on December 23rd, a few weeks ago, in speaking of the IAS study; the absence to that date of a response by CBS should not be taken as either complacency on our part nor acquiescence to the charges. And I have with me today copies of Mr. Taylor's four-page commentary on the IAS study, and I'll be happy to give it to anyone in the audience. And if there are more of you than I have copies, if you'll just leave me your name and address, I'll mail you one.

One of our main difficulties with IAS study is the failure of that group to provide us with a complete list of the CBS stories that they studied, how they were evaluated and what their methods were. The study itself, on pages 161 and 162, invite[s] CBS not to accept it uncritically and, quote, "to double-check our methods and findings." And when Mr. Salant, the president of CBS News, was sent a copy of this study by John Fisher, the President of IAS, Mr. Fisher said: "We welcome the opportunity to review the study results with you." When Mr. Fisher and Dr. Lefever unveiled the study at a Washington news conference, Dr. Lefever said: "I do say this in the book — that we invite CBS or anyone else to make an independent audit . . . to go over the material and not accept anything uncritically." But when, on November 5, Salant wrote Fisher and asked for, quote, "text of precise citation to each story analyzed or classified, along with the code or classification assigned to each," Mr. Fisher replied that explaining the different methodologies and reasons behind them would be, and I quote, "a major undertaking." Some audit!

While CBS, in the period under study, as now, does its work before any American who chooses to watch, the IAS evaluations of our stories, which stories were involved, remain locked in the files of the IAS in Boston, Virginia. Now, Fisher has suggested instead that CBS send a few people down to Boston for a one-or two-day briefing on this two-year-long study.

Salant, on December 9th, replied that this falls grievously short of a full examination of the data, but in order that our dialogue may continue, agreed to send people down. Now, that was five weeks ago. We are yet to hear from Mr. Fisher.

The study itself, as published, however, has some specifics. So let me deal with that.

First of all, we are flattered, Dr. Lefever, that you chose CBS News because we have the largest audience for our evening newscasts. By the way, when you stated that, on page 24, you said that we celebrated our 10th anniversary in 1973 — that newscast. In future attacks on us, you may want to correct that. 1973 was our tenth year as a 30-minute broadcast. *CBS Evening News* is actually 26 years old; it'll be 27 in May.

Now, I note that you used the monthly index of the Vanderbilt news archives in Nashville to isolate the items you wanted to deal with: some 260 newscasts in '72; 261 in '73. And you also throw in some editions of *60 Minutes* in 1972, but strangely not in '73. And while your Index G lists 23 CBS documentaries and specials in 1972 — and again you skipped 1973

— you deal in detail with only one of the specials, "Where We Stand", which we broadcast on May 16th, 1972.

By the way, I have a problem with the accuracy of the Vanderbilt index. On page 63 of your study, using Vanderbilt, I assume, because the language is the same, you state that on December 12th of 1973 we reported a Soviet announcement of a reduction in their military budget because of detente with the West. This was to show a "favorable to Moscow" quote by CBS. But both Vanderbilt and IAS failed to note that Walter Cronkite, when he said that, went on to point out that official Soviet military figures are not considered reliable.

In any case, from Vanderbilt, you learned of one thousand and sixty-three national security items on CBS, according to your study, and you classified them, as you've described, A, B and C. You also had a viewpoint D in the study, which you hastily go over—namely an item that had no viewpoint. Now, the A, B, C in totals, as I read your item on page 85, comes to 274 stories. Now, does that not mean that three out of four of our reports had no point of view, by your judgment, not even when carefully examined by the hard-eyed investigators of IAS? Well, if we're so biased, why do we let an opportunity go by three times out of four? The answer is: we are not biased, do not have a point of view.

Look! CBS is not one man, or even — Agnew notwithstanding — a small group of men. We are lots of different peoples. We are liberals, conservatives, and I suspect mostly down the middle; we are Democrats and Republicans and lots of independents. But most of all, we are professional news people — whose dedication to fighting bias in our work is fundamental. And we are not alone. If you examine all networks and all of the press, you will find that what we reported in '72 and '73 was little different from the press in general. Now, I would hope that we reported it better, but I know that we reported it without the infection of subjective reporting. If we ever tried to impose a point of view, our own staff would not only object violently, but they would make sure that the entire world knew of the bias suggested and their strong opposition to it.

Now, you break those 274 A, B, C stories into individual sentences, which is a good way to get bigger numbers. Your study is full of numbers. The flavor and odor [of] scientific research exudes page after page.

Well, on Vietnam, Chapter Five, quoted, you accuse us of 287 sentences reflecting viewpoint C. Well, why can't you cite all 287 for our examination. Surely, the dark files in Boston can spare that much. Now, I'm interested because Bob Simon, who I suspect many in this room have never heard of, is listed as a major offender, guilty of 44 sentences of advocacy of expressing his own direct view. Now, Bob is a gifted reporter, but he was not a major figure in our coverage of Vietnam. Forty-four expressions of bias? I'd like to see what they were.

Now, there is one place where you do get specific. That's Chapter Three, where you cite 42 stories that we failed to report. John Roche, in that article quoted earlier, cites some of them. Now, on page 29, earlier, you suggested, as you did in your opening remarks, that CBS has limited time and you said (and I quote) "We have no quarrel with the quantity of such news. We raise serious questions about how this limited time was used." Fair enough! But you devote all of Chapter Three to stories that appeared in print but not on CBS — most of them in *The New York Times*. Now, even other newspapers can't cover as much as *The New York Times*.

The St. Louis *Globe Democrat*, which loved your study, praised it editorially and it ran a lengthy series of articles that you wrote for NANA, digesting the study — but even the *Globe Democrat* ran only four of those 42 missing stories. And I'll bet it missed an awful lot of those 1,063 national security stories that did appear on our air. And the publisher of the Los Angeles *Herald Examiner*, he's a director of IAS, his paper only carried 12 of those 42 items in Chapter Three, and his newspaper has a lot more space for news than we have time for news.

Four pages of Chapter Three are devoted to our documentary "Where We Stand", which was a prelude to Nixon's 1972 visit to Moscow. Now, here again, I can deal in specifics because I have a transcript of that broadcast. It is not something anonymous in the IAS files. You called it our one ambitious look at the comparative military strengths of the U.S. and the Soviet Union. Then you spend page after page citing matters we failed to mention. Well, first of all, it was not meant to be a military comparison. It was an overall evaluation of two countries, this one and the Soviet Union, in terms of diplomatic and economic, as well as military. And we devoted only five minutes specifically to the military. Incidentally, knowing the A point of view, I'm sure you can't quarrel with the conclusion of Correspondent Charles Collingwood in that documentary, when he said: "Starting from a position of technological inferiority with only half the gross national product of the United States, Russia has, in a few years, created an arsenal of nuclear weapons comparable to that of the United States."

Let me look at some specifics. . . .

Item: You ask why didn't we mention that, according to the International Institute for Strategic Studies, about 75% of the Soviet science budget is devoted to military resources? Good question. Answer: the IISS said that in its 1973—74 edition, published over one year after our broadcast. [Final] item: You say that the most serious deficiency was the total absence [of] the point of view that the Soviets continue to be a major threat to the United States and other independent governments. Yet, on page eight of our transcript, we talk of the Soviet military influence growing most spectacularly at sea; and on page nine, that the U.S. is reducing conventional forces while the Soviets increase and modernize naval, air and ground forces; and finally, we said — and I quote — "The Soviet Union is visibly thrusting its power outward, eagerly entering into new political military alliances with nations like India, Egypt and Iraq, contributing arms, showing the flag and flexing its muscles in many directions." End of quote. Is that ignoring the Soviet threat? Of course not.

The IAS has divided the world of national security into A, B and C. Well, it isn't that simple. Even IAS has trouble sticking viewpoint B to the Administration, because sometimes the Administration is viewpoint A or viewpoint C. And anyone can develop categories to make a point. I don't think on close examination that, once you get past the scientific veneer, that IAS has proved that point.

Let me close with the words of James J. Kilpatrick. He is no enemy of conservative causes, and he wrote a newspaper column in which he praised the IAS study; but this is how he ended it: "Something more remains to be said on the nature of news and the task of editorial judgment. The Institute complains repeatedly, for example, that CBS carried little about the mission of the Air Force, the mission of the Navy and the mission of the Army. The Institute objects that CBS ignored significant news of national security, gave time instead to — on a given night to such events as the trial of Angela Davis. "Well," he said, "the trouble is that the mission isn't news." And put to a choice between reporting Admiral Moorer on Soviet submarines and the covering of the trial of Angela Davis, 99 editors out of a hundred would take the Davis trial. The Institute for American Strategy is obsessed with national defense, a useful obsession; but a thousand other outfits have a thousand other newsworthy obsessions — abortion, gun control, fluoridation, organic gardening, racial balance, busing, women's rights, historic preservation. . . . It is likely that every one of them could compile a statistical violation of the Fairness Doctrine. "On the record," said Kilpatrick, "CBS News evidently failed to meet requirements of the Fairness Doctrine in its coverage of national security news. But to some degree fairness, like beauty, lies in the eye of the beholder. If Solomon himself were sitting in for Walter Cronkite, complaints would still be heard. In the news business, alas, that's the way it is." ■

We can see that Lefever believes that network news, or at least one network's news, is politically biased, while Small is convinced that the network simply mirrors reality.

Here, now, is a third view: that TV news is shaped by organizational considerations. In the view of Edward Jay Epstein network is *neither* a mirror of reality nor a product of liberal bias. It is the product of an organization which works within a whole series of "constraints."

THE ORGANIZATION SHAPES THE NEWS

Edward Jay Epstein, from NEWS FROM NOWHERE: TELEVISION AND THE NEWS (New York, 1973)

The main finding of this study is that the pictures of society that are shown on television as national news are largely—though not entirely—performed and shaped by organizational considerations. To maintain themselves in a competitive world, the networks impose a set of prior restraints, rules and conditions on the operations of their news divisions. Budgets are set for the production of news, time is scheduled for its presentation, and general policies are laid down concerning its content. To satisfy these requirements—and keep their jobs—news executives and producers formulate procedures, systems and policies intended to reduce the uncertainties of news to manageable proportions. . . .

First, there is the budgetary requisite set by the economic logic of network television. The prevailing assumption among network executives, it will be recalled, is that increasing the budget of a news program for news gathering or production past a certain point will not bring about a commensurate increase in advertising revenues, and that the point at which these diminishing returns set in is located immediately beyond the budget necessary to produce the minimum amount of news programing of adequate technical quality to fill the news schedule. . . .

Because budget levels are fixed with an eye toward filling a specific number of minutes of news programing a week, the allocation of funds for the unseen parts of news gathering tends to be held to a minimum. For one thing, there is no economic incentive to spend money on searches for original information, or intelligence gathering, since it is not presumed that scoops, exclusives or original reporting significantly increase the audience, and hence the revenue, for network news. Instead, for advance notice of news events, the networks rely heavily on the wire services, the *New York Times* and other secondary sources. . . .

Further, since there is no economic reason regularly to employ more film crews than is necessary to produce the daily quota, coverage is generally limited to a dozen or so selected events. This, in turn, requires that the events which are selected for coverage are highly predictable and almost certain to produce a usable news story. . . .

Moreover, since it is less expensive to take a film story from some cities than from others, according to the budgetary accounting practices of the networks, the filmed news tends to be skewed toward certain geographic areas of the country—specifically, New York, Washington and, to a lesser extent, Chicago. The societal themes depicted on network news thus tend to be illustrated with a disproportionate number of visual examples taken from a few cosmopolitan centers with special problems.

A second basic requisite that network news divisions are expected to meet is that their programs maintain—or at least not significantly diminish—the networks' "audience flows." While it is presumed that network news cannot *attract* large numbers of new viewers to a channel, no matter how high the quality of its coverage, executives also generally believe that "visually unsatisfactory" news, as one NBC vice-president put it, can cause a significant number of viewers to change channels. Since any noticeable reduction in a network's audience flow during the dinnertime news seriously affects the ratings of the entire prime-time schedule—programs begin with a smaller "base" audience—network executives insist that the news be presented in its most visually satisfactory form, no matter how complex or difficult to comprehend the subject is. The effectiveness of the visual presentation is measured by a low "turn-off" rate among viewers. . . .

The first assumption made by news executives and producers is that viewers' interest is most likely to be maintained through easily recognizable and palpable images, and conversely, most likely to be distracted by unfamiliar or confusing images. . . .

A second assumption in this logic of audience maintenance is that scenes of potential conflict are more interesting to the audience than scenes of placidity. Virtually all executives and producers share this view. Situations are thus sought out in network news in which there is a high potential for violence, but a low potential for audience confusion. News events showing a violent confrontation between two easily recognizable sides in conflict— for example, blacks versus whites, uniformed police versus demonstrators, or military versus civilians— are preferable to ones in which the issues are less easily identifiable. . . .

A third closely related assumption is that the viewer's span of attention— which is presumed to be limited—is prolonged by action, or subjects in motion, and sharply reduced by static subjects, such as "talking heads." . . .This helps explain why news on television tends willy-nilly to focus on activity. . . .

Finally, government regulation of television sets a fourth basic requirement for network news: it must conform to certain outside standards of fairness in the presentation of controversial issues. Since the Federal Communication Commission defines fairness simply as the presentation of opposing views on an issue, network news commonly has satisfied this requisite by soliciting views from spokesmen of two opposing sides in a controversy—and then editing the opposing views together as a "dialogue." To avoid any apparent disparities in the presentations, equally articulate spokesmen are usually selected to present the arguments on each side. Complicated issues thus appear to be merely a point-counterpoint debate between equally matched opponents. . . .

To be sure, network news cannot be entirely explained in terms of organizational requisites. The personal opinions of newsmen color newscasts to some degree, no matter how stringent a network's controls; also, reporting and editorials in other news media, especially the *New York Times* and *Time* magazine, help crystallize issues and heavily influence the producers in their selection of news. Nonetheless, the organizational imperatives of network news, and the logics that proceed from these demands, irresistibly shape the pictures of society in consistent directions, and therefore produce a very particular, perhaps unique, version of national news. In this version, all local events tend to be transmuted to great national themes, with the inevitable loss of their local and specific character. Since the events that are used to illustrate the national themes tend to be taken from large cosmopolitan centers, which are economically and geographically the most convenient sources of news, the themes tend to follow the line of conflict in such cities as New York, Washington and Chicago. To maintain the interest of the audience, happenings involving visual conflict are routinely selected over less violent ones, and ones involving recognizable figures of authority are selected over less identifiable images. . . .

Moreover, the requirement to present conflicts as disputes between no more than two equally matched sides tends to reduce complex issues, which may have a multitude of dimensions, to a simple conflict between protesters (or nonauthorities) and authorities.

[C]onsider the conservative critique which holds that network news is politically biased in favor of the causes and leaders of the liberal-left faction. In this critique, the liberal-left bias of television is generally attributed to a small clique of newsmen in New York and Washington who share the same perspectives on politics, report preponderantly the same kinds of challenges to established authority, and then shape the news to fit their own political commitments. What emerges is seen as a consistently distorted view of a small minority which is falsely represented as the beliefs of a majority of Americans. Since in this critique network news is presumed to be highly politicized by the men who select and report it, the remedy most often suggested is to employ conservative newsmen to balance the liberal viewpoints. . . .

The organizational approach accounts for some of the same manifestations in less political terms. While most of the domestic news on the network programs does, in fact, come from a few cities—New York, Washington, and Chicago—it is because news is less expensive and more conveniently available from these cities, not because of the political preferences of any small fraternity of newsmen, as Vice-President Agnew suggested. Moreover, since a considerable portion of the efforts to change the distribution of political values and services were concentrated in Washington, New York and Chicago during the 1960s for a complex of reasons, network news reported, willy-nilly, a disproportionately large share of these activities. And since the logic of audience maintenance favors conflict between easily recognizable groups, network news almost irresistibly focuses on challenges to established authority. . . .

In short, the tendency of network news to focus their attention on certain causes to the comparative neglect of others proceeds more from organizational problems than from the political biases of individuals. . . . ■

The foregoing has examined the issue of bias in news and other public affairs programs. It hardly needs to be said however, that, in general, TV entertainment programs are much more popular than news. Entertainment often seems to be what commercial television is all about. If *it* is biased, then bias is practically everywhere on TV.

But what does bias mean in the context of entertainment? Critics contend that the plots and characterizations of TV entertainment programs carry messages, morals, and cues to behavior which teach us lessons about how to behave and how to react to the social-political environment. What lessons? Here the critics are not in full agreement, though some leading ones think that TV entertainment writers lean toward liberal ideology. Writer Ben Stein, in his THE VIEW FROM SUNSET BOULEVARD (Basic Books, 1979), thinks that the entertainment programs are incessantly anti-business. This is also the conclusion of a study published by The Media Institute, a pro-business think tank. In the expressive title of its pamphlet, businessmen on TV are *Crooks, Conmen and Clowns* (The Media Institute, 1981). Political scientist Michael Robinson is convinced that the bias of TV entertainment tended toward political conservatism in the 1970s, except on "social" issues like abortion, premarital sex, and marijuana. See Michael J. Robinson, "Prime Time Chic," *Public Opinion,* March/May 1979. Political scientists David L. Paletz and Robert M. Entman do not think that the bias of TV entertainment is liberal in any sense. In their MEDIA POWER POLITICS (Free Press, 1981) they develop the argument that television entertainment adheres "to the familiar social values and practices" while serving to stimulate business by creating false needs.

A necessary corollary to the issue of bias is the question of how much effect it has on the mind of the viewer. If we are relatively impervious to the ideological tilt of news or entertainment programs, then bias may not be so important. It may be annoying for a conservative (or liberal) to see TV programs pushing liberal (or conservative) values, but it would be consoling to know that viewers are unaffected by it. But are they? In a larger framework, the question becomes; to what extent, if at all, are we manipulated by what we see on TV? This is the question now to be debated.

CHAPTER 5

Are We Manipulated By The Media?

In 1957 Vance Packard published THE HIDDEN PERSUADERS, a book arguing that "many of us are being influenced and manipulated, far more than we realize, in the patterns of our everyday lives." TV was one of the manipulators, constantly selling us products, candidates, ways of life. Packard was particularly horrified by "the extraordinary ability of TV to etch messages on young brains." As he was working on his book he heard his own eight-year-old daughter singing a cigarette jingle: "Don't miss the fun of smoking."

Packard's book was an instant best-seller, and within eight years it went through nineteen printings. The title itself became catchy, so that people who had never opened the book were soon talking about the danger of "hidden persuaders." A market had developed for an abundance of books with similar themes, from philosophical works to treatises on "subliminal seduction."

How much truth is there in the contention that people are manipulated by their TV sets? Can normal people be made to vote for candidate A over candidate B because candidate A uses more or cleverer TV ads? Can violence, or promiscuity, or compulsive buying be elicited by the shadows on a television screen? Ordinary people tend to answer "yes" to such questions; the experts tend to say "no," or at least "we don't know." Packard's thesis is usually dismissed by social scientists as typical "pop sociology" because there is a shortage of systematic, empirical data to back it up. For the layman, however, it seems as if there must be something to the contention that candidates can be "sold"—otherwise, why would candidates spend so much money on ads? As for the sex and violence on television, they have got to have *some* effect. Common sense would seem to be on the layman's side, but the social scientist has a ready reply: common sense, which is usually nothing more than received opinion and prejudice, can be highly misleading; it is never a substitute for hard data.

While the larger questions are still unresolved (we have not gotten much further than Bernard Berelson's conclusion a generation ago that "some kinds of communication, on some kinds of issues, brought to the attention of some kinds of people, under some kinds of conditions, have some kinds of effects"), in recent years social scientists have taken up some narrower questions and tried to find data for resolving them. One of them concerns the type of TV ads used to promote political candidates. Can they be sold to the American voters like commercial products? Putting it another way, does "image" advertising work better than advertising which spells out the candidate's political program?

In THE SELLING OF THE PRESIDENT 1968 Joe McGinnis suggested that Richard Nixon was "sold" to the American public by the use of TV spots that were mindless if not outright mendacious. The "image" of Nixon was sold to us much in the same way that Coca-Cola is sold to us. We are not told the ingredients of Coke. We are not told what it does for us, or to us. We are just given images of happy people frolicking in the sun, and left to make the emotional association between Coke and happiness. Nixon's ads used the same "image" approach, McGinnis said, because Nixon's media advisors shared the typical Madison Avenue view that the American voter is an imbecile.

Here are some excerpts from McGinnis's book.

THE SELLING OF THE PRESIDENT

Joe McGinnis, from THE SELLING OF THE PRESIDENT 1968, (New York, 1970)

. . . Politics, in a sense, has always been a con game.

The American voter, insisting upon his belief in a higher order, clings to his religion, which promises another, better life; and defends passionately the illusion that the men he chooses to lead him are of finer nature than he.

It has been traditional that the successful politician honor this illusion. To succeed today, he must embellish it. Particularly if he wants to be President.

"Potential presidents are measured against an ideal that's a combination of leading man, God, father, hero, pope, king, with maybe just a touch of the avenging Furies thrown in," an adviser to Richard Nixon wrote in a memorandum late in 1967. Then, perhaps aware that Nixon qualified only as father, he discussed improvements that would have to be made—not upon Nixon himself, but upon the image of him which was received by the voter.

That there is a difference between the individual and his image is human nature. Or American nature, at least. That the difference is exaggerated and exploited electronically is the reason for this book.

Advertising, in many ways, is a con game, too. Human beings do not need new automobiles every third year; a color television set brings little enrichment of the human experience; a higher or lower hemline no expansion of consciousness, no increase in the capacity to love.

It is not surprising, then, that politicians and advertising men should have discovered one another. And, once they recognized that the citizen did not so much vote for a candidate as make a psychological purchase of him, not surprising that they began to work together.

The voter, as reluctant to face political reality as any other kind, was hardly an unwilling victim. "The deeper problems connected with advertising," Daniel Boorstin has written in THE IMAGE, "come less from the unscrupulousness of our 'deceivers' than from our pleasure in being deceived, less from the desire to seduce than from the desire to be seduced. . . .

"In the last half-century we have misled ourselves . . . about men . . . and how much greatness can be found among them. . . . We have become so accustomed to our illusions that we mistake them for reality. We demand them. And we demand that there be always more of them, bigger and better and more vivid."

The Presidency seems the ultimate extension of our error.

Advertising agencies have tried openly to sell Presidents since 1952. When Dwight Eisenhower ran for re-election in 1956, the agency of Batton, Barton, Durstine and Osborn, which had been on a retainer throughout his first four years, accepted his campaign as a regular account. Leonard Hall, national Republican chairman, said: "You sell your candidates and your programs the way a business sells its products."

The only change over the past twelve years has been that, as technical sophistication has increased, so has circumspection. The ad men were removed from the parlor but were given a suite upstairs.

What Boorstin says of advertising: "It has meant a reshaping of our very concept of truth," is particularly true of advertising on TV.

With the coming of television, and the knowledge of how it could be used to seduce voters, the old political values disappeared. Something new, murky, undefined started to rise from the mists. "In all countries," Marshall McLuhan writes, "the party system has folded like the organization chart. Policies and issues are useless for election purposes, since they are too specialized and hot. The shaping of a candidate's integral image has taken the place of discussing conflicting points of view."

Americans have never quite digested television. The mystique which should fade grows stronger. We make celebrities not only of the men who cause events but of the men who read reports of them aloud.

The televised image can become as real to the housewife as her husband,

and much more attractive. Hugh Downs is a better breakfast companion, Merv Griffin cozier to snuggle with on the couch.

Television, in fact, has given status to the "celebrity" which few real men attain. And the "celebrity" here is the one described by Boorstin: "Neither good nor bad, great nor petty . . . the human pseudo-event . . . fabricated on purpose to satisfy our exaggerated expectations of human greatness."

This is, perhaps, where the twentieth century and its pursuit of illusion have been leading us. "In the last half-century," Boorstin writes, "the old heroic human mold has been broken. A new mold has been made, so that marketable human models—modern 'heroes'—could be mass-produced, to satisfy the market, and without any hitches. The qualities which now commonly make a man or woman into a 'nationally advertised' brand are in fact a new category of human emptiness."

The television celebrity is a vessel. An inoffensive container in which someone else's knowledge, insight, compassion, or wit can be presented. And we respond like the child on Christmas morning who ignores the gift to play with the wrapping paper.

Television seems particularly useful to the politician who can be charming but lacks ideas. Print is for ideas. Newspapermen write not about people but policies; the paragraphs can be slid around like blocks. Everyone is colored gray. Columnists—and commentators in the more polysyllabic magazines—concentrate on ideology. They do not care what a man sounds like; only how he thinks. For the candidate who does not, such exposure can be embarrassing. He needs another way to reach the people.

On television it matters less that he does not have ideas. His personality is what the viewers want to share. He need be neither statesman nor crusader; he must only show up on time. Success and failure are easily measured: How often is he invited back? Often enough and he reaches his goal—to advance from "politician" to "celebrity," a status jump bestowed by grateful viewers who feel that finally they have been given the basis for making a choice.

The TV candidate, then, is measured not against his predecessors—not against a standard of performance established by two centuries of democracy—but against Mike Douglas. How well does he handle himself? Does he mumble, does he twitch, does he make me laugh? Do I feel warm inside?

Style becomes substance. The medium is the massage and the masseur gets the votes.

In office, too, the ability to project electronically is essential. We were willing to forgive John Kennedy his Bay of Pigs; we followed without question the perilous course on which he led us when missiles were found in Cuba; we even tolerated his calling of reserves for the sake of a bluff about Berlin.

We forgave, followed, and accepted because we liked the way he looked.

And he had a pretty wife. Camelot was fun, even for the peasants, as long as it was televised to their huts.

Then came Lyndon Johnson, heavy and gross, and he was forgiven nothing. He might have survived the sniping of the displaced intellectuals had he only been able to charm. But no one taught him how. Johnson was syrupy. He stuck to the lens. There was no place for him in our culture.

"The success of any TV performer depends on his achieving a low-pressure style of presentation," McLuhan has written. The harder a man tries, the better he must hide it. Television demands gentle wit, irony, understatement: the qualities of Eugene McCarthy. The TV politician cannot make a speech; he must engage in intimate conversation. He must never press. He should suggest, not state; request, not demand. Nonchalance is the key word. Carefully studied nonchalance.

Warmth and sincerity are desirable but must be handled with care. Unfiltered, they can be fatal. Television did great harm to Hubert Humphrey. His excesses—talking too long and too fervently, which were merely annoying in an auditorium—became lethal in a television studio. The performer must talk to one person at a time. He is brought into the living room. He is a guest. It is improper for him to shout. Humphrey vomited on the rug.

It would be extremely unwise for the TV politician to admit such knowledge of his medium. The necessary nonchalance should carry beyond his appearance while *on* the show; it should rule his attitude *toward* it. He should express distaste for television; suspicion that there is something "phony" about it. This guarantees him good press, because newspaper reporters, bitter over their loss of prestige to the television men, are certain to stress anti-television remarks. Thus, the sophisticated candidate, while analyzing his own on-the-air technique as carefully as a golf pro studies his swing, will state frequently that there is no place for "public relations gimmicks" or "those show business guys" in his campaign. Most of the television men working for him will be unbothered by such remarks. They are willing to accept anonymity, even scorn, as long as the pay is good.

Into this milieu came Richard Nixon: grumpy, cold and aloof. He would claim privately that he lost elections because the American voter was an adolescent whom he tried to treat as an adult. Perhaps. But if he treated the voter as an adult, it was as an adult he did not want for a neighbor.

This might have been excused had he been a man of genuine vision. An explorer of the spirit. Martin Luther King, for instance, got by without being one of the boys. But Richard Nixon did not strike people that way. He had, in Richard Rovere's words, "an advertising man's approach to his work," acting as if he believed "policies [were] products to be sold the public—this one today, that one tomorrow, depending on the discounts and the state of the market."

So his enemies had him on two counts: his personality, and the convictions—or lack of such—which lay behind. They worked him over heavily on both.

Norman Mailer remembered him as "a church usher, of the variety who would twist a boy's ear after removing him from church."

McLuhan watched him debate Kennedy and thought he resembled "the railway lawyer who signs leases that are not in the best interests of the folks in the little town."

But Nixon survived, despite his flaws, because he was tough and smart, and—some said—dirty when he had to be. Also, because there was nothing else he knew. A man to whom politics is all there is in life will almost always beat one to whom it is only an occupation.

He nearly became President in 1960, and that year it would not have been by default. He failed because he was too few of the things a President had to be—and because he had no press to lie for him and did not know how to use television to lie about himself.

It was just Nixon and John Kennedy and they sat down together in a television studio and a little red light began to glow and Richard Nixon was finished. Television would be blamed but for all the wrong reasons.

They would say it was makeup and lighting, but Nixon's problem went deeper than that. His problem was himself. Not what he said but the man he was. The camera portrayed him clearly. America took its Richard Nixon straight and did not like the taste.

The content of the programs made little difference. Except for startling lapses, content seldom does. What mattered was the image the viewers received, though few observers at the time caught the point.

McLuhan read Theodore White's THE MAKING OF THE PRESIDENT book and was appalled at the section on the debates. "White offers statistics on the number of sets in American homes and the number of hours of daily use of these sets, but not one clue as to the nature of the TV image or its effects on candidates or viewers. White considers the 'content' of the debates and the deportment of the debaters, but it never occurs to him to ask why TV would inevitably be a disaster for a sharp intense image like Nixon's and a boon for the blurry, shaggy texture of Kennedy." In McLuhan's opinion: "Without TV, Nixon had it made."

What the camera showed was Richard Nixon's hunger. He lost, and bitter, confused, he blamed it on his beard.

He made another, lesser thrust in 1962, and that failed, too. He showed the world a little piece of his heart the morning after and then he moved East to brood. They did not want him, the hell with them. He was going to Wall Street and get rich.

He was afraid of television. He knew his soul was hard to find. Beyond that, he considered it a gimmick; its use in politics offended him. It had not been part of the game when he had learned to play, he could see no reason to bring it in now. He half suspected it was an eastern liberal trick: one more way to make him look silly. It offended his sense of dignity, one of the truest senses he had.

So his decision to use it to become President in 1968 was not easy. So much of him argued against it. But in his Wall Street years, Richard Nixon had traveled to the darkest places inside himself and come back numbed. He was, as in the Graham Greene title, a burnt-out case. All feeling was behind him; the machine inside had proved his hardiest part. He would run for President again and if he would have to learn television to run well, then he would learn it.

America still saw him as the 1960 Nixon. If he were to come at the people again, as candidate, it would have to be as something new; not this scarred, discarded figure from their past.

He spoke to men who thought him mellowed. They detected growth, a new stability, a sense of direction that had been lacking. He would return with fresh perspective, a more unselfish urgency.

His problem was how to let the nation know. He could not do it through the press. He knew what to expect from them, which was the same as he had always gotten. He would have to circumvent them. Distract them with coffee and doughnuts and smiles from his staff and tell his story another way.

Television was the only answer, despite its sins against him in the past. But not just any kind of television. An uncommitted camera could do irreparable harm. His television would have to be controlled. He would need experts. They would have to find the proper settings for him, or if they could not be found, manufacture them. These would have to be men of keen judgment and flawless taste. He was, after all, Richard Nixon, and there were certain things he could not do. Wearing love beads was one. He would need men of dignity, who believed in him and shared his vision. But more importantly, men who knew television as a weapon: from broadest concept to most technical detail. This would be Richard Nixon, the leader, returning from exile. Perhaps not beloved, but respected. Firm but not harsh; just but compassionate. With flashes of warmth spaced evenly throughout. . . .

Harry Treleaven, hired as creative director of advertising in the fall of 1967, immediately went to work on the more serious of Nixon's personality problems. One was his lack of humor.

"Can be corrected to a degree," Treleaven wrote, "but let's not be too obvious about it. Romney's cornball attempts have hurt him. If we're going to be witty, let a pro write the words."

Treleaven also worried about Nixon's lack of warmth but decided that "he can be helped greatly in this respect by how he is handled. . . . Give him words to say that will show his *emotional* involvement in the issues. . . . Buchanan wrote about RFK talking about the starving children in Recife. *That's* what we have to inject. . . .

"He should be presented in some kind of 'situation' rather than cold in a studio. The situation should look unstaged even if it's not."

Some of the most effective ideas belonged to Raymond K. Price, a former editorial writer for the *New York Herald Tribune,* who became Nixon's best and most prominent speech writer in the campaign. Price later composed much of the inaugural address.

In 1967, he began with the assumption that, "The natural human use of reason is to support prejudice, not to arrive at opinions." Which led to the conclusion that rational arguments would "only be effective if we can get the people to make the *emotional* leap, or what theologians call [the] 'leap of faith.' "

Price suggested attacking the "personal factors" rather than the "historical factors" which were the basis of the low opinion so many people had of Richard Nixon.

"These tend to be more a gut reaction," Price wrote, "unarticulated, non-analytical, a product of the particular chemistry between the voter and the *image* of the candidate. *We have to be very clear on this point; that the response is to the image, not to the man.* . . . It's not what's *there* that counts, it's what's projected—and carrying it one step further, it's not what *he* projects but rather what the voter receives. It's not the man we have to change, but rather the *received impression.* And this impression often depends more on the medium and its use than it does on the candidate himself."

So there would not have to be a "new Nixon." Simply a new approach to television.

"What, then, does this mean in terms of our uses of time and of media?" Price wrote.

"For one thing, it means investing whatever time RN needs in order to work out firmly in his own mind that vision of the nation's future that he wants to be identified with. This is crucial. . . ."

So, at the age of fifty-four, after twenty years in public life, Richard Nixon was still felt *by his own staff* to be in need of time to "work out firmly in his own mind that vision of the nation's future that he wants to be identified with."

"Secondly," Price wrote, "it suggests that we take the time and the money to experiment, in a controlled manner, with film and television techniques, with particular emphasis on pinpointing those *controlled* uses of the television medium that can *best* convey the *image* we want to get across. . . .

"The TV medium itself introduces an element of distortion, in terms of its effect on the candidate and of the often subliminal ways in which the image is received. And it inevitably is going to convey a partial image—thus ours is the task of finding how to control its use so the part that gets across is the part we want to have gotten across. . . .

"Voters are basically lazy, basically uninterested in making an *effort* to understand what we're talking about . . . ," Price wrote. "Reason requires a high degree of discipline, of concentration; impression is easier. Reason pushes the viewer back, it assaults him, it demands that he agree or disagree; impression can envelop him, invite him in, without making an intellectual demand. . . . When we argue with him we demand that he make the effort of replying. We seek to engage his intellect, and for most people this is the most difficult work of all. The emotions are more easily roused, closer to the surface, more malleable. . . . "

So, for the New Hampshire primary, Price recommended "saturation with a film, in which the candidate can be shown better than he can be shown in person because it can be edited, so only the best moments are shown; then a quick parading of the candidate in the flesh so that the guy they've gotten intimately acquainted with on the screen takes on a living presence—not saying anything, just being seen. . . .

"[Nixon] has to come across as a person larger than life, the stuff of legend. People are stirred by the legend, including the living legend, not by the man himself. It's the aura that surrounds the charismatic figure more than it is the figure itself, that draws the followers. Our task is to build that aura. . . .

"So let's not be afraid of television gimmicks . . . get the voters to like the guy and the battle's two-thirds won."

So this was how they went into it. Trying, with one hand, to build the illusion that Richard Nixon, in addition to his attributes of mind and heart, considered, in the words of Patrick K. Buchanan, a speech writer, "communicating with the people . . . one of the great joys of seeking the Presidency"; while with the other they shielded him, controlled him, and controlled the atmosphere around him. It was as if they were building not a President but an Astrodome, where the wind would never blow, the temperature never rise or fall, and the ball never bounce erratically on the artificial grass.

They could do this, and succeed, because of the special nature of the man. There was, apparently, something in Richard Nixon's character which sought this shelter. Something which craved regulation, which flourished best in the darkness, behind clichés, behind phalanxes of antiseptic advisers. Some part of him that could breathe freely only inside a hotel suite that cost a hundred dollars a day.

And it worked. As he moved serenely through his primary campaign, there was new cadence to Richard Nixon's speech and motion; new confidence in his heart. And, a new image of him on the television screen.

TV both reflected and contributed to his strength. Because he was winning he looked like a winner on the screen. Because he was suddenly projecting well on the medium he had feared, he went about his other tasks with assurance. The one fed upon the other, building to an astonishing peak in August as the Republican convention began and he emerged from his regal isolation, traveling to Miami not so much to be nominated as coronated. On live, but controlled, TV. . . . ■

McGinnis's revelations make depressing reading, because we know that this sort of manipulation was not confined to the Nixon campaign of 1968. It is a common feature of campaigns today. Who has not seen those 30-second spots showing shirtsleeved candidates walking through blighted streets looking "concerned"? Or candidates pledging to "get tough on criminals" without saying how they would do it? Or a candidate listening sympathetically to "ordinary Americans" telling him their woes, while a voiceover assures us that "he cares"? Nixon For President in '68 may have been the paradigm of "image" campaigning; was far from being unique.

Yet there may be grounds for hope. What is conspicuously lacking in McGinnis's book is any real discussion of causality. Is there any proof that Nixon was elected *because* of his cynically-motivated advertising campaign? Other factors may better explain Nixon's victory: a deep schism in the Democratic Party brought on by the Vietnam war, the spectacle of violent confrontations at the Democratic convention in Chicago that year, antipathy of many antiwar Democrats toward the candidacy of Hubert Humphrey. The suspicion that Nixon's ads had little or nothing to do with his electoral success is strengthened by the fact that Nixon's popularity decreased and Humphrey's increased as election day approached—this *in spite* of the increased use of the Nixon commercials during the same time period.

At any rate, during Nixon's re-election campaign four years later, two political scientists, Thomas Patterson and Robert McClure, were carefully watching (and re-watching, on video tape), interviewing voters, and laying the groundwork for some interesting conclusions about television news coverage and television commercials. As regards commercials, their conclusion was that political image-making simply does not work, for voters have a perverse way of seeing what they want to see: if they don't like a candidate's platform they can't be made to like his image.

Patterson and McClure began circulating some of their findings in mimeographed form as early as the spring of 1973. In 1976 they published them in a scholarly but highly readable book, THE UNSEEING EYE, from which the following is excerpted:

IMAGE-MAKING DOESN'T WORK

Patterson and McClure, from THE UNSEEING EYE: THE MYTH OF TELEVISION POWER IN NATIONAL ELECTIONS (New York, 1976)

. . . One minute after a product commercial fades from the television screen, most viewers have forgotten what was advertised. They cannot recall whether the ad trumpeted aspirin, shaving cream, or automobiles. A particularly clever or amusing commercial may draw some notice, and linger in their thoughts, but most product ads pass from the mind as quickly as from the screen.

Presidential ads affect viewers differently. On television only a month or two every four years, their novelty attracts attention. Also their subject matter. They picture and discuss men seeking the nation's highest office, and most Americans feel that choosing a President deserves more consideration than selecting a brand of antacid. A clear indication of presidential advertising's attention-getting ability is that most viewers can rather fully recall the message of a presidential spot. When asked to describe a commercial they had seen during the 1972 election, 56 percent of the viewers gave a remarkably full and complete description of one, and only 21 percent were unable to recall anything at all from political ads. In market research, any product whose commercials are recalled with half this accuracy is considered to have had a very successful advertising campaign.

People also evaluate presidential advertising differently than product advertising. A study conducted for the American Association of Advertising Agencies in the 1960's discovered that television viewers judge product commercials more on *how* they communicate their message than on *what* they say about a product. A commercial for a soft drink or a paper towel is regarded as good or bad by the television audience more on whether it is enjoyable to watch than on the truthfulness of its message or the value of the information it contains. People judge presidential ads, on the other hand, primarily on *what* they say, not *how* they say it. Whether the techniques used in presidential spots are visually appealing or unappealing seems to matter little. Viewers seem concerned mainly with whether the advertising message is truthful and worth knowing. Where the American Association of Advertising Agencies' study found that only 46 percent of viewer reactions to product ads related to the information communicated, 74 percent of viewer reactions to presidential commercials shown in 1972 centered on the information contained in the message.

Thus, presidential spots get noticed, and the attention centers on the message. But to what end? Does the viewer learn anything about the candidates? Does he find out anything about the issues?

For years, most political observers have been certain they knew the answers: Advertising builds false political images and robs the American electorate of important issue information. On both counts, this orthodox view is wrong. In a presidential campaign, spot commercials do much more to educate the public about the issues than they do to manipulate the public about the candidates.

ADVERTISING'S IMAGE IMPACT

In presidential politics, advertising image-making is a wasted effort. All the careful image planning—the coaching, the camera work, the calculated plea—counts for nothing. Just as with network news appearances, people's feelings about the candidate's politics—his party, past actions, and future policies—far outweigh the influence of televised commercials.

Strong evidence for advertising's ineffectiveness comes from a look at *changes* in voters' images during the 1972 campaign. Just before presidential ads began appearing on television and again when the candidates' ad campaigns were concluding, the same people were asked to judge the images of Nixon and McGovern. They evaluated each candidate on seven traits associated with personality and leadership. Because the same people were questioned each time, an exact measure exists of how their images changed during the time when the candidates' ads were appearing on television.

These changes in voters' images indicate that advertising image-making had no effect. Among people who preferred Nixon, his image showed a 35 percent improvement and McGovern's image a 28 percent decline. This happened among people exposed to many of the candidates' ads and to those seeing few commercials, if any. Among people backing McGovern, however, his image made a 20 percent improvement and Nixon's had an 18 percent decline. And again, no significant difference occurred in the image changes of people heavily and lightly exposed to presidential advertising.

Thus, whether people watched television regularly, and constantly saw the advertised images of Nixon and McGovern, had no influence on their impressions of the two candidates. Whatever people were getting from political spots, it was not their images of the candidates.

As it did when examining the influence of network news on images, this conclusion gains significance from McGovern's candidacy. The South Dakota Senator was the classic little-known nominee. In his campaign, he depended heavily on televised political advertising, and in the vast majority of spots, he appeared on the screen to communicate his message directly to the viewers. If ever a valid test of advertising's image power existed, it was the McGovern campaign. His image should have become uniformly better or worse as a result of spot exposure. Yet, it became both better and worse, dependent solely on people's politics, not on their exposure to McGovern's advertising.

By projecting their political biases, people see in candidates' commercials pretty much what they want to see. Ads sponsored by the candidate who shares their politics get a good response. They like what he has to say. And they like him. Ads sponsored by the opposing candidate are viewed negatively. They object to what he says. And they object to him.

A sampling of viewers' reactions to the series of image commercials used by George McGovern throughout the general election campaign illustrates how strongly political bias affects viewers. These spots pictured McGovern among small groups of people in natural settings, discussing their problems and promising to help them if elected. The commercials were intended to project an image of McGovern as a man who cared about people. Whether viewers received this image, however, had little to do with what happened on the television screen. It was all in their minds:

> He really cares what's happened to disabled vets. They told him how badly they've been treated and he listened. He will help them.
> —37-year-old, pro-McGovern viewer

> McGovern was talking with these disabled vets. He doesn't really care about them. He's just using them to get sympathy.
> —33-year-old, pro-Nixon viewer

> It was honest, down-to-earth. People were talking and he was listening.
> —57-year-old, pro-McGovern viewer

> Those commercials are so phoney. He doesn't care.
> —45-year-old, pro-Nixon viewer

> McGovern had his coat off and his tie was hanging down. It was so relaxed, and he seemed to really be concerned with those workers.
> —31-year-old, pro-McGovern viewer

> He is trying hard to look like one of the boys. You know, roll up the shirt sleeves and loosen the tie. It's just too much for me to take.
> —49-year-old, pro-Nixon viewer

> I have seen many ads where McGovern is talking to common people. You know, like workers and the elderly. He means what he says. He'll help them.
> —22-year-old, pro-McGovern viewer

> He's with all these groups of people. Always making promises. He's promising more than can be done. Can't do everything for everyone.
> —41-year-old, pro-Nixon viewer

These people were watching the same George McGovern, listening to the same words, and yet they were receiving vastly different impressions of the Democratic presidential nominee.

Even undecided voters are not influenced by advertising image-making. Just like partisans, the candidate images of undecided voters fluctuate with vote choice, not advertising exposure. In 1972, undecided voters' images changed very little and fit no definite pattern until after they had picked their candidate. Among those choosing Nixon, and only after they had done so, his image had a 35 percent improvement and McGovern's a 35 percent decline. This pattern of image change was the rule for those seeing many presidential ads and those seeing few or none. Likewise, for those picking McGovern, his image showed a 40 percent improvement and Nixon's a 55 percent decline. Again, there was no difference in this pattern based on the undecided voter's exposure to televised political commercials.

Spot ads do not mold presidential images because voters are not easily misled. They recognize that advertising imagery is heavily laden with something that is not intrinsically related to personal character at all—how the candidate looks on camera. This pseudocharacter, to some extent coached, posed, and created by the best media talent money can buy, is a "look" built into spots that is totally unreal. And viewers recognize its meaninglessness. Even the candid portrayals of presidential aspirants that sometimes appear in image appeals are ineffective. People's guards go up when a spot goes on. So no matter the style of presentation, when only 60 seconds are used to say that a candidate is big enough to handle the presidency, voters find the message skimpy, debatable, and unconvincing. They know that the candidate will display his strengths and mask his weaknesses and that a 60-second glimpse does not provide much of an insight into a man's fitness for the nation's highest office.

Symbolic manipulation through televised political advertising simply does not work. Perhaps the overuse of symbols and stereotypes in product advertising has built up an immunity in the television audience. Perhaps the symbols and postures used in political advertising are such patently obvious attempts at manipulation that they appear more ridiculous than reliable. Whatever the precise reason, television viewers effectively protect themselves from manipulation by staged imagery.

ADVERTISING'S ISSUE IMPACT

But where image appeals fail, issue appeals work. Through commercials, presidential candidates actually inform the electorate. In fact, the contribution of advertising campaigns to voter knowledge is truly impressive.

During the 1972 presidential election, people who were heavily exposed to political spots became more informed about the candidates' issue positions. On every single issue emphasized in presidential commercials, persons with high exposure to television advertising showed a greater increase in knowledge than persons with low exposure. And on the typical issue, individuals who happened to see many commercials were nearly half again as likely to become more knowledgeable as people who saw few, if any, televised spots. Issue knowledge among people with considerable advertising exposure achieved a 36 percent increase compared with a 25 percent increase among those with minimal exposure. Persons heavily exposed to advertising were particularly aided in their knowledge about Nixon's position on China and military spending and about McGovern's position on military spending and taxes.

This information gain represents no small achievement. Televised political advertising has been widely maligned for saying nothing of consequence. Although the issue material contained in spots is incomplete and oversimplified, it also is abundant. So abundant in fact, that presidential advertising contributes to an informed electorate.

Advertising also educates voters because of the powerful way it transmits its issue content. Three basic advertising strategies—simplicity, repetition, and sight-sound coordination—combine to make presidential spots good communicators. Ads contain such simple messages that they leave almost no room for misunderstanding. . . .

THE MYTH THAT LONGER IS BETTER

Most political observers are highly critical of televised spots and wish that presidential candidates would forsake them for broadcasts at least 30 minutes long. On its face, their argument appears reasonable. According to the critics, political spots are so short they reduce complex campaign issues to trivial and misleading nonsense. Therefore, since longer broadcasts permit more extended and meaningful political discussion, they are obviously preferable to the shorter political spots.

The argument, however, has two flaws. First, and most important, it overlooks a crucial difference between advertising spots and longer broadcasts. People watch spots. Longer programs get turned off. Second, it exaggerates the consequences of commercial brevity.

A 30-minute political discussion must compete for an audience with other prime-time shows, and candidate-sponsored broadcasts are no match for television's entertainment programming. Faced with watching *All in the Family* or a half-hour political show, few Americans choose politics. Overwhelmingly, Archie Bunker would outpoll George McGovern. Just as overwhelmingly, he would outdraw George Wallace. Paid political broadcasts consistently wind up at the bottom of television's audience ratings. By their own admission, only one in twenty adults bothered to watch the typical 30-minute candidate broadcast during the 1972 election. Regardless of how much information they contain, longer broadcasts cannot inform people who do not watch. A message unheard has to be a message unheeded.

Just as importantly, the people who watch these programs are more likely to be those who follow the campaign closely in the newspaper. Infrequent newspaper readers, precisely those people who usually are the least informed, are less likely to spend the time viewing a 30-minute broadcast—during the 1972 election, only one in thirty-five of these people watched the typical lengthy political telecast. For them, *any* entertainment program beats watching *any* presidential candidate for 30 minutes.

Longer broadcasts, because they attract only the highly partisan, have become the television equivalent of the traditional political rally. They are a gathering point for the faithful few, and a means for raising funds. (For a brief period after George McGovern's first 30-minute telecast, which contained a lengthy plea for financial help, small contributions to his campaign tripled.) But longer broadcasts are *not* the means to communicate with a cross section of the American electorate.

And finally, critics of commercial brevity exaggerate the comparison between the content in television spots and the content in other forms of political communication. Just because they may contain more words, do other forms of political communication contain more real content than political commercials? How many political messages in any medium outline an issue point-by-point, indicate the candidate's position, and then discuss whether the position is realistic, moral, and just. Almost none. It is seldom done at a campaign rally, in a direct-mail letter, or in the flyer stuck in the door. Regardless of the method of candidate communication, political argument is seldom academic dialogue.

Even when the candidate does not control the communication, political information usually flows, as Walter Lippmann described it, in bits and pieces. Except in long magazine articles, lengthy pieces of newspaper analysis, or half-hour television broadcasts, issue information filters to the voters a little bit at a time. The typical newspaper story packs more issue material than a 60-second spot, but the 5-minute ad is a close rival. And without doubt, many 60-second spots contain as much relevant content as the basic issue blurb on network news. Indeed, the 5-minute ad is far more informative than almost any issue report on the nightly network news broadcasts.

Nor is it appropriate to evaluate advertising by looking at the contents of a single commercial. Any single spot is only one part of an entire ad campaign. Lumped together, the total advertising package of a presidential candidate contains a fair amount of information on a variety of issues, information which actually reaches millions of Americans over and over again. So in the final analysis, it is the short spot, not the 30-minute broadcast, that is able to have some cumulative effect on the broad electorate's sum total or political information. . . . ■

The Case of Ronney Zamora

On June 9, 1977 a fifteen-year-old boy named Ronney Albert Zamora was burglarizing the house of a neighbor, Elinor Haggart, an eighty-two year old widow. When Mrs. Haggart walked in and caught him in the act, young Zamora shot her in the stomach. She died shortly afterwards and the youth was put on trial for murder.

What makes this case interesting to us is that the defense attorney claimed that his client was not legally responsible for his act because "at the moment of this crime" he "could not distinguish if he was in a television play, acting it out, or whether it was cold-blooded, premeditated murder." In short, Ronney Zamora, brought to this country from Costa Rica at the age of five and placed all day in front of a TV set while his mother went to work, was "a television addict." He lived so completely in the world of *Baretta* and *Kojak* and *Police Woman* that he could not understand the difference between watching make-believe violence on TV and doing the real thing.

Appropriately enough, the trial was televised. Excerpts of it were later broadcast on educational television in a program entitled *TV on Trial*, with editor and writer Richard Reeves serving as the program host.

Was TV indeed on trial, and was its violent programming in some way to blame for the death of Elinor Haggart? Whatever the jury's thoughts may have been on these questions, it found Ronney Zamora guilty of first-degree murder.

Here is Mrs. Zamora's testimony about her son's video experiences, followed by defense attorney Ellis Rubin's summation and the prosecutor's reply.

MRS. ZAMORA'S TESTIMONY

From, *TV On Trial*, PBS, May 23, 1978

YOLANDA ZAMORA: The way he learned English actually was watching TV from the time he got up in the morning until he went to sleep, from the time he got here, because he came here on April and he didn't have to go to school until September.

RUBIN: So who thought of television as a way to teach him English?

MRS. ZAMORA: Well, there was nothing else he could do. I had to go out and work, my husband had to go out and work, and we asked this lady if she could watch him. So she would come from time to time to keep an eye on him, but it was nothing else to do. He was very active, and I was afraid he would run away or something. You know, open the door and let anybody in the apartment. So I thought of watching TV, and for him watching TV was the greatest thing in the world, because he was not used to watch TV when he came here.

RUBIN: And did there come a time when he started to imitate what he saw on television?

MRS. ZAMORA: Yes. He was just crazy about Superman, and there were times when he would drop a towel around his neck and ask my husband to open the window from the fourth floor, that he could jump out, because he wanted to try if he could do the same thing that Superman was doing. So we tried to tell him that it was not true that, you know, it's just something that goes on TV or in the books or whatever. But I remember that when he went—when we went to the beach, he used to take a plastic bag and just wrap it around his neck, and the air will get in the plastic bag and give him like—like . . .

RUBIN: Wings?

MRS. ZAMORA: Right. And he used to run back and forth and as a matter of fact, that I have pictures of him doing that.

RUBIN: And was he imitating somebody?

MRS. ZAMORA: Yes. He was imitating Superman. He thought he could do the same thing that Superman was doing.

RUBIN: And did he graduate from elementary school?

MRS. ZAMORA: Yes. In fourth grade, I had to take him out of the Catholic school because they thought his behavior was not good.

RUBIN: Well, what was wrong with it?

MRS. ZAMORA: Well, he would—he got into arguments with the nuns.

RUBIN: With the nuns?

MRS. ZAMORA: Yes, and I just . . .

RUBIN: Did you learn of this by the nuns calling you to school?

MRS. ZAMORA: Yes, I used to be in school whenever they called me, and they just told me that he was too active, and they couldn't keep him. So they asked me if I could place him in another school, so I did. And he was very happy. He wanted to leave there. He went to public school and that year, especially, he did very well.

RUBIN: What year was that?

MRS. ZAMORA: Fifth grade.

RUBIN: And how old was he by that time?

MRS. ZAMORA: By that time he was—let me see—eleven—eleven years old.

RUBIN: Now what were his—what were his television habits by this time? Was he starting to watch different kinds of programs than Superman and Batman?

MRS. ZAMORA: Well, he knew every single thing that was on TV.

RUBIN: Did you?

MRS. ZAMORA: I never been a TV watcher.

RUBIN: Did you know what he was watching?

MRS. ZAMORA: Yes, I know he loved the scary movies, which I hate. I know he likes all the police movies, because he could talk about them very, very well.

RUBIN: Did you allow him to see these?

MRS. ZAMORA: No.

RUBIN: Well then, how did he see them?

MRS. ZAMORA: Well, I used to lay down about eight o'clock because I had to get up at ten-thirty to go to work.

RUBIN: You mean at night?

MRS. ZAMORA: Yes.

RUBIN: Did he talk about television or watch television or—well, what were his daily habits?

MRS. ZAMORA: Well, last year in September of '76, I registered him in the Youth Center in Miami Beach. It was just opening up, the tuition or the fee was very low and they had all kinds of like swimming and basketball and all that. So I thought it was a good place for him to go. But after we got the report from school and his marks were so bad, both my husband and I agreed that he should stay out of the Youth Center. So he was not allowed to go to the Youth Center. So he would stay home and watch TV. There was nothing else to do. He didn't want to do his homework. He didn't want to read. He just—he would just watch TV.

RUBIN: By this time, did you know what kind of programs he was watching?

MRS. ZAMORA: Yes. I know very well, because a lot of times when my husband was not home he asked me many, many times to—he actually begged me to convince my husband to shave his head like Kojak. It's silly, but he had that in his mind. And . . .

RUBIN: Ronney wanted his father to shave his head like Kojak?

MRS. ZAMORA: To look like Kojak, yes.

RUBIN: Well, what happened when Ronney told his father that, or you told your husband?

MRS. ZAMORA: Well . . .

RUBIN: How did it happen?

MRS. ZAMORA: For a while there, he was going to do it. My husband was going to do it, but then one day he was mad and he said forget about it. "I won't please him." So Ronney was very upset because we almost had him convinced that he was going to shave his head like Kojak.

RUBIN: Did he talk about the program at all?

MRS. ZAMORA: Oh yes. He knew every single one. He just thought that the way Kojak works and his TV series, he is the greatest of them all. Like whatever he did there, it was the real thing, like it was nobody else could do it better.

RUBIN: Kojak kind of became his idol?

MRS. ZAMORA: Yes.

RUBIN: Did there come a time, Mrs. Zamora, when Ronney ran away from home?

MRS. ZAMORA: Yes. One Saturday my husband beat him up because his school—his report from school that week was very bad. Every single one of the teachers said that he was not listening, that he wasn't doing his homework, and he would just not do it. So finally, I got an appointment with Dr. Jacobs. He's the head of a psychological division in the Catholic Charities.

RUBIN: Did anything happen concerning Ronney?

MRS. ZAMORA: Yes. I understood that Ronney was suicidal. He had thoughts in his mind that he wanted to commit suicide.

RUBIN: Did you talk to the boy about this?

MRS. ZAMORA: Yes. We talked a lot of times and he told me that he just couldn't help it, that we were very strict at home, that we had taken him away from the Youth Center, that my husband punished him continuously, that he was not allowed to go out with—you know, to the movies and some other things, that he felt that there was nothing else for him to do but kill himself.

RUBIN: What did your husband do?

MRS. ZAMORA: Well, my husband never believed that. He said that was just a kid talk, that he wasn't meaning that, that he was—that he knew how much I suffered, so he wanted me to suffer more. But I'm—I don't—I never believed that, because Ronney was never being mean before. He was very, very warm, and I just couldn't understand how—how he had changed in a matter of a year. Now he was complaining because he said, well, "If you don't let me go out, I'm just going to put my head in the TV and I'm going to memorize every single pro—TV there is and maybe one day I'll get to Hollywood. The only thing you have to stop me from doing," he said, "Is stop breathing, because I got nothing else to do, just stay home, walk around, watch TV. And you don't let me go out and you don't let me do anything else."

SUMMATION FOR THE DEFENSE

Naturally, I'm fighting for Ronney Zamora. Of course, Ronney knew right from wrong, but I don't think that any doctor has told you that he wasn't a sociopathic personality who could not refrain from doing wrong, and he didn't care whether he did wrong. And from thousands and thousands and thousands of murders that he has seen, this was a reaction that he imitated, or a conditioned reflex. I'm not concerned with those scientific words. You and I are going to talk common sense. I couldn't understand half of what these doctors were talking about. That's why they're experts and they want to make us experts, because you're going to go in that little room, you're going to have to tell which psychiatrist was guessing correctly. It's a heavy burden.

Dr. Gilbert said that because of the saturation of the repeat and the repeat and the repeat of thousands of times seeing a murder—how many of us have ever seen one real murder? God forbid. This boy and children like him—how many people have seen thousands of murders? How many people has Kojak killed in upholding the law? Baretta, in upholding the law? Police Woman, the good girl, in upholding the law, kills with guns, so that you will buy the product that is sponsoring that program. You see, the more real the program, the more people want to see it. And the more violence in the program, the more people want to see it, because it's abnormal. It's bizarre. It's insane. And somehow man wants to see that violence.

It's almost six o'clock. Normally, that is supper time. But there are millions of people who don't eat supper at six o'clock anymore, because that's the time for the news on television. You see, television can change our habits. It used to be that people went to bed when the sun went down and got up when the sun got up. And then into the nineteenth century and the twentieth century, the Industrial Revolution and modern civilization and all of the conveniences that you and I enjoy. In the 1940's and '50's, along came this movie set in your own home. Why? So they started to produce programs which would draw attention and viewers, because the more viewers you get the more the producer of the program can charge the sponsors of the products that are advertised. So our sleeping habits started changing too. Television has changed when we eat and when we sleep and when we kill and when we don't kill, and how to kill, and the good guys can kill, and the bad guys can kill, and it all comes on the tube again next week, same time, same station. And we're getting so civilized now and so sophisticated and so great in our wealth and in our luxury that they even have murder and rape on giant screens in your own home, and that isn't good enough. Now, they've invented a machine that, in case there's a murder on one channel, and you want to see a rape on another channel, you can hook up this machine, and it records the channel that you're not watching, so that when you're not saturated with the murder, that isn't good enough, you can then go in your bedroom and hook up this machine and see the rape also. You don't miss a thing.

It's time we did something. It's time we did something for Elinor Haggart. Your verdict which says that Ronney Zamora is not guilty by reason of insanity—because if he were to be guilty of murder, television would be an accessory to the crime—your verdict is going to say this woman's life was not taken in vain, because your verdict is the day that it began to stop.

Thank you very much. ∎

SUMMATION FOR THE PROSECUTION

What has the defense offered as a reason for you not to hold this defendant accountable and responsible for what he did? The reason they've offered is, "I'm not guilty by reason of insanity, because I watch too much television."

My God. Where have we gotten when someone can come into a court of law and, with a straight face, ask you to excuse the death of a human being because the killer watched television? The defense in this case could have just as easily have been too much violence from reading the Bible; too much violence from reading history books; too much violence from reading the papers. Unfortunately, we do have violence in this world and we're exposed to it. But exposure to that violence does not make you legally insane, or we're going to have free license to do whatever. And what did the defense offer to establish their defense? Did you hear the efforts Mrs. Zamora went to help this defendant? She worked hard. She tried to make something of herself. She tried to help this defendant. Unfortunately and regrettably, he became a murderer. I suggest it was not Mrs. Zamora's fault.

∎

Ronney Zamora's case was not the only one in which TV was alleged to have induced violent behavior in young people. Shortly after the broadcast of a TV drama portraying youths burning a woman alive by pouring gasoline on her and igniting it, a group of teenagers did precisely that to a woman in Boston, with fatal results. Another case, this one involving the gang rape of a nine-year-old girl, reached the courts in the summer of 1978. The parents of the girl had sued NBC for $11 million, claiming that her attackers had been inspired by a TV movie, "Born Innocent," which depicted a similar scene. NBC won the suit, but some people fear that the TV industry may be subjected to a growing number of suits blaming TV for every antisocial act from speeding to rape and murder.

Stephen Rhode, a lawyer for the entertainment industry, is one of those who worries about what such suits could do to First Amendment freedoms.

DON'T BLAME TV FOR VIOLENCE

Stephen, Rohde, from "Fairytales and Game Shows," *The Los Angeles Times,* **1978**

Saddling TV networks with responsibility for crimes committed by emotionally disturbed minors is like killing a messenger who bears bad tidings; it runs contrary to the principles that determine civil liability for personal conduct, and violates First Amendment guarantees of freedom of expression. For this reason, the courts have never accepted the notion that, because some people may react violently to what they see or read, a given book or movie can be censored or its creator made to pay damages.

To do otherwise would be absurd, for there is no telling who will be provoked to violence by exposure to the most unlikely of stimuli. For example, it is reported that Heinrich Pommerenke, a German rapist and mass slayer of women, carried out his ghastly deeds after seeing—of all things—Cecil B. DeMille's "The Ten Commandments." During the scene in which Jewish women dance around the golden calf, all his suspicions about the opposite sex were confirmed; women, he decided, were indeed the source of the world's troubles, and it was his mission to execute them. Leaving the theater, he slew his first victim in a nearby park.

Similarly, John George Haigh, the British vampire who sucked his victims' blood through soda straws, claims he first experienced a thirst for blood on watching a "voluptuous" procedure—the drinking of the "blood" of Christ—in an Anglican communion service. There was also the case, earlier this year, of a 58-year-old Frenchman who confessed that he had killed his uncle by poisoning a bottle of red wine, using a recipe from an Agatha Christie murder mystery.

Can anyone seriously contend that Cecil B. DeMille, the Anglican church, or Dame Agatha Christie is civilly liable for having "incited" these disturbed criminals? Yet that is exactly what the cases against the TV networks allege. The only difference is that the target of the suits is television—the whipping boy of everyone from Spiro Agnew to the PTA.

This wrongheaded legal assault on the networks, if it prevails, could result in de facto censorship. Unless our Constitution assures authors, producers, and actors that the exposition of any idea—including depictions of the seamy side of human existence—will not subject them to multimillion-dollar jury verdicts, we will eventually find nothing but game shows on the air and fairy tales in the bookstores.

Only the most rabid censor would seriously contend that TV networks and producers have intentionally directed their programs in order to provoke criminal action. And no responsible critic of television would argue that the networks actually advocate using force or violating the law (though even such advocacy would be protected by the Constitution).

People who urge stronger censorship over television than is permitted with other media usually justify their position with the theory that television has a much greater effect because we are somehow "involuntarily" subjected to it, right in our own homes. But the very fact that television is broadcast into our living rooms gives viewers, particularly parents, more control, not less, over the violence to which their children are exposed. At the first suggestion of a violent or disturbing scene, parents can simply switch off the set.

Similarly specious is the argument that television programming should be subject to government censorship because TV stations (unlike, say, book publishers) are licensed by the Federal Communications Commission, which requires them to operate in the "public interest." However, this "public-interest" requirement does not grant government the right to judge the worth, social utility, or possible adverse consequences of broadcasting particular TV programs.

The paternalism of those who would use the FCC as a handy vehicle to censor the content of television programs out of professed concern for our children is misguided, to say the least; for it places the primary responsibility for a child's upbringing with the government or the courts, rather than with parents.

If the television industry has a responsibility to help improve our society, that is a responsibility that we all share. Indeed, the First Amendment protects every citizen's right to criticize and condemn the medium whenever it strays from what he conceives of as the "public interest." But not on pain of huge monetary judgments or government censorship. Solutions to difficult problems are never found in the repression of ideas.

■

One of the most exhaustive studies of television's effects was the five-volume staff report to the U.S. Surgeon General's Scientific Advisory Committee in 1972 summarizing the results of 23 separate research projects. (TELEVISION AND SOCIAL BEHAVIOR—A Technical Report to the Surgeon General's Scientific Advisory Committee on Television and Social Behavior, 1972.)

If the question of violence on TV is a controversial topic, the issue of sexual content is even more so. In 1981 the Rev. Donald Wildmon, a Methodist minister, formed an organization called the Coalition for Better Television, whose purpose was to put pressure on advertisers to stop sponsoring shows with too much profanity, sex and violence. After his group threatened a boycott, a number of advertisers met with Wildmon and agreed to help "clean up" TV. The boycott was then called off.

The reaction to televised portrayals of sex and violence raises a larger question about the rights and responsibilities of the mass media, which will be studied in the next chapter.

CHAPTER 6

What Are the Media's Rights and Responsibilities?

We live today in an age of loudspeakers, and those who control access to those loudspeakers are often the ones who determine what will be heard by the public at large. The unamplified human voice is no match for a coast-to-coast network of electronic communication or a national chain of newspapers. That is why today, soapbox oratory seems so quaint. The circle of listeners is small (unless a TV camera is present) and Americans are no longer tuned in to local oratory; they are wired to the nation and the world. Those who control those communication channels are the ones whose free speech has the greatest influence.

Public Access: The Need for Reply

Liberty in today's world has to be seen as more than the absence of restraint. Liberty of speech has to be defined affirmatively as *the right to communicate through the media from which Americans customarily receive news and opinion.*

In the past those media were mainly two: the vocal cords (more or less equally distributed throughout the population) and the printing press (to which it was easy to gain access). Today, when the media of communication serve mass audiences through wire services, sophisticated printing equipment, audio and visual electronics, the problem is to find some way of opening these up to all who wish to communicate.

Such a goal may never be fully attained, but it can hardly be forgotten if we are to realize the true meaning of freedom of speech: freedom of *effective* speech, which means access to those forums where an appreciable audience can be found. People seeking to influence opinion have no desire simply to talk to themselves.

The Tornillo Case

The Supreme Court has said that the First Amendment rests upon "the principle that debate on issues should be uninhibited, robust, and wide-open." But what if uninhibited and robust debate is squelched by the mass media? Imagine that a town's only newspaper prints a scorching criticism of a political candidate shortly before the election, and the aggrieved candidate requests space for a reply. If the newspaper refuses, has it not replaced "uninhibited, robust, and wide-open" debate with controlled, unhealthy, and one-sided debate—that is to say, by no debate at all?

Such a case is not purely hypothetical. In Miami in 1972, Pat L. Tornillo, Jr., a candidate for the Florida state legislature, asked the *Miami Herald* for space to reply to editorial attacks on him. When he was refused, he sued under a Florida "right of reply" statute, and won in the Florida courts. In *Miami Herald v. Tornillo* (1974), however, the U.S. Supreme Court reversed, upholding the newspaper.

In his opinion, Chief Justice Burger spoke for a unanimous court. Here are some excerpts from that opinion.

THE *TORNILLO* CASE: NEWSPAPERS NEED NOT PRINT REPLIES

Chief Justice Burger, from *Miami Herald Publishing Co. v. Tornillo,* 1974

Access advocates submit that although newspapers of the present are superficially similar to those of 1791 the press of today is in reality very different from that known in the early years of our national existence. In the past half century a communications revolution has seen the introduction of radio and television into our lives, the promise of a global community through the use of communications satellites, and the spectre of a "wired" nation by means of an expanding cable television network with two-way capabilities. The printed press, it is said, has not escaped the effects of this revolution. Newspapers have become big business and there are far fewer of them to serve a larger literate population. Chains of newspapers, national newspapers, national wire and news services, and one-newspaper towns, are the dominant features of a press that has become noncompetitive and enormously powerful and influential in its capacity to manipulate popular opinion and change the course of events. Major metropolitan newspapers have collaborated to establish news services national in scope. Such national news organizations provide syndicated "interpretive reporting" as well as syndicated features and commentary, all of which can serve as part of the new school of "advocacy journalism."

The elimination of competing newspapers in most of our large cities, and the concentration of control of media that results from the only newspaper's being owned by the same interests which own a television station and a radio station, are important components of this trend toward concentration of control of outlets to inform the public.

The result of these vast changes has been to place in a few hands the power to inform the American people and shape public opinion. Much of the editorial opinion and commentary that is printed is that of syndicated columnists distributed nationwide and, as a result, we are told, on national and world issues there tends to be a homogeneity of editorial opinion, commentary, and interpretive analysis. The abuses of bias and manipulative reportage are, likewise, said to be the result of the vast accumulations of unreviewable power in the modern media empires. In effect, it is claimed, the public has lost any ability to respond or to contribute in a meaningful way to the debate on issues. The monopoly of the means of communication allows for little or no critical analysis of the media except in professional journals of very limited readership. . . .

Proponents of enforced access to the press take comfort from language in several of this Court's decisions which suggests that the First Amendment acts as a sword as well as a shield, that it imposes obligations on the owners of the press in addition to protecting the press from government regulation. . . .

In New York Times Co. v. Sullivan, 376 U.S. 254, 270, 84 S.Ct. 710, 721, 11 L.Ed.2d 686 (1964), the Court spoke of "a profound national commitment to the principle that debate on public issues should be uninhibited, robust, and wide-open." It is argued that the "uninhibited, robust" debate is not "wide-open" but open only to a monopoly in control of the press. . . .

. . . However much validity may be found in these arguments, at each point the implementation of a remedy such as an enforceable right of access necessarily calls for some mechanism, either governmental or consensual. If it is governmental coercion, this at once brings about a confrontation with the express provisions of the First Amendment and the judicial gloss on that Amendment developed over the years.

[In previous cases] the Court has expressed sensitivity as to whether a restriction or requirement constituted the compulsion exerted by government on a newspaper to print that which it would not otherwise print. The clear implication has been that any such compulsion to publish that which " 'reason' tells them should not be published" is unconstitutional. A responsible press is an undoubtedly desirable goal, but press responsibility is not mandated by the Constitution and like many other virtues it cannot be legislated.

Appellee's argument that the Florida statute does not amount to a restriction of appellant's right to speak because "the statute in question here has not prevented the *Miami Herald* from saying anything it wished" begs the core question. Compelling editors or publishers to publish that which "'reason' tells them should not be published" is what is at issue in this case. The Florida statute operates as a command in the same sense as a statute or regulation forbidding appellant to publish specified matter. Governmental restraint on publishing need not fall into familiar or traditional patterns to be subject to constitutional limitations on governmental powers. . . .

The Florida statute exacts a penalty on the basis of the content of a newspaper. The first phase of the penalty resulting from the compelled printing of a reply is exacted in terms of the cost in printing and composing time and materials and in taking up space that could be devoted to other material the newspaper may have preferred to print. It is correct, as appellee contends, that a newspaper is not subject to the finite technological limitations of time that confront a broadcaster but it is not correct to say that, as an economic reality, a newspaper can proceed to infinite expansion of its column space to accommodate the replies that a government agency determines or a statute commands the readers should have *available.*

Faced with the penalties that would accrue to any newspaper that published news or commentary arguably within the reach of the right-of-access statute, editors might well conclude that the safe course is to avoid controversy. Therefore, under the operation of the Florida statute, political and electoral coverage would be blunted or reduced. Government-enforced right of access inescapably "dampens the vigor and limits the variety of public debate," New York Times Co. v. Sullivan, *supra,* 376 U.S., at 279, 84 S.Ct., at 725. The Court, in Mills v. Alabama, 384 U.S. 214, 218, 86 S. Ct. 1434, 1437 (1966), stated:

> "[T]here is practically universal agreement that a major purpose of [the First] Amendment was to protect the free discussion of governmental affairs. This of course includes discussions of candidates. . . ."

Even if a newspaper would face no additional costs to comply with a compulsory access law and would not be forced to forgo publication of news or opinion by the inclusion of a reply, the Florida statute fails to clear the barriers of the First Amendment because of its intrusion into the function of editors. A newspaper is more than a passive receptacle or conduit for news, comment, and advertising. The choice of material to go into a newspaper, and the decisions made as to limitations on the size and content of the paper, and treatment of public issues and public officials—whether fair or unfair—constitute the exercise of editorial control and judgment. It has yet to be demonstrated how governmental regulation of this crucial process can be exercised consistent with First Amendment guarantees of a free press as they have evolved to this time. Accordingly, the judgment of the Supreme Court of Florida is reversed.

Not all commentators agree on the ramifications of the courts decision. Professor Lewis Wolfson is not so sure that the *Tornillo* decision should be hailed as a victory for civil liberties. It may have opened the way for a heightened mood of arrogance and self-congratulation by the nation's press.

NEWSPAPERS MUST SERVE THE PEOPLE

Lewis Wolfson, from "Whose First Amendment", *The Progressive,* **January 1975**

The American press is in a self-congratulatory mood these days, after it exposed Watergate and other government ills while resisting the Nixon Administration's repeated attempts to chip away at its First Amendment rights. But, in their sweetest moments of victory, newspapers find too few friends to celebrate with. Instead, they are being assailed and even taken into court by politicians, frustrated advocates of various causes, and even by average readers who mistrust the power of the press and question whether newspapers in actual fact do speak for the people, as they claim they do.

The press's recent vindication of its First Amendment freedom has been worth crowing about. Journalists' persistence in good part helped to oust the President and Vice President who had furiously attacked their independence. The Supreme Court upheld the right of newspapers to publish the Pentagon Papers. And most recently the high Court, in another landmark decision, has ruled that no one—especially not the Government—can tell a newspaper what it must print.

[In summer of 1974] the Supreme Court unanimously overturned a Florida Supreme Court ruling which had upheld a state right-of-reply law that guaranteed candidates free space to answer editorial attacks during a political campaign. The U.S. Supreme Court's decision turned back the challenge of Pat L. Tornillo Jr. who, as a candidate for the Florida state legislature in 1972, had petitioned the *Miami Herald* for space to respond to editorial attacks on him.

Noted communications lawyer Floyd Abrams called the decision in *Miami Herald v. Tornillo* "one of the great reaffirmations of the First Amendment in this century." The press editorialized glowingly about the outcome. But some newspapers also conceded that *Tornillo* was no reaffirmation of the press's credibility with the public. Thoughtful journalists recognize that the case was no isolated episode, but rather the most serious manifestation to date of reader unhappiness with newspapers. For surveys show that the Nixon Administration's attacks fell on fertile ground. Many people feel that the press speaks less and less for their hopes and needs, and they would just as soon have government do something to curb the press's independent power, no matter what the First Amendment says.

The First Amendment says that "Congress shall make no law . . . abridging the freedom of speech, or of the press. . . ." Through the years, the courts invariably have seen the press as the principal guarantor of free expression and the guardian against government attempts to abridge it. But the public interest lawyers who fought for *Tornillo* favor a new interpretation of the First Amendment which would provide legally guaranteed space for people to speak out in their local newspaper, regardless of how the newspaper itself felt about it.

This would mean that government, in effect, could tell its own watchdog what to print. Few press or legal experts expected that the Supreme Court would accept this argument. Indeed, Chief Justice Warren Burger, in his opinion in the *Tornillo* case, said the purpose of the First Amendment is to keep government out of the editor's chair. But, even as it upheld the press's independence, the Court also seemed to be warning newspapers to look to their public sins. Burger recounted at length the access advocates' arguments that newspaper readers are frustrated because, as newspaper chains and media conglomerates grow, their own voice seems to diminish, and they feel powerless to call the monopoly press to account for its abuses of power or judgment.

The problem of access and newspapers' accountability to the public is not a new one. At least two Presidential commissions and countless independent study groups have warned the press in recent years about the possible consequences of the public's mistrust. As far back as 1947, the Hutchins Commission on Freedom of the Press was saying that the press "must know that its faults and errors have ceased to be private vagaries and have become public dangers." Foreshadowing the *Tornillo* threat, the Hutchins Commission concluded that journalists "should put forth every effort to make the press accountable, for it does not become so of its own motion, the power of government will be used to force it to be so."

Now the press is more than ever under siege. Despite their victory in court, newspapers must contemplate fresh assaults on their credibility and fairness: from politicians irked about the press's power, from antitrust officials eying the growth of the media monopolies, and from a growing cadre of groups and individuals who feel their message is being shut out. Faced with these pressures, editors have experimented in recent years with ways to make the newspapers more accountable. But, critics warn, with the specter of more court decisions, government actions, and escalating reader unrest, the press will have to move more decisively to earn readers' trust and support—or risk new erosion of its First Amendment freedom.

Public interest lawyers contend that America's newspaper owners, especially chain "press lords" who often have a supermarket mentality about buying and selling newspapers, should not be able to dominate so fully the public's chief channels of communication. The First Amendment, they say, belongs to the people, not to an increasingly monopolistic press; the Constitution did not provide "a grant of press immunity" for whatever newspapers want to do, but "a mandate for press responsibility" to guarantee a voice for many points of view.

Justice Oliver Wendell Holmes set the basis for court interpretation of press freedom when he envisioned a marketplace of ideas that would flourish under the First Amendment's safeguard for the press. The access advocates maintain that there are millions of people today who cannot get a ticket into the marketplace unless the big daily newspaper—and in more and more cases the only newspaper—in their hometown will give them a say. A Tom Paine with a ditto machine in Brooklyn or a Malcolm X on a street corner in Harlem doesn't stand a chance against a majestic utterance from the editorial page of *The New York Times.*

But if monopoly ownership of the means of mass communication implies a new brand of censorship, does that justify bringing in government to decide what is a "fair" award of news or advertising space in order to ensure a flourishing marketplace?

It is a difficult question for liberals. Even the American Civil Liberties Union found itself split in conflict over two not necessarily compatible libertarian values—freedom of the press and assured public access to the marketplace. Members of its Communications Media Committee favored a form of guaranteed public entree, at least to newspaper advertising space. But ACLU legal director Melvin Wulf campaigned against this view; he circulated a fiery memo that said such an interpretation of the First Amendment would be "an invitation to constitutional disaster." As Ben Bagdikian, respected journalist and press critic, puts it, the "disease"—lack of access to big newspapers—is a serious one, but the proposed cure of calling on government to judge is "more dangerous than the disease."

The Supreme Court agreed. Justice Burger, in *Tornillo,* wrote that whatever the merits to the arguments of advocates of a right of reply or any other kind of mandatory press access, "such an enforceable right of access necessarily calls for some mechanism, either governmental or consensual. If it is governmental coercion, this at once brings about a confrontation with the express provisions of the First Amendment and the judicial gloss on that amendment developed over the years." The Court concluded that "a responsible press is an undoubtedly desirable goal, but press responsibility is not mandated by the Constitution and like many other virtues it cannot be legislated."

But, if the press had beaten back the public interest lawyers in this case, it had not stilled other voices which question its power. Spiro Agnew may be gone, but his ghost still haunts American journalism. He unleashed the resentment that many people in public life feel about what they see as press license, and the anger is unlikely to be capped back in the bottle by a few favorable court decisions. . . .

While the press has been able to rebuff its adversaries, it cannot always expect the courts to see its First Amendment freedom as an unalloyed right. Some judges already have warned newspapers to that effect. In upholding the right-of-reply in the *Tornillo* case, the Florida Supreme Court argued vigorously that government has an obligation to do what it could to offset media monopoly power. It said, "The First Amendment did not create a privileged class which, through a monopoly of instruments of the newspaper industry, would be able to deny people the freedom of expression which the First Amendment guaranteed." Some lower Federal courts have made similar arguments that government should encourage public access in broadcasting cases. . . .

The paradoxes do not go unnoticed by the public. The "free" press stands impeached in the minds of many Americans. Surveys show that, to many, the local paper is just one more big, impersonal institution that is not sensitive to them, though it claims to be the public's voice. Blacks in the South or in northern ghettos do not believe that their big city papers speak for them. Environmentalists often feel that newspapers have a conservative bias that makes them defer to community business interests which are the worst polluters. Conservative crusaders accuse the big city press—especially *The New York Times* and *The Washington Post*—of giving a "liberal lining" slant to reporting of government and choking out contrary views. . . .

For years, critics have been warning the newspaper industry to listen, and to be more open with the people before government moves into the editor's chair with the public's acquiescence. If the *Tornillo* case had gone against the press, newspapers would now be in the biggest fight of their lives to preserve their freedom, facing government intervention with the people's approval. They may be in that fight anyway. But the public's anger will not be answered by pious declarations about press rights, nor by victories in court. The best response for the press would be to be more accessible, more accountable, more outgoing about its practices. . . . ■

A counterpart to the *Tornillo* case, except that it involved a radio station instead of a newspaper, was the case of *Red Lion Broadcasting Co. v. FCC,* decided by the Supreme Court in 1969. A right-wing radio station in the town of Red Lion, Pennsylvania, had broadcast an attack on Fred Cook, a liberal journalist. Cook demanded air time to reply, and was refused. He appealed to the Federal Communications Commission, which then ordered the station to broadcast Cook's reply. The station appealed to the Supreme Court. But in that case, unlike *Tornillo,* the Court agreed that the government could enforce a right to reply. Why?

The essential difference, at least as the Supreme Court views it, is that broadcasting—unlike publishing—is a licensed medium. And it is licensed because it is a "limited access" medium.

By the mid-1920s there were so many radio stations operating that they were interfering with each other's signals. The result in many areas was that when Americans turned on their radios they heard nothing but a babble of voices and sounds. The Congress responded to this crisis by passing the Radio Act of 1927, which assigned certain frequencies in which each broadcaster was supposed to operate, thus keeping them from cutting in on each other. This was done more systematically by the Communications Act of 1934. It set up a system for licensing broadcasters.

The problem was that there were only so many frequencies to go around. Thus, to obtain this sole right to operate at a certain frequency was to be granted a very exclusive privilege. Congress wanted to make sure that those who operated in the assigned frequencies did not abuse the privilege. So the Communications Act contained two sections of particular relevance to the issue we are considering. First, it stipulated that those who operate radio and television stations are to do so in "the public interest, convenience, and necessity." Second, while leaving the above language undefined, it created a Federal Communications Commission (whose members were to be appointed by the President) to interpret and enforce the law.

In spelling out the meaning of "public interest, convenience, and necessity" the FCC, in 1949, laid down what has come to be called "the Fairness Doctrine." Among the provisions of the Fairness Doctrine is the requirement that broadcasters give "balanced" coverage to controversial issues. If one side of an issue is presented, the station has an obligation—at some reasonable time, not necessarily the same day—to present an opposing view. Failure to present that view would open a licensee to a complaint hearing before the FCC. If the FCC, acting now as a judge, decided in favor of the complainant, it would compel the station to broadcast the reply.

That is what happened when journalist Fred Cook brought his complaint about Red Lion's radio station before the FCC. Cook won, and the station responded by challenging the constitutionality of the Fairness Doctrine. The station claimed that the doctrine interfered with free speech and thus violated the First Amendment. But the Supreme Court, speaking through Justice Byron White, upheld the Fairness Doctrine and replied to the radio station's argument as follows.

THE *RED LION* CASE: BROADCASTERS MUST ALLOW REPLIES

From Red Lion Broadcasting Co. v. Federal Communications Commission, 1969

. . . A license permits broadcasting, but the licensee has no constitutional right to be the one who holds the license or to monopolize a radio frequency to the exclusion of his fellow citizens. There is nothing in the First

Amendment which prevents the Government from requiring a licensee to share his frequency with others and to conduct himself as a proxy or fiduciary with obligations to present those views and voices which are representative of his community and which would otherwise, by necessity, be barred from the airwaves.

This is not to say that the First Amendment is irrelevant to public broadcasting. On the contrary, it has a major role to play as the Congress itself recognized in section 326, which forbids FCC interference with "the right of free speech by means of radio communication." Because of the scarcity of radio frequencies, the Government is permitted to put restraints on licensees in favor of others whose views should be expressed on this unique medium. But the people as a whole retain their interest in free speech by radio and their collective right to have the medium function consistently with the ends and purposes of the First Amendment. It is the right of the viewers and listeners, not the right of the broadcasters, which is paramount. . . .

It is the purpose of the First Amendment to preserve an uninhibited marketplace of ideas in which truth will ultimately prevail, rather than to countenance monopolization of that market, whether it be by the Government itself or a private licensee. . . . It is the right of the public to receive suitable access to social, political, esthetic, moral, and other ideas and experiences which is crucial here. That right may not constitutionally be abridged either by Congress or by the FCC. . . .

Nor can we say that it is inconsistent with the First Amendment goal of producing an informed public capable of conducting its own affairs to require a broadcaster to permit answers to personal attacks occurring in the course of discussing controversial issues, or to require that the political opponents of those endorsed by the station be given a chance to communicate with the public. Otherwise, station owners and a few networks would have unfettered power to make time available only to the highest bidders, to communicate only their own views on public issues, people and candidates, and to permit on the air only those with whom they agreed. There is no sanctuary in the First Amendment for unlimited private censorship operating in a medium not open to all. "Freedom of the press from governmental interference under the First Amendment does not sanction repression of that freedom by private interests." *Associated Press v. United States,* 326 U.S. 1, 20 (1945).

. . . It does not violate the First Amendment to treat licensees given the privilege of using scarce radio frequencies as proxies for the entire community, obligated to give suitable time and attention to matters of great public concern. To condition the granting or renewal of licenses on a willingness to present representative community views on controversial issues is consistent with the ends and purposes of those constitutional provisions forbidding the abridgment of freedom of speech and freedom of the press. Congress need not stand idly by and permit those with licenses to ignore the problems which beset the people or to exclude from the airways anything but their own views of fundamental questions. . . . ■

Edwin Diamond is one writer on the mass media who thinks that the Fairness Doctrine as outlined in this opinion is in fact unfair. He believes that it relegates broadcasters to the status of second-class citizens, and does so on the basis of a whole set of misunderstandings, or "myths," about the broadcasting industry.

RED LION DISCRIMINATES AGAINST BROADCASTERS

Edwin Diamond, from "Media Myths That Limit Free Speech", *TV Guide,* November 5, 1977

When the Federal Government started regulating broadcasting, its function was primarily that of a traffic cop. There's only so much room on the radio dial, a limited number of frequencies. And a lot of people wanted to use them. If they all used them at once, no one would be heard clearly.

In the early days of radio, back in the 1920s, signals wandered all over. A police call in Albany might interfere with a musical interlude from Pittsburgh, and vice versa. One central authority was therefore needed to assign space on the dial to the various competing claimants . . . and so the Federal Radio Commission, precursor of the FCC, was born. . . .

If the Florida reply law was unconstitutional, then why is the Fairness Doctrine, as well as other limits on broadcasters' rights, still on the books? The fact is, as Eric Sevareid suggests, broadcast journalists are treated as second-class journalists; newspapers have free-speech rights that television stations don't have.

This inequality exists, at least in part, because of the persistence of certain myths of the media. In no particular order of importance, these are:

The show-business myth. Broadcasting is, primarily, an "entertainment" medium and therefore only a qualified form of "the press." But surely newspapers and magazines seek to entertain as well as to educate or to sell ads.

The myth of television's persuasive powers. Television-watching is intellectually "passive"—they can sell you anything—while reading requires more critical skills, and therefore little will be "put over" on the reader. Pure bunkum. Viewers/listeners are not idiots; neither does all of television speak with one voice on every issue.

The myth that newspapers are private-business enterprises, but broadcast stations are public utilities. In law school, this is known as a circular argument; if the Government got out of broadcasting, then broadcasting would also be a private enterprise.

The myth that broadcasters operate a monopoly business while newspapers are highly competitive. More nonsense. The latest figures show that there are some 9200 broadcast outlets in the United States (8240 AM and FM radio stations; 984 VHF and UHF TV stations) and only 1762 daily newspapers. Moreover, of all localities with daily newspapers in the U.S., nearly nine out of 10 have only one newspaper, a good definition of monopoly.

The myth of spectrum scarcity. Since the wavelengths are limited, Government has to ration their use to ensure that everyone is heard. Cable television will spell the end to that notion, though it hasn't held up very well in recent years in any case. Newspapers also have limited resources—newsprint, delivery trucks, distribution points—but the private market is allowed to operate without Government control.

The myth that, without Government, only the monied interests would be heard. Who's kidding whom? *With* Government now, the richest people in town—the bankers, insurance-company owners, real-estate operators, what Kansas editor William Allen White called the "country-club set"—own both newspapers and broadcast stations (if the even wealthier chains haven't yet taken over).

The myth that Government rules ensure diversity of ideas, the airing of controversy and the chance for "both sides" to be heard on television. In practice, many broadcasters worry about broadcasting *anything* that might interfere with the nice sounds of their ringing cash registers. They don't like controversy because it gets in the way of profits. Also, where is it written that all issues have two sides, and two sides only? There may be more than two sides, or there may be only one.

Very few people who have thought about it will disagree that the present broadcasting nonsystem in the U.S. is confusing, contradictory, a legal hybrid: a private enterprise licensed by the State, with some of the First Amendment protections of the Constitution, except when it comes to "controversy," political campaigns, ideological ads and other exceptions.

Some prefer this jerry-built structure, with the FCC or the courts mediating the clashing interests of various pressure groups: the broadcast journalists who want their full First Amendment rights; the Hollywood artists who want creative freedom; the parents and teachers who exercise their free speech, demanding an end to violence on TV. Texaco clamors to be heard, and so do environmentalists, political parties and Presidential candidates. That's one form of democracy, the "squeaky-wheel" theory where the loudest—or most powerful—claimants get the attention.

Suppose we take as desirable a broadcast system embracing everyone's goals, no matter how conflicting: a press that is free *and* fair, open *and* ideological, private *and* public, creative *and* clean. That's another, more democratic form of democracy. I think it's possible. How do we get there from here?

A first step is suggested in Fred Friendly's 1975 study of the Fairness Doctrine. Friendly would keep the FCC, he would keep the Fairness Doctrine, he would keep the private character of station ownership. The proprietors would still have to come before the Commission when their broadcast licenses were up for renewal. Private citizens and public-interest groups—from the antisex and violence forces to the prodivestiture lobby—would still be encouraged to bring their complaints about content and bias to the FCC. But the FCC would review immediately only those complaints involving broadcasts of a political nature, where timing of any rebuttal would be crucial. Beyond that, the FCC's role would be limited to judging complaints in the context of the station's total performance at license-renewal time. As Friendly writes:

"With this approach, a licensee that broadcast a substantial number of programs on controversial issues and therefore had received a large number of complaints would not be punished [for devoting a reasonable amount of time to discussion of controversial issues]; indeed, the station would be encouraged to continue to broadcast controversial programs, and at the renewal hearing it would be considered an affirmative indication that the licensee was living up to its obligations as a public trustee."

Another sensible legislative step has been proposed by Sen. William Proxmire of Wisconsin. His First Amendment Clarification Act of 1977 would have the Congress specifically go on record as telling the FCC that it has no role, direct or indirect, in program content. Proxmire says he hopes to stop the "raised-eyebrow effect" that FCC actions or pronouncements may have on already timid broadcasters.

If Government gets its censorious nose out of day-to-day broadcasting decisions, there will still be the question of biased broadcasters. Some kind of close check is needed: Friendly proposes a system of voluntary public access on a regular basis, a form of "letters-to-the-editor" column for television and radio.

We would still have the question of clashing tastes and program content—one man's (or woman's) "action-adventure" series may be another's poisonous pornography. ABC is broadcasting a new series called *Soap*, described by some as "sex-saturated." The *Soap* writer's freedom to speak sexually clashes with the home viewer's freedom not to hear, especially if choices are limited. Here, I think, cable-television technology will soon overtake the argument and settle it. Cable TV is, of course, pay-TV. The watcher pays, monthly or hourly, for the programs delivered. But with pay-cable TV, large, undifferentiated audiences can be broken down into smaller, more homogeneous, more targeted demographic groups as the number of channels grows. So more diversity is possible.

Star Trek and *The Lawrence Welk Show,* to take two examples, were dropped from network television because they drew audiences in the low millions—too small and "unviable" by network standards. On pay-TV, however, seven to eight million people, at one dollar a household, is a box-office winner.

But then won't the poor, who watch more television on the average than the middle and upper classes, suffer disproportionately by having to pay for their major form of entertainment? Columnist Nicholas von Hoffman, half seriously, suggests that the poor be given entertainment stamps, just as they are given food stamps. If watching television is deemed a necessity by our society, then the Department of Health, Education and Welfare can see to it that people get their minimum daily requirement.

It is an outrageous idea, of course, but think for a moment; is it any more outrageous than the present situation in broadcasting? Entertainment stamps aren't unconstitutional. And that statement cannot be made with certainty about the antics of the FCC, the Congress, and the courts, as they go about the dubious task of regulating broadcasting in the United States.

■

Naturally, broadcasters themselves have a view of the Red Lion case. Radio Station WCBS is a CBS-owned station in New York City, with an all-news format. Its powerful signal reaches nine million potential listeners in New York, New Jersey, and Connecticut.

Late in 1980 WCBS addressed the issue of "right to reply" laws.

A WCBS RADIO EDITORIAL: DON'T SHOOT THE MESSENGER

Broadcast, November 6 and 7, 1980

If you are like most Americans, you probably think that freedom of the press is not your right, but ours—the right of broadcasters and newspaper publishers to air and print what they want. That's only part of the story. Freedom of the press is also your right to have access to the facts and opinions which help keep you informed. If we lose it, you lose it, and the whole fabric of our society would be diminished.

It is surprising then that a kind of "shoot the messenger" attitude is growing in the country. Late last month the Public Agenda Foundation released results of a national survey on press fairness which had to do with coverage of political candidates and controversial issues. Eighty-two percent of those questioned thought newspapers should, by law, be required to give major party candidates equal amounts of coverage. Sixty-three percent thought there should be laws requiring newspapers to cover major third party candidates. Nearly seventy-five percent of those polled thought newspapers should by law have to give equal space to both sides of a controversial issue. It is laws the people favored, in spite of the fact that the Constitution clearly states that Congress shall make no laws abridging the freedom of the press. The men who wrote the Bill of Rights [knew] what they were doing. Our country has survived for two centuries with the press printing what it saw fit. Indeed, at times in our history, papers were biased to an extent we would find unbelievable now. But the people ferreted that out and still made decisions that kept the country thriving. With no laws telling them what to print and how, newspapers do their job very well.

We hope there never will be laws regulating newspapers. It is terrifying to think what a short step it is from telling papers and broadcasters what they can print and air to telling you what you can read and hear. ■

Taking full advantage of the government-guaranteed right to reply to broadcast media, the author attempted a rebuttal to the WCBS editorial. It was broadcast a few weeks later, with only a stutter edited out.

THE NEED FOR COMPETING VIEWS

George McKenna, from editorial reply broadcast November 13 and 14, 1980

My name is George McKenna. I teach at City College of New York. Not long ago WCBS broadcast an editorial which began by stating that freedom of the press is important not just for the press but for us as well because it insures that we have access to the facts and opinions which keep us informed. The editorial then went on to deplore the fact that the overwhelming majority of Americans would approve of laws forcing newspapers to give equal space to opposing points of view.

Here we have a classic case of a conclusion not following from a premise. If the purpose of the press is to keep us informed, how could that purpose be ill-served by requiring the press to give us both sides of an argument? Isn't that the best way of keeping people well-informed? Who among us has not noticed the tendency of newspapers to give massive coverage to the points of view they support, while burying, or not covering at all, the statements of the opposition?

WCBS is correct to note that such bias was even more blatant a century ago. But a century ago there was a splendid variety of newspapers in America, while today, between newspaper bankruptcies and newspaper chains, we are left with only a few giant press monopolies. To give these monopolies unlimited freedom is actually contrary to the spirit of the First

Amendment: it does not increase information but constricts it; it does not promote competition but smothers it.

Most Americans know this intuitively, which is why they want our newspapers to open their pages to competing points of view. The majority may not always be right, but it is in this case. ■

The author of the WCBS editorial was Susan Veatch, the station's editorial director. In the following exchange with the editor, she spells out more fully her views on access—views which, she made clear at the outset, are her own and not necessarily those of WCBS Radio.

AN INTERVIEW WITH SUSAN VEATCH

MCKENNA: The point that you made in your editorial on WCBS was that there is a danger to civil liberties when the government gets into the business of ordering replies to the mass media. My question is, isn't it also somewhat of a danger to the free trade in ideas if there are media monopolies, and if that is a problem—the problem of shrinking newspapers, for example, and lack of competition in newspapers—is there any way that you would propose to deal with the problem of lack of competition in the media?

VEATCH: Well, as I understand it, there was a time when there were more newspapers—thirty years ago to two hundred years ago—and everyone who had an opinion had a newspaper, so people didn't feel they were prejudiced, because someone with any opinion could find his opinion in one of the newspapers. Today, people can write to newspapers, and the letters get published—I don't know in what proportion to the number of letters sent in, but some of them are always in there, and as you know some of them are so critical. But the best argument that can be made for newspapers is the one that broadcasters make all the time, and that is, if you don't like it, don't buy it. If you don't like it, you can turn the set off, or you can turn the radio off. I imagine that it's been for economic reasons rather than ideological reasons that newspapers have gone out of business, but others will go out of business if you stop buying them, if you think they're so prejudiced. And that's the heart of it. The consumer always has that option. Don't buy it.

MCKENNA: Well, of course, with radio and TV we can do more than that.

What Are the Media's Rights and Responsibilities?

We can have the government guarantee the right to reply on the media. Do you think that the Fairness Doctrine of the FCC and the Court case that upheld it, the *Red Lion* case, are good law, or do you think that—

VEATCH: I don't think they're necessary, and I don't think they're necessary for the same reasons, if I remember correctly, that I argued about the newspapers in the editorial. Any station worth its salt which is doing news coverage, or certainly that is doing editorials, will be fair. There's a difference, obviously, between the news and editorial part. It would not be in a television or radio station's best interest to give only one side of the news. People would sneer at them. People know that there are two sides, or ten sides, or eight sides, and they would see that. If the network news went on and gave only one side of any story, people would turn it off, or watch another channel or station, because people know better. They're smarter than that.

MCKENNA: So, even in the absence of a Fairness Doctrine, there would probably be, in the interest of the stations themselves, provision for editorial reply?

VEATCH: Well, sure. And, it would not be unreasonable to say that most broadcasters resent the ruling. I obviously can't speak for everybody, but it just seems so unnecessary. We're not irresponsible. And the idea that we would take to the air and give only one side of the story—I mean, even if we were that biased, even if we were that prejudiced, there are people at television and radio stations whose bottom line is money. They wouldn't let the news people get that far out of line so that everybody would turn the station off.

MCKENNA: So commercial considerations would take the place of government coercion?

VEATCH: Well, good sense, . . . If we were going to take to the air with only our biases, then we'd have all-editorial radio or all-editorial television. Broadcasters aren't silly, they know better. They know how to differentiate between a news story and an editorial. And they're always going to let other people have something to say about it.

MCKENNA: The idea behind the *Red Lion* decision and the justification for the Fairness Doctrine was that radio and TV, unlike newspapers, are limited-access media, so that the consumer, if that's the right word, really in fact doesn't have as much choice as he would have with newspapers. This is, after all, a licensed medium, [in which] channels are portioned out. The medallion is awarded to a station and no other station may interfere with it.

Therefore the consumer or the listener doesn't find it easy to turn channels and find another one.

VEATCH: In some of the more rural areas of the country, sometimes, there's more difficulty in picking up stations. A city might have three or four television stations to choose from, maybe six or eight radio stations rather than the fifty which people might find in a big city market. But I've always found the argument specious. It's true that the bands are limited, but who has the money to buy enough of God's green trees to start a newspaper? I mean, practically, it doesn't make sense any more.

MCKENNA: Right. A.J. Liebling said, "Freedom of the press is limited to those who own one."

VEATCH: Sure. It may have been that, when Tom Paine was doing his work, anyone could start up a pamphlet with a little printing press, but for heaven's sake nobody could start up a *New York Times* now any more easily than someone could start up an ABC Network News. A regular consumer couldn't.

MCKENNA: Right. I agree. But doesn't that argument really prove too much? Isn't that really an argument for extending the principle of the Fairness Doctrine to newspapers?

VEATCH: Well, I understand that argument and I know how it can be made. I just don't agree with it because, I would go back to my point, if we're not doing the job right we'll be put out of business. Any of us. And I think broadcasters and newspapers are way too responsible to count everybody out. Even if broadcasters had absolutely no conscience, they wouldn't be dumb enough—financially or in a business sense—to alienate everybody who might be a listener or a buyer.

* * * *

Toward the end of the interview Veatch said that she was surprised that she had not been asked about the equal-time law. Unlike the Fairness Doctrine, equal-time did not emerge from an FCC ruling but is written into the Communications Act itself. Section 315 of the law requires that any station which provides time for a political candidate must provide the same amount of time for every other candidate for office. If there are thirty candidates running for office, including candidates from the Vegetarian, Prohibitionist, and Communist parties, each must be given equal time.

What particularly annoyed Veatch about the equal-time requirement was its application to editorial endorsements of candidates. When a station broadcasts an editorial endorsement, it then has the responsibility of locating every other candidate for the office and sending each an invitation to reply. It must provide equal air time to each reply, and it may not censor or edit them, no matter how outlandish or mendacious they may be. Often it is difficult even to locate all of the minor party candidates, some of whom may be running their campaigns from their kitchens.

On top of it all, said Veatch, listeners often get upset when the stations run these replies, especially when the replies come from the candidates of radical parties. A station ends up getting abused by listeners for doing what the law requires it to do.

VEATCH: The best anecdote of my whole professional life was in Chicago when I was doing one of the elections. Someone called up, beside herself because we allowed a Socialist Worker's Party spokesman on, and she said, "I'm gonna write the FCC, you got no business having that Communist on the air." And I said, "Oh, I'll give you the address."

MCKENNA: So there's massive irony there.

VEATCH: Yes. And her parting shot was, "The *Chicago Tribune* would never allow this!" Now that's the constraint we're under.

MCKENNA: But I think that makes you better than the *Chicago Tribune*. I think it makes you, in the estimation of people who care about civil liberties, a better medium than the *Chicago Tribune*, because you do have these replies and you're forced to have these replies, and maybe it's a good thing that you do.

VEATCH: Some, I would say, sure. You can take the top four parties, they could have five parties, but not all these parties. There's someone who has his own party in New Jersey and his sole message is that people should love one another. Nobody really cares what he says. If they liked him, they'd vote for him.

MCKENNA: Well, their argument is that they don't get the votes because they don't get the coverage, because the news media, when they're not bound by equal-time but by Fairness, give them short shrift.

VEATCH: But they don't get news coverage because nobody's interested. I know it's chicken-and-egg, but if someone has something to say—

MCKENNA: What about the example of Barry Commoner, who has substantial things to say and who got so few votes in the last election. Whether one agrees with him or not, he's a person who has things of substance to say. If the news media were not obliged to give equal time, he would have [had] absolutely no coverage.

VEATCH: If nobody is interested in what he has to say, then that's his problem. People were informed about him, or at least informed about the issue he was talking about. Obviously nobody gave a damn.

MCKENNA: His charge, of course, was that nobody gave a damn because so little coverage was given to him by the news media that hardly anyone knew he was running. Now when you go back in history, are there not minority causes which, for the time, seem bizarre—women's suffrage seemed bizarre at one time—and which have few adherents, but which need to be heard?

VEATCH: Well, yes. But it's not our business to make their cause, either. If nobody else is interested in Barry Commoner, why the hell should we be?

The question of Governmental or legal interference in the free operation of the media has several other dimensions. If one finds his views being ignored by the media, or is a victim of negative publicity, his attitude toward regulation of the media may take shape accordingly.

Slander suits present one such issue. Professional journalists live under the shadow of slander suits, and contend that their reporting is correspondingly superficial. The question then must be asked; *should* the media be free to print or broadcast whatever they see fit? What protection do we have from the tremendous power of the mass media? Can we fairly seek restitution for damage that may be caused by lies that are repeated and amplified by the media? This question is examined from different perspectives in the following section.

SLANDER SUITS: HOW MUCH IMMUNITY?

There was cheering in Hollywood in the spring of 1981 when comedienne Carol Burnett won her libel suit against *The National Enquirer* for falsely implying that she had made a drunken nuisance of herself in a Washington restaurant. There were few who could resist the conclusion that the old "scandal sheet" finally got what was coming to it—a $1.3 million judgment against it, half of its stated net worth. For years it had been trafficking in what seemed to many to be malicious gossip and getting away with it because of the reluctance of celebrities to call any more negative attention to themselves by suing, even if the gossip were untrue. But Carol Burnett had the determination to force a confrontation with the magazine and win. Even though the amount of damages was later cut in half, it was still substantial enough to be a crushing blow to the *Enquirer* and a warning to similar magazines.

But even as the celebrities were celebrating the ruling against the *Enquirer*, civil libertarians were wondering whether libel suits were not starting to become a threat to press freedom. *The National Enquirer* may appear to be totally bereft of socially redeeming value, but what about other magazines and newspapers, including those which more clearly serve the public's need for information? If they make an occasional misstatement of fact, will they risk getting sued for huge sums? And if judges and juries award those sums, as they did in the Burnett case, will that not serve to intimidate newspapers or anyone who would speak in public? Could this make them unwilling to expose wrongdoing or criticize public officials? There were enough actual cases to make these questions more than speculative ones. A California citizen who protested a land development project in a letter to a newspaper was sued for $3 million. Another man who criticized a Dallas police investigator was fined $4,000 in damages. In Illinois a court ordered a small daily newspaper, the *Alton Telegraph,* to pay $9.2 million to a businessman who claimed he was defamed in a memo which two reporters sent to the local U.S. attorney. In California, a court ordered the *San Francisco Examiner* and two reporters to pay $4.2 million to an assistant district attorney and two homicide inspectors for writing a story that the prosecution was pressuring witnesses to perjure themselves, even though the story was based on signed affidavits from witnesses. In Louisiana, a small daily newspaper was successfully sued by a city attorney for venturing to say that "no bond-buyer would buy a nickel's worth of securities" based on the attorney's opinion. Some of these cases would be overturned on appeal, but the legal fees themselves constituted a kind of penalty for speaking out.

Of course, innocent people are sometimes very badly hurt by defamatory and untrue stories spread by newspapers and other publications. It is only fair that they be able to recover damages when they are victims of deliberate character assassination and that such practices be discouraged, by punitive fines if necessary. Even though freedom of the press is protected by the First Amendment, the Framers never intended to abolish libel laws. (They passed some of their own.) Throughout our history American courts have never recognized libel against individuals as something which enjoys the protection of the First Amendment.

Never, that is, until the case of *New York Times v. Sullivan* (1964). The case arose from the following circumstances: Martin Luther King's organization, the Southern Christian Leadership Conference (SCLC), put an ad in the *New York Times* alleging that black students protesting segregation were maltreated by city officials in Montgomery, Alabama. Some of the particulars in the allegations turned out to be factually incorrect, and Sullivan, Montgomery's commissioner of public affairs, sued for libel; he won a $500,000 judgment against the *Times* and the SCLC. After losing in the Alabama courts the *Times* succeeded in carrying its case to the U.S. Supreme Court, where it won a reversal.

The Court's opinion, written by Justice William Brennan, turned upon a crucial distinction—a distinction between private individuals and public officials. For a private individual to win a libel suit he need only prove that what was said about him was false and defamatory (damaging to his reputation). But a public official has an additional burden: he must prove that the statement was made with "actual malice," that is, "with knowledge that it was false or with reckless disregard" of its truth or falsity. Since Sullivan had not met this last burden of proof, the judgment against the *Times* was reversed.

The Court's double standard for libel was based on the premise that public officials are different from private individuals in at least three respects. First, they wield power; to make it too easy for them to sue their critics might inhibit criticism of the government. Justice Brennan said that public debate must be "uninhibited, robust, and wide-open." Second, public officials, because their words can command attention in the media, are better able than most of us to set the record straight if they have been slandered. Third, public officials have chosen voluntarily to enter the limelight. "If you can't stand the heat, get out of the kitchen," former President Harry Truman used to say. Justice Brennan used different words but with much the same meaning in quoting from an earlier Court opinion: "public men are, as it were, public property."

Here are excerpts from the *Sullivan* opinion:

DEBATE SHOULD BE "UNINHIBITED, ROBUST, AND WIDE-OPEN"

Justice Brennan, from *New York Times v. Sullivan*, 1964

We are required for the first time in this case to determine the extent to which the constitutional protections for speech and press limit a State's power to award damages in a libel action brought by a public official against critics of his official conduct. . . .

Respondent's complaint alleged that he had been libeled by statements in a full-page advertisement that was carried in the New York Times on March 29, 1960. Entitled "Heed Their Rising Voices," the advertisement began by stating that "As the whole world knows by now, thousands of Southern Negro students are engaged in widespread non-violent demonstrations in positive affirmation of the right to live in human dignity as guaranteed by the U.S. Constitution and the Bill of Rights." It went on to charge that "in their efforts to uphold these guarantees, they are being met by an unprecedented wave of terror by those who would deny and negate that document which the whole world looks upon as setting the pattern for modern freedom. . . ."

Of the 10 paragraphs of text in the advertisement, the third and a portion of the sixth were the basis of respondent's claim of libel. They read as follows:

Third paragraph:

> In Montgomery, Alabama, after students sang "My Country 'Tis of Thee" on the State Capitol steps, their leaders were expelled from school, and truckloads of police armed with shotguns and tear-gas ringed the Alabama State College Campus. When the entire student body protested to state authorities by refusing to re-register, their dining hall was padlocked in an attempt to starve them into submission. . . .

Although neither of these statements mentions respondent by name, he contended that the word "police" in the third paragraph referred to him as the Montgomery Commissioner who supervised the Police Department, so that he was being accused of "ringing" the campus with police. He further claimed that the paragraph would be read as imputing to the police, and hence to him, the padlocking of the dining hall in order to starve the students into submission. As to the sixth paragraph, he contended that since arrests are ordinarily made by the police, the statement "They have arrested [Dr. King] seven times" would be read as referring to him; he further contended that the "They" who did the arresting would be equated with the "They" who committed the other described acts and with the "Southern violators.". . .

We hold that the rule of law applied by the Alabama courts is constitutionally deficient for failure to provide the safeguards for freedom of speech and of the press that are required by the First and Fourteenth Amendments in a libel action brought by a public official against critics of his official conduct. We further hold that under the proper safeguards the evidence presented in this case is constitutionally insufficient to support the judgment for respondent. . . .

We may dispose at the outset of two grounds asserted to insulate the judgment of the Alabama courts from constitutional scrutiny. The first is the proposition relied on by the State Supreme Court—that "The Fourteenth Amendment is directed against State action and not private action." That proposition has no application to this case. Although this is a civil lawsuit between private parties, the Alabama courts have applied a state rule of law which petitioners claim to impose invalid restrictions on their constitutional freedoms of speech and press. It matters not that that law has been applied in a civil action and that it is common law only, though supplemented by statute. The test is not the form in which state power has been applied but, whatever the form, whether such power has in fact been exercised. . . .

The publication here was not a "commercial" advertisement. It communicated information, expressed opinion, recited grievances, protested claimed abuses, and sought financial support on behalf of a movement whose existence and objectives are matters of the highest public interest and concern. . . . That the Times was paid for publishing the advertisement is as immaterial in this connection as is the fact that newspapers and books are sold. . . .

Any other conclusion would discourage newspapers from carrying "editorial advertisements" of this type, and so might shut off an important outlet for the promulgation of information and ideas by persons who do not themselves have access to publishing facilities—who wish to exercise their freedom of speech even though they are not members of the press. . . . The effect would be to shackle the First Amendment in its attempt to secure "the widest possible dissemination of information from diverse and antagonistic sources.". . . To avoid placing such a handicap upon the freedoms by expression, we hold that if the allegedly libelous statements would otherwise be constitutionally protected from the present judgment, they do not forfeit that protection because they were published in the form of a paid advertisement. . . .

Respondent relies heavily, as did the Alabama courts, on statements of this Court to the effect that the Constitution does not protect libelous publications. Those statements do not foreclose our inquiry here. None of the cases sustained the use of libel laws to impose sanctions upon expression critical of the official conduct of public officials. The dictum in *Pennekamp v. Florida,* 328 U.S. 331, 348-349, . . . that "when the statements amount to defamation, a judge has such remedy in damages for libel as do other public servants," implied no view as to what remedy might constitutionally be afforded to public officials. In *Beauharnais v. Illinois,* 343 U.S. 250, . . . the Court sustained an Illinois criminal libel statute as applied to a publication held to be both defamatory of a racial group and "liable to cause violence and disorder." But the Court was careful to note that it "retains and exercises authority to nullify action which encroaches on freedom of utterance under the guise of punishing libel"; for "public men, are, as it were, public property," and "discussion cannot be denied and the right, as well as the duty, of criticism must not be stifled." . . . In the only previous case that did present the question of constitutional limitations upon the power to award damages for libel of a public official, the Court was equally divided and the question was not decided. *Schenectady Union Pub. Co. v. Sweeney,* 316 U.S. 642. . . . In deciding the question now, we are compelled by neither precedent nor policy to give any more weight to the epithet "libel" than we have to other "mere labels" of state law. . . . Like "insurrection," contempt, advocacy of unlawful acts, breach of the peace, obscenity, solicitation of legal business, and the various other formulae for the repression of expression that have been challenged in this Court, libel can claim no talismanic immunity from constitutional limitations. It must be measured by standards that satisfy the First Amendment.

The general proposition that freedom of expression upon public questions is secured by the First Amendment has long been settled by our decisions. The constitutional safeguard, we have said, "was fashioned to assure the unfettered interchange of ideas for the bringing about of political and social changes desired by the people." *Roth v. United States,* 354 U.S. 476. . . . "The maintenance of the opportunity for free political discussion to the end that government may be responsive to the will of the people and that changes may be obtained by lawful means, an opportunity essential to the security of the Republic, is a fundamental principle of our constitutional system." *Stromberg v. California,* 283 U.S. 359, 369. . . . "[I]t is a prized American privilege to speak one's mind, although not always with perfect good taste, on all public institutions," *Bridges v. California,* 314 U.S. 252, 270, . . . and this opportunity is to be afforded for "vigorous advocacy" no less than "abstract discussion." *N.A.A.C.P. v. Button,* 371 U.S. 415. . . .

Thus we consider this case against the background of a profound national commitment to the principle that debate on public issues should be uninhibited, robust, and wide-open, and that it may well include vehement, caustic, and sometimes unpleasantly sharp attacks on government and public officials. . . . The present advertisement, as an expression of grievance and protest on one of the major public issues of our time, would seem clearly to qualify for the constitutional protection. The question is whether it forfeits that protection by the falsity of some of its factual statements and by its alleged defamation of respondent. . . .

Authoritative interpretations of the First Amendment guarantees have consistently refused to recognize an exception for any test of truth, whether administered by judges, juries, or administrative officials—and especially not one that puts the burden of proving truth on the speaker. . . . The constitutional protection does not turn upon "the truth, popularity, or social utility of the ideas and beliefs which are offered." *N.A.A.C.P. v. Button,* 371 U.S. 415, 445. . . . As Madison said, "Some degree of abuse is inseparable from the proper use of every thing; and in no instance is this more true than in that of the press." 4 Elliot's Debates on the Federal Constitution (1876) p. 571. . . .

That erroneous statement is inevitable in free debate, and that it must be protected if the freedoms of expression are to have the "breathing space" that they "need . . . to survive," *N.A.A.C.P. v. Button,* 371 U.S. 415. . . .

Just as factual error affords no warrant for repressing speech that would otherwise be free, the same is true of injury to official reputation. Where judicial officers are involved, this Court has held that concern for the dignity and reputation of the courts does not justify the punishment as criminal contempt of criticism of the judge or his decision. *Bridges v. California* 314 U.S. 252. . . . This is true even though the utterance contains "half-truths" and "misinformation.". . . Such repression can be justified, if at all, only by a clear and present danger of the obstruction of justice. If judges are to be treated as "men of fortitude, able to thrive in a hardy climate,". . . surely the same must be true of other government officials, such as elected city commissioners. Criticism of their official conduct does not lose its constitutional protection merely because it is effective criticism and hence diminishes their official reputations.

If neither factual error nor defamatory content suffices to remove the constitutional shield from criticism of official conduct, the combination of the two elements is no less inadequate. . . .

A rule compelling the critic of official conduct to guarantee the truth of all his factual assertions—and to do so on pain of libel judgments virtually unlimited in amount—leads to a comparable "self-censorship." Allowance of the defense of truth, with the burden of proving it on the defendant, does not mean that only false speech will be deterred. Even courts accepting this defense as an adequate safeguard have recognized the difficulties of adducing legal proofs that the alleged libel was true in all its factual particulars. . . .

Under such a rule would-be critics of official conduct may be deterred from voicing their criticism, even though it is believed to be true and even though it is in fact true, because of doubt whether it can be proved in court or fear of the expense of having to do so. They tend to make only statements which "steer far wider of the unlawful zone.". . . The rule thus dampens the vigor and limits the variety of public debate. It is inconsistent with the First and Fourteenth Amendments.

The constitutional guarantees require, we think, a federal rule that prohibits a public official from recovering damages for a defamatory falsehood relating to his official conduct unless he proves that the statement was made with "actual malice"—that is, with knowledge that it was false or with reckless disregard of whether it was false or not. . . .

We hold today that the Constitution delimits a State's power to award damages for libel in actions brought by public officials against critics of their official conduct. Since this is such an action, the rule requiring proof of actual malice is applicable. While Alabama law apparently requires proof of actual malice for an award of punitive damages, where general damages are concerned malice is "presumed." Such a presumption is inconsistent with the federal rule. "The power to create presumptions is not a means of escape from constitutional restrictions," *Bailey v. Alabama,* 219 U.S. 219, . . . "the showing of malice required for the forfeiture of the privilege is not presumed but is a matter for proof by the plaintiff. . . ." Since the trial judge did not instruct the jury to differentiate between general and punitive damages, it may be that the verdict was wholly an award of one or the other. But it is impossible to know, in view of the general verdict returned. Because of this uncertainty, the judgment must be reversed and the case remanded.

This Court's duty is not limited to the elaboration of constitutional principles; we must also in proper cases review the evidence to make certain that those principles have been constitutionally applied. This is such a case, particularly since the question is one of alleged trespass across "the line between speech unconditionally guaranteed and speech which may legitimately be regulated.". . . In cases where that line must be drawn, the rule is that we "examine for ourselves the statements in issue and the circumstances under which they were made to see . . . whether they are of a character which the principles of the First Amendment, as adopted by the Due Process Clause of the Fourteenth Amendment, protect." *Pennekamp* v. *Florida,* 328 U.S. 331, 335. . . . We must "make an independent examination of the whole record," . . . so as to assure ourselves that the judgment does not constitute a forbidden intrusion on the field of free expression.

Applying these standards, we consider that the proof presented to show actual malice lacks the convincing clarity which the constitutional standard demands, and hence that it would not constitutionally sustain the judgment for respondent under the proper rule of law. The case of the individual petitioners requires little discussion. Even assuming that they could constitutionally be found to have authorized the use of their names on the advertisement, there was no evidence whatever that they were aware of any erroneous statements or were in any way reckless in that regard. The judgment against them is thus without constitutional support.

As to the Times, we similarly conclude that the facts do not support a finding of actual malice. . . . We think the evidence against the Times supports at most a finding of negligence in failing to discover the misstatements, and is constitutionally insufficient to show the recklessness that is required for a finding of actual malice. . . . ∎

Two key terms in the *Sullivan* case have opened up new areas of controversy.

The first of these is the term "public official." What is there about a "public official" which makes him fair game for "uninhibited, robust, and wide-open" criticism? Is it his "public-ness" or his official status? What about a "public figure"—someone who is a celebrity but who wields no official power? Is it necessary for such a person to assume the *Sullivan* burden of proving "actual malice" in a libel suit? The Supreme Court's answer would seem to be yes. In two 1967 cases reviewing libel suits brought by well-known individuals (one of them a University of Georgia football coach) who did not hold public office, narrow Court majorities extended the *Sullivan* doctrine beyond "public officials" to "public figures," people who have thrust themselves into the limelight of publicity.

For a time it looked as if the Court was extending the *Sullivan* burden of proving "actual malice" even further, to individuals involved "in an event of public or general interest." A man named Rosenbloom who had been acquitted on pornography charges sued a radio network for broadcasting reports about his "smut literature racket." He won in the lower courts, but the Supreme Court reversed in 1971 *(Rosenbloom v. Metromedia)* on grounds that the *Sullivan* standard had not been used. Justice William Brennan, writing a plurality opinion, said that even though the plaintiff was not a "public figure," the matter involved was "a subject of public or general interest." But the Court reversed itself three years later in *Gertz v. Robert Welch, Inc.* (1974) when it ruled that a private individual involved in a public controversy could sue and win a judgment without having to prove "actual malice." However, the Court added, in the absence of such proof the plaintiff is entitled only to "compensation for actual injury," not punitive fines against the libeler.

The second term in the *Sullivan* case that has spawned new controversy in recent years is the term "actual malice."

There is an irony here. The *Sullivan* opinion was widely hailed in the media as a landmark in civil liberties. By making public officials (later broadened to "public figures") have to prove "actual malice," it seemed to guarantee the press almost total immunity against successful libel suits by the powerful and the well-known. After all, how could such plaintiffs possibly prove that a newspaper printed a defamatory falsehood "with knowledge that it was false or with reckless disregard of whether it was false or not"? How could anyone prove such intent? How does one get into the minds of reporters and editors?

But there are ways, and therein lies the irony of *Sullivan.* This great landmark of press freedom pointed the way, with a logic which seemed inescapable, to *Herbert v. Lando* (1979), a decision which produced howls of pain and dismay in press rooms all over the country.

Justice Byron White, who delivered the Court's 6-3 majority opinion in the case, also set forth the facts leading up to it.

DETERMINING THE PRESS'S "STATE OF MIND"

Justice White, from *Herbert v. Lando,* 1979

By virtue of the First and Fourteenth Amendments, neither the Federal nor a State Government may make any law "abridging the freedom of speech, or of the press. . . ." The question here is whether those Amendments should be construed to provide further protection for the press when sued for defamation than has hitherto been recognized. More specifically, we are urged to hold for the first time that when a member of the press is alleged to have circulated damaging falsehoods and is sued for injury to the plaintiff's reputation, the plaintiff is barred from inquiring into the editorial processes of those responsible for the publication, even though the inquiry would produce evidence material to the proof of a critical element of his cause of action.

Petitioner, Anthony Herbert, is a retired Army officer who had extended war-time service in Vietnam and who received widespread media attention in 1969-1970 when he accused his superior officers of covering up reports of atrocities and other war crimes. Three years later, on February 4, 1973, respondent Columbia Broadcasting System, Inc. (CBS), broadcast a report on petitioner and his accusations. The program was produced and edited by respondent Barry Lando and was narrated by respondent Mike Wallace. Lando later published a related article in Atlantic Monthly magazine. Herbert then sued Lando, Wallace, CBS, and Atlantic Monthly for defamation in Federal District Court, basing jurisdiction on diversity of citizenship. In his complaint, Herbert alleged that the program and article falsely and maliciously portrayed him as a liar and a person who had made war-crimes charges to explain his relief from command, and he requested substantial damages for injury to his reputation and to the literary value of a book he had just published recounting his experiences.

. . . Although his cause of action arose under New York State defamation law, Herbert conceded that because he was a "public figure" the First and Fourteenth Amendments precluded recovery absent proof that respondents had published a damaging falsehood "with 'actual malice'— that is, with knowledge that it was false or with reckless disregard of whether it was false or not." This was the holding of *New York Times v. Sullivan*, 376 U.S. 254, 280, 84 S.Ct. 710, 726, 11 L.Ed.2d 686 (1964), with respect to alleged libels of public officials, and extended to "public figures" by *Curtis Publishing Co. v. Butts*, 388 U.S. 130, 87 S.Ct. 1975, 18 L.Ed.2d 1094 (1967). Under this rule, absent knowing falsehood, liability requires proof of reckless disregard for truth, that is, that the defendant "in fact entertained serious doubts as to the truth of his publication." *St. Amant v. Thompson*, 390 U.S. 727, 731, 88 S.Ct. 1323, 1325, 20 L.Ed.2d 262 (1968). Such "subjective awareness of probable falsity," *Gertz v. Robert Welch, Inc.*, 418 U.S. 323, 335 n. 6, 94 S.Ct. 2997, 3004, 41 L.Ed.2d 789 (1974), may be found if "there are obvious reasons to doubt the veracity of the informant or the accuracy of his reports." *St. Amant v. Thompson, supra*, 390 U.S., at 732, 88 S.Ct., at 1326.

In preparing to prove his case in light of these requirements, Herbert deposed Lando at length and sought an order to compel answers to a variety of questions to which response was refused on the ground that the First Amendment protected against inquiry into the state of mind of those who edit, produce or publish, and into the editorial process. Applying the standard of Fed. Rule Civ. Proc. 26(b), which permits discovery of any matter "relevant to the subject matter involved in the pending action" if it would either be admissible in evidence or "appears reasonably calculated to lead to the discovery of admissible evidence," the District Court ruled that because the defendant's state of mind was of "central importance" to the issue of malice in the case, it was obvious that the questions were relevant and "entirely appropriate to Herbert's efforts to discover whether Lando had any reason to doubt the veracity of certain of his sources, or, equally significant, to prefer the veracity of one source over another." 73 F.R.D. 387, 395, 396 (S.D. N.Y. 1977). The District Court rejected the claim of constitutional privilege because it found nothing in the First Amendment or the relevant cases to permit or require it to increase the weight of the injured plaintiff's already heavy burden of proof by in effect creating barriers "behind which malicious publication may go undetected and unpunished." *Id.*, at 394. The case was then certified for an interlocutory appeal under 28 U.S.C. § 1292(b), and the Court of Appeals agreed to hear the case.

A divided panel reversed the District Court. 568 F.2d 974 (CA2 1977). Two judges, writing separate but overlapping opinions, concluded that the First Amendment lent sufficient protection to the editorial processes to protect Lando from inquiry about his thoughts, opinions, and conclusions with respect to the material gathered by him and about his conversations with his editorial colleagues. The privilege not to answer was held to be absolute. We granted certiorari because of the importance of the issue involved. 435 U.S. 922, 98 S.Ct. 1483, 55 L.Ed.2d 515 (1978). We have concluded that the Court of Appeals misconstrued the First and Fourteenth Amendments and accordingly reverse its judgment. . . .

As respondents would have it, the defendant's reckless disregard of the truth, a critical element, could not be shown by direct evidence through inquiry into the thoughts, opinions and conclusions of the publisher but could be proved only by objective evidence from which the ultimate fact could be inferred. It may be that plaintiffs will rarely be successful in proving awareness of falsehood from the mouth of the defendant himself, but the relevance of answers to such inquiries, which the District Court recognized and the Court of Appeals did not deny, can hardly be doubted. To erect an impenetrable barrier to the plaintiff's use of such evidence on his side of the case is a matter of some substance, particularly when defendants themselves are prone to assert their good-faith belief in the truth of their publications, and libel plaintiffs are required to prove knowing or reckless falsehood with "convincing clarity." *New York Times v. Sullivan,* 376 U.S., at 285-286, 84 S.Ct., at 729.

Furthermore, the outer boundaries of the editorial privilege now urged are difficult to perceive. The opinions below did not state, and respondents do not explain, precisely when the editorial process begins and when it ends. Moreover, although we are told that respondent Lando was willing to testify as to what he "knew" and what he had "learned" from his interviews, as opposed to what he "believed," it is not at all clear why the suggested editorial privilege would not cover knowledge as well as belief about the veracity of published reports. It is worth noting here that the privilege as asserted by respondents would also immunize from inquiry the internal communications occurring during the editorial process and thus place beyond reach what the defendant participants learned or knew as the result of such collegiate conversations or exchanges. If damaging admissions to colleagues are to be barred from evidence, would a reporter's admissions made to third parties not participating in the editorial process also be immune from inquiry? We thus have little doubt that Herbert and other defamation plaintiffs have important interests at stake in opposing the creation of the asserted privilege.

Nevertheless, we are urged by respondents to override these important interests because requiring disclosure of editorial conversations and of a reporter's conclusions about the veracity of the material he has gathered will have an intolerable chilling effect on the editorial process and editorial decisionmaking. But if the claimed inhibition flows from the fear of damages liability for publishing knowing or reckless falsehoods, those effects are precisely what *New York Times* and other cases have held to be consistent with the First Amendment. Spreading false information in and of itself carries no First Amendment credentials. "[T]here is no constitutional value in false statements of fact." *Gertz v. Robert Welch, Inc.*, 418 U.S., at 340, 94 S.Ct., at 3007.

Realistically, however, some error is inevitable; and the difficulties of separating fact from fiction convinced the Court in *New York Times, Butts, Gertz,* and similar cases to limit liability to instances where some degree of culpability is present in order to eliminate the risk of undue self-censorship and the suppression of truthful material. Those who publish defamatory falsehoods with the requisite culpability, however, are subject to liability, the aim being not only to compensate for injury but also to deter publication of unprotected material threatening injury to individual reputation. Permitting plaintiffs such as Herbert to prove their cases by direct as well as indirect evidence is consistent with the balance struck by our prior decisions. If such proof results in liability for damages which in turn discourages the publication of erroneous information known to be false or probably false, this is no more than what our cases contemplate and does not abridge either freedom of speech or of the press.

Of course, if inquiry into editorial conclusions threatens the suppression not only of information known or strongly suspected to be unreliable but also of truthful information, the issue would be quite different. But as we have said, our cases necessarily contemplate examination of the editorial process to prove the necessary awareness of probable falsehood, and if indirect proof of this element does not stifle truthful publication and is consistent with the First Amendment, as respondents seem to concede, we do not understand how direct inquiry with respect to the ultimate issue would be substantially more suspect. Perhaps such examination will lead to liability that would not have been found without it, but this does not suggest that the determinations in these instances will be inaccurate and will lead to the suppression of protected information. On the contrary, direct inquiry from the actors, which affords the opportunity to refute inferences that might otherwise be drawn from circumstantial evidence, suggests that more accurate results will be obtained by placing all, rather than part, of the evidence before the decision-maker. Suppose, for example, that a reporter has two contradictory reports about the plaintiff, one of which is false and damaging, and only the false one is published. In resolving the issue whether the publication was known or suspected to be false, it is only common sense to believe that inquiry from the author, with an opportunity to explain, will contribute to accuracy. If the publication is false but there is an exonerating explanation, the defendant will surely testify to this effect. Why should not the plaintiff be permitted to inquire before trial? On the other hand, if the publisher in fact had serious doubts about accuracy, but published nevertheless, no undue self-censorship will result from permitting the relevant inquiry. Only knowing or reckless error will be discouraged; and unless there is to be an absolute First Amendment privilege to inflict injury by knowing or reckless conduct, which respondents do not suggest, constitutional values will not be threatened.

It is also urged that frank discussion among reporters and editors will be dampened and sound editorial judgment endangered if such exchanges, oral or written, are subject to inquiry by defamation plaintiffs. We do not doubt the direct relationship between consultation and discussion on the one hand and sound decisions on the other; but whether or not there is liability for the injury, the press has an obvious interest in avoiding the infliction of harm by the publication of false information, and it is not unreasonable to expect the media to invoke whatever procedures that may be practicable and useful to that end. Moreover, given exposure to liability when there is knowing or reckless error, there is even more reason to resort to prepublication precautions, such as a frank interchange of fact and opinion. Accordingly, we find it difficult to believe that error-avoiding procedures will be terminated or stifled simply because there is liability for culpable error and because the editorial process will itself be examined in the tiny percentage of instances in which error is claimed and litigation ensues. Nor is there sound reason to believe that editorial exchanges and the editorial process are so subject to distortion and to such recurring misunderstanding that they should be immune from examination in order to avoid erroneous judgments in defamation suits. The evidentiary burden Herbert must carry to prove at least reckless disregard for the truth is substantial indeed, and we are unconvinced that his chances of winning an undeserved verdict are such that an inquiry into what Lando learned or said during editorial process must be foreclosed.

This is not to say that the editorial discussions or exchanges have no constitutional protection from casual inquiry. There is no law that subjects the editorial process to private or official examination merely to satisfy curiosity or to serve some general end such as the public interest; and if there were, it would not survive constitutional scrutiny as the First Amendment is presently construed. No such problem exists here, however, where there is a specific claim of injury arising from a publication that is alleged to have been knowing or recklessly false.

. . . Evidentiary privileges in litigation are not favored, and even those rooted in the Constitution must give way in proper circumstances. The President, for example, does not have an absolute privilege against disclosure of materials subpoenaed for a judicial proceeding. *United States v. Nixon,* 418 U.S. 683, 94 S.Ct. 3090, 41 L.Ed.2d 1039 (1974). In so holding, we found that although the President has a powerful interest in confidentiality of communications between himself and his advisers, that interest must yield to a demonstrated specific need for evidence. As we stated, in referring to existing limited privileges against disclosure, "[w]hatever their origins, these exceptions to the demand for every man's evidence are not lightly created nor expansively construed, for they are in derogation of the search for truth." *Id.,* at 710, 94 S.Ct., at 3108.

. . . With these considerations in mind, we conclude that the present construction of the First Amendment should not be modified by creating the evidentiary privilege which the respondents now urge. ■

Some of the press reaction to the *Lando* decision bordered on the hysterical. There was talk about the courts "rummaging through the minds" of news people, warnings about "thought police," and calls for new safeguards against an "imperial judiciary." A more thoughtful, though strongly-worded, protest against the decision came from Tom Wicker of the *New York Times.*

A CHILLING DECISION

Tom Wicker, from "A Chilling Court," *New York Times,* 1979

The Supreme Court has generally upheld the right of the press to publish or broadcast what it knows. But whether or not by design, the Court seems to be moving on two tracks toward a position that editors and reporters have little—if any—constitutional protection when engaged in gathering the news.

First, in a series of decisions, the Court has held that reporters have no constitutional right to protect the identity of their sources, and has effectively undermined the legislative privilege to do so that numerous states had extended.

Now, in its remarkable ruling in Herbert v. Lando, the Court has undoubtedly "chilled" the willingness of the press to go after and make public controversial material that might result in an expensive and time-consuming libel suit.

The six-justice majority ruled that a public figure trying to prove that an article or a broadcast had defamed him or her could constitutionally inquire into the "state of mind" of the editors and reporters responsible. Such an inquiry, they held, was relevant, perhaps vital, to an attempt to show that the material had been published or broadcast "with knowledge that it was false or with reckless disregard of whether it was false or not."

The Court acknowledged that this would amount to an inquiry into the "editorial process" but it denied that this process was constitutionally protected by the First Amendment in libel cases. Yet, as essentially the same Court said in another case (that of Richard Nixon's tapes), "human experience teaches us that those who expect public dissemination of their remarks may well temper candor with a concern for appearances . . ."

That palpable fact led Justice Marshall, dissenting vigorously, to observe that "society's interest in enhancing the accuracy of coverage of public events is ill-served by procedures tending to muffle expression of uncertainty. To preserve a climate of free interchange among journalists, the confidentiality of their conversation must be guaranteed."

But in addition to chilling the exchange of information and opinion among reporters and editors (a vital part of the "editorial process"), the Herbert decision will inhibit journalists in another important fashion. When the question is whether to make public a controversial story about a public figure and risk a libel suit that the Herbert ruling makes far more likely, many newspapers and broadcasters will decide to drop the story.

On occasion, this may well prevent an inaccurate or misleading story from appearing. Far more often, it is likely to mean the public will be deprived of legitimate and important information believed to be accurate but perhaps not probably so in court—or not without expense and effort that a newspaper or broadcaster cannot afford.

It was to avoid just such self-censorship that the Warren Court ruled in the 1964 Sullivan case that public figures could be defamed only if material about them had been disseminated "with knowledge that it was false or with reckless disregard of whether it was false or not." This heavy burden gave the press effective immunity, as the Warren Court intended, from libel suits in all but the most palpable cases of defamation.

The Herbert ruling ends that immunity by making the "editorial process" and the "state of mind" of reporters and editors legitimate targets of inquiry by public figures claiming libel. Not only will more libel suits be encouraged; they will be lengthier and costlier and more harassing as plaintiffs delve endlessly into the elements of even the most confidential and crucial editorial decisions.

The Burger Court did show concern for the First Amendment implications of its decision. Justice Powell wrote in a concurring opinion that district courts "must ensure that the values protected by the First Amendment, though entitled to no constitutional privilege in a case of this kind, are weighed carefully in striking a proper balance."

That is a weak reed for journalists to lean on in dealing with such public-figure cases as Watergate or the current inquiry into President Carter's peanut business. As Justice Marshall put it, journalistic self-censorship is all too likely "so long as any plaintiff with a deep pocket and a facially sufficient complaint is afforded unconstrained discovery of the editorial process."

But Justice White, for the majority that imposed this new chill on the free press, seemed to give more weight to discouraging publication of "false or probably false" information than to encouraging free and robust public debate. "Only knowing or reckless error will be discouraged," he wrote, by inquiry into the editorial process.

The problem with that confident assertion is that it can never be proved. Just as no one will ever know how many important sources do *not* give information because their confidentiality cannot be guaranteed, so no one will know how many important stories do not get published or broadcast because of the revived threat of hamstringing libel suits. ■

Is it fair for journalists to demand immunities for themselves—such as immunity to being questioned about one's "state of mind"—without demanding similar immunities for the rest of us who are not journalists? This was the issue raised by the *New Republic*'s managing editor, Michael Kinsley, in the wake of the press protests against the *Lando* decision.

THE PRESS DOESN'T OWN THE FIRST AMENDMENT

Michael Kinsley, from "Journalists' Privilege," *The New Republic,* 1979

Despite what you read in the papers, the biggest threat to the First Amendment roaming loose in Washington these days is not Justice Byron White of the United States Supreme Court. It is Jack Landau, the monomaniacal head of the Reporters Committee for Freedom of the Press. Following a fairly minor Supreme Court decision last month reaffirming the state of the libel laws as they have existed for the past 15 years, Landau set the tone for much of the press coverage by declaring, "The courts can take your notes, the Government can take your telephone records, and the police can march into the newsroom. Now libel lawyers can go into your brain. I'd like to know what's left." Talk like this—besides being simply deceitful—is crying wolf. Journalists are uniquely able to make their screams of pain heard. They should hoard these screams for maximum impact when the First Amendment really is threatened. Raising the roof about every minor imposition also reveals a contempt for other important social values—including the First Amendment rights of non-journalists—that can only undermine public (and judicial) empathy for the news business.

Here is what the most recent fuss was about. The Supreme Court has ruled that the First Amendment places some limits on state libel laws. Statements about public figures—even false statements that cause harm or humiliation—are immune from the libel laws unless they were made with "reckless disregard for the truth." Mere carelessness about the facts is not enough. To win a libel case against you, a public figure must prove that you were consciously lying or at the very least that you "in fact entertained serious doubts as to the truth" of what you said when you said it. This is a valuable protection of the press. As envious journalists from other countries will tell you, the fear that every fact of a controversial article might have to be proved in court has a real chilling effect.

In 1973 a segment of the CBS television show "60 Minutes" accused Colonel Anthony Herbert of making up stories about atrocities in Vietnam. Herbert sued for libel. He conceded he was a public figure, and began trying to prove that CBS had shown reckless disregard for the truth. Herbert's lawyers subjected the producer, Barry Lando, to hours of grilling about how the show was prepared. Lando's lawyers objected to some of the questions, arguing that the First Amendment protects the editorial process of the press from this kind of public scrutiny.

Justice White, writing for a six-man majority, ruled that Lando has to answer the questions. His basic reasoning was that you cannot have your cake and eat it too. It is unreasonable to insist that the First Amendment requires a libel plaintiff to prove the state of a journalist's knowledge and beliefs, and also to insist that the First Amendment prevents the plaintiff from acquiring this very information.

You would think from the press coverage that this was a major setback for press freedom. "Court Opens Press To Questioning on Writing of Stories," was the *Washington Star* headline. The news story by *Star* Supreme Court reporter Lyle Denniston called the decision "a sweeping defeat for the nation's media." The *Washington Post* headlined, "High Court Opens Newsroom Editing To Libel Inquiry." In fact, what was new was the suggestion that journalists should *not* be subject to questioning about the editorial process, just as the parties to any lawsuit must answer their opponents' questions about the matter in controversy. Several of the celebrated Supreme Court opinions protecting journalists from libel laws were based on detailed examinations of the editorial process. Nobody

What Are the Media's Rights and Responsibilities?   149

objected to this at the time or since. What CBS was asserting in the Herbert case was a *new* "journalist's privilege."

Of course even the failure to get a new privilege might be unfortunate. First Amendment junkies argue that forcing journalists to answer questions about how they put together a story will "chill" them in the exercise of their First Amendment rights. It is not clear from the ravings how this "chill" is supposed to work. Is it the increased risk of losing a libel suit that will give a journalist pause before expressing himself? Or is it simply that further erosion of the privacy of notes, sources, first drafts, etc. will make the reporter's job harder to do?

If the problem is fear of libel suits, the short answer is that this is the whole point. The Supreme Court *wants* to chill journalists from acting with reckless disregard for the truth. This is still what a public figure must prove in order to win a libel suit. It is not a terribly stringent standard of behavior. The Supreme Court has made lesser misbehavior immune from libel suits by public figures in order to give the pursuit of truth, and comment upon it, a bit of breathing room. There is an honorable argument—persuasive to me, not persuasive to any present member of the Supreme Court—that discussion about matters of public controversy, at least, should be totally immune from libel suits. But it is not honorable to argue that a partial immunity should be expanded on the sly by making crucial information impossible to obtain.

If the problem is that a lack of guaranteed secrecy will thwart the editorial process, then there is a difference between a journalist's private thoughts and things a journalist may have said or written down. All nine justices agreed that it is hard to imagine how a journalist can be "chilled in the very process of thought" (as the lower court decision by Judge Irving Kaufman colorfully suggested) by a fear of having to answer questions in a later lawsuit. The justices decorously failed to point out that private thoughts, though hard to restrain, are *easy to lie about*. All the demonic talk about how the Court is inviting libel lawyers to "go into your brain" (or, as columnist Marquis Childs put it, to "explore the deepest recesses of editors' and reporters' minds") simply means that plaintiffs' lawyers can ask reporters questions and hope they say something self-incriminating. Reporters' lawyers can ask plaintiffs questions too. That's how lawsuits work.

A more serious issue is the right of libel plaintiffs to demand documentary evidence such as notes, first drafts and internal memos, and also to ask reporters and editors to recall conversations they had while preparing a story. Unlike thoughts, these things really can be "chilled" by fear of exposure. Knowing that they can be kept private does indeed grease the wheels of a free press. Increasing the risk that they will become public does make the journalist's job harder. By discouraging journalists from expressing their doubts, the risk of exposure may even *increase* the amount of misinformation that gets published.

The problem is one of simple fairness. Journalists defending libel suits naturally will say that they have been very careful about the facts. If they have any documents, or recall any conversations, that bolster this claim, they certainly will produce these items. Indeed, journalists are taught early on to save all interview notes and other documents in case some story is challenged in a lawsuit. What if the same stockpile of materials contains evidence that the journalist has been quite cavalier about the facts? How can you make a journalist's degree of care a central issue in a lawsuit, and then give one side exclusive access to the best evidence concerning this key issue, both in the name of the First Amendment?

This sort of anomaly does not bother First Amendment junkies like the Reporters Committee for Freedom of the Press. They believe the First Amendment provides absolute protection for all the activities of journalists—gathering the news as well as publishing it—and any conflicting interest must simply give way. But by seeing every intrusion of the law into their working lives as an assault on the First Amendment, reporters are missing a central truth about modern American society, which is that the law is intruding on everybody's lives in a way that makes important work harder to do.

The Herbert case provides a good example of this. When Barry Lando, the CBS producer, refused to answer any more questions from Colonel Herbert's lawyers, he already had answered enough questions to fill 26 volumes of transcript, containing 3000 pages and 240 exhibits. This was just one small part of a "discovery" process—as these pre-trial orgies of information gathering are called—that had been going on for more than a year. Lando already had answered dozens of questions about the editorial process. It looks as if his real reason for refusing to answer any more was simply a feeling that "enough is enough."

The rules encouraging elaborate "discovery" in civil lawsuits were considered a great innovation when they first appeared during the 1930s. By preventing either side from keeping secrets from the other, they were supposed to avoid "trial by surprise." By revealing all the crucial evidence before trial, they were supposed to encourage settlements out of court. American courts place almost no limit on how much time and information one side of a lawsuit can demand of the other before trial. But this tradition, combined with the almost unique American rule that the loser of a lawsuit needn't pay the winner's legal costs, has made the mere threat of a lawsuit a powerful blackmail tool. And even legitimate lawsuits cost far more time, money and inconvenience than the cause of justice reasonably demands. Libel suits are the principal occasions when reporters get caught up in the awful machinery of the law. Instead of reflecting on what this kind of harassment means for the society they are supposed to be reporting on, too many journalists instead demand a special exemption on the grounds that their own job is too important to be subject to such intrusions.

Another recent example of journalists' myopia was their presentation of last year's notorious Supreme Court decision in *Zurcher* v. *Stanford Daily,* also written by Justice White. This is the one that generated all the hysteria about police marching through newsrooms and ransacking files, etc. What the Court held was that the press has no absolute exemption from search warrants. You would not know from the evocations of jackboots this ruling induced in the press that *everybody's* house and office can be invaded by police with a search warrant looking for evidence of a crime. The Constitution requires that the police convince some judicial officer that they have "probable cause" to suspect they'll find valuable evidence before they can get a search warrant. But in practice search warrants often are issued pretty automatically. This is not good. Some legal scholars argue that the police shouldn't be able to get search warrants against people not suspected of a crime; that police should have to get information from non-suspects either voluntarily or by subpoena. The Reporters Committee brief in the *Stanford Daily* case mentioned this argument in a footnote. (In the Farber case, it argued that reporters should be exempt from subpoenas too.) The rest of the brief demonstrated complete indifference to whether police can "march through" and "ransack" other people's offices and homes. So did most of the editorial comment afterward.

In both his recent anti-press decisions, Justice White said that the press's legitimate need for privacy is entitled to consideration. But press fanatics insist this need is entitled to *absolute* consideration, and absolute priority. They like to note that the First Amendment says nothing about balancing freedom of expression against other rights and values. Indeed it doesn't. But these controversies over notes and files don't involve the press's right to publish information. Quite the contrary: the issue is the press's right to keep information *secret.* When the Court has agreed that some secrecy is a valuable part of the publishing process, and is entitled to important consideration under the Constitution, it is foolish to insist that the press's right to secrecy is absolute. Such claims cheapen the rhetorical currency, which should be saved up for occasions when the actual right to *publish* is threatened. . . .

When the press fights against direct interference with the right to speak out, it is defending a right that is available equally to all citizens. When it claims immunity for preliminary steps in the editorial process, it is asking for privileges that apply only to the press as an institution. It is asking in these cases for special exemptions from the ordinary duties and risks of citizenship. It would be tactful to make such requests in a more humble spirit than what is usually displayed.

The day the Supreme Court decided the "60 Minutes" case, there was an article buried inside the *Washington Post* about a New York court's ruling that book authors are not entitled to the same consideration as newspaper reporters when a judge is deciding whether to subpoena their notes. This is an important victory for reporters' rights. Obviously *somebody* must have to obey subpoenas. A "First Amendment right" such as immunity from subpoenas—or from search warrants or from pre-trial discovery—by its nature must be exclusive. The more exclusive it can be made, the easier it will be for the legal system to tolerate. A few days later, the *Post* ran a resentful editorial comparing the Supreme Court's concern about news leaks to a Court decision about bugging devices. The two events, the *Post* said, "reveal how deeply the justices feel about their own privacy and how casually a majority of them regard the privacy of others." The same can be said about the official voices of the press, not only concerning privacy but also concerning the First Amendment itself. ■

If the Government is allowed to "get its foot in the door," through slander and "right of reply" laws, where is the line to be drawn? Should reporters be forced to divulge their sources of information?

It can be argued that one of our most critical constitutional rights is the right to confront any witnesses or evidence against us. If information gathered by a reporter is used in an accusation against us, should we know the source of that information so we can defend ourselves against it?

Another, critical right to be considered is the freedom of the press. If sources are made public, all sorts of coercion or intimidation might follow. If the sources of sensitive information dry up, who will expose the abuses of the Government to the light of public scrutiny? These opposed, but equally indispensible rights are the subject of the following section.

Must Reporters Identify Their Sources?

The issue of "reporter's privilege"—the question of whether a reporter has the right to refuse to reveal information given him under the promise of confidentiality—has been the subject of considerable confusion. It is not true, as defenders of reporter's privilege have sometimes alleged, that it is an ancient right. It is found nowhere in the United States Constitution, and American courts have never recognized the right of reporters to be exempt from a citizen's duty to tell law-enforcement authorities all one knows about matters related to the commission of a crime. (The only right of silence recognized by the Constitution is the Fifth Amendment's prohibition against coerced self-incrimination, which protects all of us.) What can be said on behalf of the press's claims is that law-enforcement officials began to make unprecedented demands upon newsmen by the end of the 1960s. From Justice Department officials to local district attorneys there came a flurry of subpoenas for reporters' notes, tapes, film, and testimony about things said to them in confidence. Not content to rely on their own investigations, these officials seemed to be trying to annex the press to their offices.

What brought about this threat to the historical independence of the press? Some observers noted that it coincided with the arrival of the Nixon Administration and a general mood of conservative backlash. The more likely cause is bound up with the history of the preceding decade. During the Sixties the American media suddenly took on unprecedented importance. The coverage of the civil rights confrontations in the South, the coverage of President Kennedy's funeral, the coverage of the urban riots and the burning American cities, the coverage of the Vietnam war and the reaction to it at home, the coverage of the assassinations of Martin Luther King and Robert Kennedy, the coverage of the blood-spattered 1968 Democratic convention, and then the investigative journalism—the exposure of everything from the massacres of civilians in Vietnam to the lies and plots of politicians in Washington—all combined to make the press seem a "progressive" institution, independent of, and frequently opposed to, the political "establishment." The press came to be perceived as a friend of underdogs: its facilities served as giant amplifiers for otherwise powerless voices and reporters became increasingly sympathetic to those voices. Political radicals, counterculturists, and ordinary felons began seeking access to the facilities of the press for delivering harangues, sociological lectures, and taunts to their enemies in the "establishment." In consequence, the police and other law enforcement authorities began serving the press with subpoenas.

Branzburg v. Hayes (1972) exemplified the new symbiosis of journalists and lawbreakers. It was one of three decided by the Supreme Court on the same day, since all three concerned the same issue of whether journalists should enjoy the privilege of not having to testify or give names before grand juries. The other two cases were *United States v. Caldwell* and *In re Pappas*.

Branzburg grew out of a story by a reporter for the *Courier-Journal* of Louisville, Kentucky describing in detail the reporter's observations of two young men synthesizing hashish from marijuana, an activity which, one of them boasted, earned them about $5,000 in three weeks. "I don't know why I'm letting you do this story," one of them was quoted as saying. "To make the narcs mad, I guess." The "narcs" were indeed provoked, and the reporter was asked to appear before a grand jury investigating the illegal use of narcotics. He appeared, but refused to identify the individuals involved, claiming the protection of a Kentucky reporters' privilege statute, the Kentucky constitution, and the First Amendment. Losing his case in the state courts, he petitioned the Supreme Court.

United States v. Caldwell arose from the following circumstances. In 1969 Earl Caldwell, then a *New York Times* reporter, was assigned to cover the Black Panther Party and other militant black organizations. Not long after some of Caldwell's articles on the Black Panthers appeared in the *Times*, he was subpoenaed to appear before a grand jury to answer questions about their aims, purposes, and activities. One of their officers had announced on television that "we will kill Richard Nixon" (the threat was repeated in three subsequent issues of their newspaper), and Caldwell quoted their "chief of staff" as urging "the very direct overthrow of the Government by way of force and violence." Yet, when the inevitable subpoena was issued to Caldwell, he refused even to appear before a grand jury, arguing that his appearance might drive "a wedge of distrust and silence between the news media and the militants" and thus "suppress vital First Amendment freedoms." Caldwell lost in the lower courts, but won in the Court of Appeals, so it was the government that petitioned the Supreme Court.

In re Pappas also involved the rhetorical activities of the Black Panthers. During a time of serious civil disturbance in New Bedford, Massachusetts, a television newsman gained entrance to their headquarters and recorded a prepared statement of one of their leaders. When called before a grand jury investigating the disturbances, Pappas refused to appear and answer any questions about what he saw and heard within the headquarters, citing the protection of the First Amendment. Pappas lost in Massachusetts courts, then petitioned the Supreme Court.

By 5 to 4 the Court voted to deny any special reporters' privilege in these cases. Since one member of the majority wrote a separate concurring opinion, Justice Byron White was really delivering the opinion of himself and three other Justices when he wrote the official "opinion of the Court."

THE DUTY OF A CITIZEN

Justice White, from *Branzburg v. Hayes,* 1972

The issue in these cases is whether requiring newsmen to appear and testify before state or federal grand juries abridges the freedom of speech and press guaranteed by the First Amendment. We hold that it does not. . . .

Petitioners Branzburg and Pappas and respondent Caldwell press First Amendment claims that may be simply put: that to gather news it is often necessary to agree either not to identify the source of information published or to publish only part of the facts revealed, or both; that if the reporter is nevertheless forced to reveal these confidences to a grand jury, the source so identified and other confidential sources of other reporters will be measurably deterred from furnishing publishable information, all to the detriment of the free flow of information protected by the First Amendment. Although petitioners do not claim an absolute privilege against official interrogation in all circumstances, they assert that the reporter should not be forced either to appear or to testify before a grand jury or at trial until and unless sufficient grounds are shown for believing that the reporter possesses information relevant to a crime the grand jury is investigating, that the information the reporter has is unavailable from other sources, and that the need for the information is sufficiently compelling to override the claimed invasion of First Amendment interests occasioned by the disclosure. Principally relied upon are prior cases emphasizing the importance of the First Amendment guarantees to individual development and to our system of representative government, decisions requiring that official action with adverse impact on First Amendment rights be justified by a public interest that is "compelling" or "paramount," and those precedents establishing the principle that justifiable governmental goals may not be achieved by unduly broad means having an unnecessary impact on protected rights of speech, press, or association. The heart of the claim is that the burden on newsgathering resulting from compelling reporters to disclose confidential information outweighs any public interest in obtaining the information.

We do not question the significance of free speech, press, or assembly to the country's welfare. Nor is it suggested that newsgathering does not qualify for First Amendment protection; without some protection for seeking out the news, freedom of the press could be eviscerated. But this case involves no intrusions upon speech or assembly, no prior restraint or restriction on what the press may publish, and no express or implied command that the press publish what it prefers to withhold. No exaction or tax for the privilege of publishing, and no penalty, civil or criminal, related to the content of published material is at issue here. The use of confidential sources by the press is not forbidden or restricted; reporters remain free to seek news from any source by means within the law. No attempt is made to require the press to publish its sources of information or indiscriminately to disclose them on request.

The sole issue before us is the obligation of reporters to respond to grand jury subpoenas as other citizens do and to answer questions relevant to an investigation into the commission of crime. Citizens generally are not constitutionally immune from grand jury subpoenas; and neither the First Amendment nor other constitutional provision protects the average citizen from disclosing to a grand jury information that he has received in confidence. The claim is, however, that reporters are exempt from these obligations because if forced to respond to subpoenas and identify their sources or disclose other confidences, their informants will refuse or be reluctant to furnish newsworthy information in the future. This asserted burden on newsgathering is said to make compelled testimony from newsmen constitutionally suspect and to require a privileged position for them.

It is clear that the First Amendment does not invalidate every incidental burdening of the press that may result from the enforcement of civil or criminal statutes of general applicability. Under prior cases, otherwise valid laws serving substantial public interests may be enforced against the press as against others, despite the possible burden that may be imposed. The Court has emphasized that "[t]he publisher of a newspaper has no special immunity from the application of general laws. He has no special privilege to invade the rights and liberties of others." [*Associated Press v. NLRB*, 1937.] It was there held that the Associated Press, a newsgathering and disseminating organization, was not exempt from the requirements of the National Labor Relations Act. The holding was reaffirmed in *Oklahoma Press Publishing Co. v. Walling* (1946), where the Court rejected the claim that applying the Fair Labor Standards Act to a newspaper publishing business would abridge the freedom of press guaranteed by the First Amendment. *Associated Press v. United States* (1945) similarly overruled assertions that the First Amendment precluded application of the Sherman Act to a newsgathering and disseminating organization. Likewise, a newspaper may be subjected to nondiscriminatory forms of general taxation.

The prevailing view is that the press is not free with impunity to publish everything and anything it desires to publish. Although it may deter or regulate what is said or published, the press may not circulate knowing or reckless falsehoods damaging to private reputation without subjecting itself to liability for damages, including punitive damages, or even criminal prosecution. A newspaper or a journalist may also be punished for contempt of court, in appropriate circumstances.

It has generally been held that the First Amendment does not guarantee the press a constitutional right of special access to information not available to the public generally. In *Zemel v. Rusk* ([1965], for example, the Court sustained the Government's refusal to validate passports to Cuba even though that restriction "rendered less than wholly free the flow of information concerning that country." The ban on travel was held constitutional, for "[t]he right to speak and publish does not carry with it the unrestrained right to gather information."

Despite the fact that newsgathering may be hampered, the press is regularly excluded from grand jury proceedings, our own conferences, the meetings of other official bodies gathered in executive session, and the meetings of private organizations. Newsmen have no constitutional right of access to the scenes of crime or disaster when the general public is excluded, and they may be prohibited from attending or publishing information about trials if such restrictions are necessary to assure a defendant a fair trial before an impartial tribunal. . . .

It is thus not surprising that the great weight of authority is that newsmen are not exempt from the normal duty of appearing before a grand jury and answering questions relevant to a criminal investigation. At common law, courts consistently refused to recognize the existence of any privilege authorizing a newsman to refuse to reveal confidential information to a grand jury.

In 1958, a newsgatherer asserted for the first time that the First Amendment exempted confidential information from public disclosure pursuant to a subpoena issued in a civil suit [*Garland v. Torre*], but the claim was denied, and this argument has been almost uniformly rejected since then, although there are occasional dicta that, in circumstances not presented, a newsman might be excused. These courts have applied the presumption against the existence of an asserted testimonial privilege [*United States v. Bryan,* 1950], and have concluded that the First Amendment interest asserted by the newsman was outweighed by the general obligation of a citizen to appear before a grand jury or at trial, pursuant to a subpoena, and give what information he possesses. The opinions of the state courts in *Branzburg* and *Pappas* are typical of the prevailing view, although a few recent cases, such as *Caldwell,* have recognized and given effect to some form of constitutional newsman's privilege.

The prevailing constitutional view of the newsman's privilege is very much rooted in the ancient role of the grand jury, which has the dual function of determining if there is probable cause to believe that a crime has been committed and of protecting citizens against unfounded criminal prosecutions. . . . Because its task is to inquire into the existence of possible criminal conduct and to return only well-founded indictments, its investigative powers are necessarily broad. "It is a grand inquest, a body with powers of investigation and inquisition, the scope of whose inquiries is not to be limited narrowly by questions of propriety or forecasts of the probable result of the investigation, or by doubts whether any particular individual will be found properly subject to an accusation of crime." [*Blair v. United States,* 1919.] Hence the grand jury's authority to subpoena witnesses is not only historic, [sic] but essential to its task. Although the powers of the grand jury are not unlimited and are subject to the supervision of a judge, the long-standing principle that "the public has a right to every man's evidence," except for those persons protected by a constitutional, common law, or statutory privilege, is particularly applicable to grand jury proceedings.

A number of states have provided newsmen a statutory privilege of varying breadth, but the majority have not done so, and none has been provided by federal statute. Until now the only testimonial privilege for unofficial witnesses that is rooted in the federal Constitution is the Fifth Amendment privilege against compelled self-incrimination. We are asked to create another by interpreting the First Amendment to grant newsmen a testimonial privilege that other citizens do not enjoy. This we decline to do. Fair and effective law enforcement aimed at providing security for the person and property of the individual is a fundamental function of government, and the grand jury plays an important, constitutionally mandated role in this process. On the records now before us, we perceive no basis for holding that the public interest in law enforcement and in ensuring effective grand jury proceedings is insufficient to override the consequential, but uncertain, burden on newsgathering which is said to result from insisting that reporters, like other citizens, respond to relevant questions put to them in the course of a valid grand jury investigation or criminal trial.

This conclusion itself involves no restraint on what newspapers may publish or on the type or quality of information reporters may seek to acquire, nor does it threaten the vast bulk of confidential relationships between reporters and their sources. Grand juries address themselves to the issues of whether crimes have been committed and who committed them. Only where news sources themselves are implicated in crime or possess information relevant to the grand jury's task need they or the reporter be concerned about grand jury subpoenas. Nothing before us indicates that a large number or percentage of *all* confidential news sources fall into either category and would in any way be deterred by our holding that the Constitution does not, as it never has, exempt the newsman from performing the citizen's normal duty of appearing and furnishing information relevant to the grand jury's task.

The preference for anonymity of those confidential informants involved in actual criminal conduct is presumably a product of their desire to escape criminal prosecution, and this preference, while understandable, is hardly deserving of constitutional protection. It would be frivolous to assert—and no one does in these cases—that the First Amendment, in the interest of securing news or otherwise, confers a license on either the reporter or his news sources to violate otherwise valid criminal laws. Although stealing documents or private wiretapping could provide newsworthy information, neither reporter nor source is immune from conviction for such conduct, whatever the impact on the flow of news. Neither is immune, on First Amendment grounds, from testifying against the other, before the grand jury or at a criminal trial. . . .

There remain those situations where a source is not engaged in criminal conduct but has information suggesting illegal conduct by others. Newsmen frequently receive information from such sources pursuant to a tacit or express agreement to withhold the source's name and suppress any information that the source wishes not published. Such informants presumably desire anonymity in order to avoid being entangled as a witness in a criminal trial or grand jury investigation. They may fear that disclosure will threaten their job security or personal safety or that it will simply result in dishonor or embarrassment.

The argument that the flow of news will be diminished by compelling reporters to aid the grand jury in a criminal investigation is not irrational, nor are the records before us silent on the matter. But we remain unclear how often and to what extent informers are actually deterred from furnishing information when newsmen are forced to testify before a grand jury. The available data indicate that some newsmen rely a great deal on confidential sources and that some informants are particularly sensitive to the threat of exposure and may be silenced if it is held by this Court that, ordinarily, newsmen must testify pursuant to subpoenas, but the evidence fails to demonstrate that there would be a significant constriction of the flow of news to the public if this Court reaffirms the prior common law and constitutional rule regarding the testimonial obligations of newsmen. Estimates of the inhibiting effect of such subpoenas on the willingness of informants to make disclosures to newsmen are widely divergent and to a great extent speculative. It would be difficult to canvass the views of the informants themselves; surveys of reporters on this topic are chiefly opinions of predicted informant behavior and must be viewed in the light of the professional self-interest of the interviewees.

Reliance by the press on confidential informants does not mean that all such sources will in fact dry up because of the later possible appearance of the newsman before a grand jury. The reporter may never be called and if he objects to testifying, the prosecution may not insist. Also, the relationship of many informants to the press is a symbiotic one which is unlikely to be greatly inhibited by the threat of subpoena: quite often, such informants are members of a minority political or cultural group which relies heavily on the media to propagate its views, publicize its aims, and magnify its exposure to the public. Moreover, grand juries characteristically conduct secret proceedings, and law enforcement officers are themselves experienced in dealing with informers and have their own methods for protecting them without interference with the effective administration of justice. There is little before us indicating that informants whose interest in avoiding exposure is that it may threaten job security, personal safety, or peace of mind, would in fact be in a worse position, or would think they would be, if they risked placing their trust in public officials as well as reporters. We doubt if the informer who prefers anonymity but is sincerely interested in furnishing evidence of crime will always or very often be deterred by the prospect of dealing with those public authorities characteristically charged with the duty to protect the public interest as well as his.

Accepting the fact, however, that an undetermined number of informants not themselves implicated in crime will nevertheless, for whatever reason, refuse to talk to newsmen if they fear identification by a reporter in an official investigation, we cannot accept the argument that the public interest in possible future news about crime from undisclosed, unverified sources must take precedence over the public interest in pursuing and prosecuting those crimes reported to the press by informants and in thus deterring the commission of such crimes in the future.

We note first that the privilege claimed is that of the reporter, not the informant, and that if the authorities independently identify the informant, neither his own reluctance to testify nor the objection of the newsman would shield him from grand jury inquiry, whatever the impact on the flow of news or on his future usefulness as a secret source of information. More important, it is obvious that agreements to conceal information relevant to commission of crime have very little to recommend them from the standpoint of public policy. . . .

Of course, the press has the right to abide by its agreement not to publish all the information it has, but the right to withhold news is not equivalent to a First Amendment exemption from the ordinary duty of all other citizens to furnish relevant information to a grand jury performing an important public function. . . .

Neither are we now convinced that a virtually impenetrable constitutional shield, beyond legislative or judicial control, should be forged to protect a private system of informers operated by the press to report on criminal conduct, a system that would be unaccountable to the public, would pose a threat to the citizen's justifiable expectations of privacy, and would equally protect well-intentioned informants and those who pay or otherwise betray their trust to their employer or associates. . . .

We are admonished that refusal to provide a First Amendment reporter's privilege will undermine the freedom of the press to collect and disseminate news. But this is not the lesson history teaches us. As noted previously, the common law recognized no such privilege, and the constitutional argument was not even asserted until 1958. From the beginning of our country the press has operated without constitutional protection for press informants, and the press has flourished. The existing constitutional rules have not been a serious obstacle to either the development or retention of confidential news sources by the press.

It is said that currently press subpoenas have multiplied, that mutual distrust and tension between press and officialdom have increased, that reporting styles have changed, and that there is now more need for confidential sources, particularly where the press seeks news about minority cultural and political groups or dissident organizations suspicious of the law and public officials. These developments, even if true, are treacherous grounds for a far-reaching interpretation of the First Amendment fastening a nationwide rule on courts, grand juries, and prosecuting officials everywhere. The obligation to testify in response to grand jury subpoenas will not threaten these sources not involved with criminal conduct and without information relevant to grand jury investigations, and we cannot hold that the Constitution places the sources in these two categories either above the law or beyond its reach.

The argument for such a constitutional privilege rests heavily on those cases holding that the infringement of protected First Amendment rights must be no broader than necessary to achieve a permissible governmental purpose. We do not deal, however, with a governmental institution that has abused its proper function, as a legislative committee does when it "expose[s] for the sake of exposure." [*Watkins v. United States*, 1957.] Nothing in the record indicates that these grand juries were "prob[ing] at will and without relation to existing need." [*DeGregory v. Attorney General of New Hampshire*, 1966.] Also, there is no attempt here by the grand juries to invade protected First Amendment rights by forcing wholesale disclosure of names and organizational affiliations for a purpose which is not germane to the determination of whether crime has been committed, and the characteristic secrecy of grand jury proceedings is a further protection against the undue invasion of such rights. The investigative power of the grand jury is necessarily broad if its public responsibility is to be adequately discharged.

The requirements of those cases, which hold that a state's interest must be "compelling" or "paramount" to justify even an indirect burden on First Amendment rights, are also met here. As we have indicated, the investigation of crime by the grand jury implements a fundamental governmental role of securing the safety of the person and property of the citizen, and it appears to us that calling reporters to give testimony in the manner and for the reasons that other citizens are called "bears a reasonable relationship to the achievement of the governmental purpose asserted as its justification." If the test is that the Government "convincingly show a substantial relation between the information sought and a subject of overriding and compelling state interest," it is quite apparent (1) that the state has the necessary interest in extirpating the traffic in illegal drugs, in forestalling assassination attempts on the President, and in preventing the community from being disrupted by violent disorders endangering both persons and property; and (2) that, based on the stories Branzburg and Caldwell wrote and Pappas' admitted conduct, the grand jury called these reporters as they would others—because it was likely that they could supply information to help the Government determine whether illegal conduct had occurred and, if it had, whether there was sufficient evidence to return an indictment. . . .

The privilege claimed here is conditional, not absolute; given the suggested preliminary showings and compelling need, the reporter would be required to testify. Presumably, such a rule would reduce the instances in which reporters could be required to appear, but predicting in advance when and in what circumstances they could be compelled to do so would be difficult. Such a rule would also have implications for the issuance of compulsory process to reporters at civil and criminal trials and at legislative hearings. If newsmen's confidential sources are as sensitive as they are claimed to be, the prospect of being unmasked whenever a judge determines the situation justifies it is hardly a satisfactory solution to the problem. For them, it would appear that only an absolute privilege would suffice.

We are unwilling to embark the judiciary on a long and difficult journey to such an uncertain destination. The administration of a constitutional newsman's privilege would present practical and conceptual difficulties of a high order. Sooner or later, it would be necessary to define those categories of newsmen who qualified for the privilege, a questionable procedure in light of the traditional doctrine that liberty of the press is the right of the lonely pamphleteer who uses carbon paper or a mimeograph just as much as of the large metropolitan publisher who utilizes the latest photocomposition methods. Cf. *In re Grand Jury Witnesses,* 322 F. Supp. 573, 574 (ND

Cal. 1970). Freedom of the press is a "fundamental personal right" which "is not confined to newspapers and periodicals. It necessarily embraces pamphlets and leaflets. . . . The press in its historic connotation comprehends every sort of publication which affords a vehicle of information and opinion." The informative function asserted by representatives of the organized press in the present cases is also performed by lecturers, political pollsters, novelists, academic researchers, and dramatists. Almost any author may quite accurately assert that he is contributing to the flow of information to the public, that he relies on confidential sources of information, and that these sources will be silenced if he is forced to make disclosures before a grand jury.*

In each instance where a reporter is subpoenaed to testify, the courts would also be embroiled in preliminary factual and legal determinations with respect to whether the proper predicate had been laid for the reporters' appearance: Is there probable cause to believe a crime has been committed? Is it likely that the reporter has useful information gained in confidence? Could the grand jury obtain the information elsewhere? Is the official interest sufficient to outweigh the claimed privilege?

Thus, in the end, by considering whether enforcement of a particular law served a "compelling" governmental interest, the courts would be inextricably involved in distinguishing between the value of enforcing different criminal laws. By requiring testimony from a reporter in investigations involving some crimes but not in others, they would be making a value judgment which a legislature had declined to make, since in each case the criminal law involved would represent a considered legislative judgment, not constitutionally suspect, of what conduct is liable to criminal prosecution. The task of judges, like other officials outside the legislative branch is not to make the law but to uphold it in accordance with their oaths.

At the federal level, Congress has freedom to determine whether a statutory newsman's privilege is necessary and desirable and to fashion standards and rules as narrow or broad as deemed necessary to address the evil discerned and, equally important, to refashion those rules as experience from time to time may dictate. There is also merit in leaving state legislatures free, within First Amendment limits, to fashion their own standards in light of the conditions and problems with respect to the relations between law enforcement officials and press in their own areas. It

*Such a privilege might be claimed by groups that set up newspapers in order to engage in criminal activity and to therefore be insulated from grand jury inquiry, regardless of Fifth Amendment grants of immunity. It might appear that such "sham" newspapers would be easily distinguishable, yet the First Amendment ordinarily prohibits courts from inquiring into the content of expression, except in cases of obscenity or libel, and protects speech and publications regardless of their motivation, orthodoxy, truthfulness, timeliness, or taste. *New York Times Co. v. Sullivan*, 376 U.S. 254, 269-270 (1964); *Kingsley Pictures Corp. v. Regents*, 360 U.S. 684, 689 (1959); *Winters v. New York*, 333 U.S. 507, 510 (1948); *Thomas v. Collins*, 323 U.S. 516, 537 (1945). By affording a privilege to some organs of communication but not to others, courts would inevitably be discriminating on the basis of content.

goes without saying, of course, that we are powerless to erect any bar to state courts responding in their own way and construing their own constitutions so as to recognize a newsman's privilege, either qualified or absolute.

In addition, there is much force in the pragmatic view that the press has at its disposal powerful mechanisms of communication and is far from helpless to protect itself from harassment or substantial harm. Furthermore, if what the newsmen urged in these cases is true—that law enforcement cannot hope to gain and may suffer from subpoenaing newsmen before grand juries—prosecutors will be loath to risk so much for so little. Thus, at the federal level the Attorney General has already fashioned a set of rules for federal officials in connection with subpoenaing members of the press to testify before grand juries or at criminal trials. These rules are a major step in the direction petitioners desire to move. They may prove wholly sufficient to resolve the bulk of disagreements and controversies between press and federal officials.

Finally, as we have earlier indicated, newsgathering is not without its First Amendment protections, and grand jury investigations if instituted or conducted other than in good faith, would pose wholly different issues for resolution under the First Amendment. Official harassment of the press undertaken not for purposes of law enforcement but to disrupt a reporter's relationship with his news sources would have no justification. Grand juries are subject to judicial control and subpoenas to motions to quash. We do not expect courts will forget that grand juries must operate within the limits of the First Amendment as well as the Fifth. . . . ■

Among the four dissenters in these cases was Justice Potter Stewart. In an opinion joined by Justices William Brennan and Thurgood Marshall, Stewart argued for a qualified reporters' privilege. He would not rule out compelling reporters to testify, but he would first make the government show "that there is probable cause" that the reporter knows something relating to a specific crime, that the government cannot find the information in any other way than by compelling the reporter's testimony, and that there is a "compelling and overriding interest" in obtaining the information.

THE RIGHT TO GATHER NEWS

Justice Stewart's dissent, from *Branzburg v. Hayes*, 1972

The Court's crabbed view of the First Amendment reflects a disturbing insensitivity to the critical role of an independent press in our society. The question whether a reporter has a constitutional right to a confidential relationship with his source is of first impression here, but the principles which should guide our decision are as basic as any to be found in the Constitution. . . .

The Court in these cases holds that a newsman has no First Amendment right to protect his sources when called before a grand jury. The Court thus invites state and federal authorities to undermine the historic [sic] independence of the press by attempting to annex the journalistic profession as an investigative arm of government. Not only will this decision impair performance of the press' constitutionally protected functions, but it will, I am convinced, in the long run, harm rather than help the administration of justice.

I respectfully dissent. . . .

. . . In no previous case have we considered the extent to which the First Amendment limits the grand jury subpoena power. But the Court has said that the "Bill of Rights is applicable to investigations as to all forms of governmental action. Witnesses cannot be compelled to give evidence against themselves. They cannot be subjected to unreasonable searches and seizures. Nor can the First Amendment freedoms of speech, press . . . or political speech and association be abridged." *Watkins v. United States,* 354 U.S. 178, 188. And in *Sweezy v. New Hampshire,* 354 U.S. 234, it was stated: "it is particularly important that the exercise of the power of compulsory process be carefully circumscribed when the investigative process tends to impinge upon such highly sensitive areas as freedom of speech or press, freedom of political association, and freedom of communication of ideas." *Id.,* at 245 (plurality opinion).

The established method of "carefully" circumscribing investigative powers is to place a heavy burden of justification on government officials when First Amendment rights are impaired. The decisions of this Court have "consistently held that only a compelling state interest in the regulation of a subject within the state's constitutional power to regulate can justify limiting First Amendment freedoms." *NAACP v. Button,* 371 U.S. 415, 438. And "it is an essential prerequisite to the validity of an investigation which intrudes into the area of constitutionally protected rights of speech, press, association and petition that the state *show a substantial relation between the information sought and a subject of overriding and compelling state interest."* *Gibson v. Florida Legislative Investigation Committee,* 372 U.S. 539, 546 (emphasis supplied). See also *DeGregory v. Attorney General of New Hampshire,* 383 U.S. 825; *NAACP v. Alabama,* 357 U.S. 449; *Sweezy, supra; Watkins, supra.*

Thus, when an investigation impinges on First Amendment rights, the government must not only show that the inquiry is of "compelling and overriding importance" but it must also "convincingly" demonstrate that the investigation is "substantially related" to the information sought.

Government officials must, therefore, demonstrate that the information sought is *clearly* relevant to a *precisely* defined subject of governmental inquiry . . . They must demonstrate that it is reasonable to think the witness in question has that information. . . . And they must show that there is not any means of obtaining the information less destructive of First Amendment liberties. . . .

These requirements, which we have recognized in decisions involving legislative and executive investigations, serve established policies reflected in numerous First Amendment decisions arising in other contexts. The requirements militate against vague investigations which, like vague laws, create uncertainty and needlessly discourage First Amendment activity. They also insure that a legitimate governmental purpose will not be pursued by means that "broadly stifle fundamental personal liberties when the end can be more narrowly achieved." . . . As we said in *Gibson, supra,* "Of course, a legislative investigation—as any investigation—must proceed 'step by step,' . . . but step by step or in totality, an adequate foundation for inquiry must be laid before proceeding in such a manner as will substantially intrude upon and severely curtail or inhibit constitutionally protected activities or seriously interfere with similarly protected associational rights." . . .

I believe the safeguards developed in our decisions involving governmental investigations must apply to the grand jury inquiries in these cases. Surely the function of the grand jury to aid in the enforcement of the law is no more important than the function of the legislature, and its committees, to make the law. We have long recognized the value of the role played by legislative investigations, . . . for the "power of Congress to conduct investigations is broad . . . [encompassing] surveys of defects in our social, economic or political system for the purpose of enabling Congress to remedy them." *Watkins, supra,* at 187. Similarly, the associational rights of private individuals, which have been the prime focus of our First Amendment decisions in the investigative sphere, are hardly more important than the First Amendment rights of mass circulation newspapers and electronic media to disseminate ideas and information, and of the general public to receive them. Moreover, the vices of vagueness and overbreadth which legislative investigations may manifest are also exhibited by grand jury inquiries, since grand jury investigations are not limited in scope to specific criminal acts, . . . and since standards of materiality and relevance are greatly relaxed. . . . For, as the United States notes in its brief in *Caldwell,* the grand jury "need establish no factual basis for commencing an investigation, and can pursue rumors which further investigation may prove groundless."

Accordingly, when a reporter is asked to appear before a grand jury and reveal confidences, I would hold that the government must (1) show that there is probable cause to believe that the newsman has information which is clearly relevant to a specific probable violation of law; (2) demonstrate that the information sought cannot be obtained by alternative means less destructive of First Amendment rights; and (3) demonstrate a compelling and overriding interest in the information. . . .

The crux of the Court's rejection of any newsman's privilege is its observation that only "where news sources themselves are implicated in crime or possess information *relevant* to the grand jury's task need they or the reporter be concerned about grand jury subpoenas." . . . (Emphasis supplied). But this is a most misleading construct. For it is obviously not true that the only persons about whom reporters will be forced to testify will be those "confidential informants involved in actual criminal conduct" and those having "information suggesting illegal conduct by others.". . . As noted above, given the grand jury's extraordinarily broad investigative powers and the weak standards of relevance and materiality that apply during such inquiries, reporters, if they have no testimonial privilege, will be called to give information about informants who have neither committed crimes nor have information about crime. It is to avoid deterrence of such sources and thus to prevent needless injury to First Amendment values that I think the government must be required to show probable cause that the newsman has information which is clearly relevant to a specific probable violation of criminal law.

Similarly, a reporter may have information from a confidential source which is "related" to the commission of crime, but the government may be able to obtain an indictment or otherwise achieve its purposes by subpoenaing persons other than the reporter. It is an obvious but important truism that when government aims have been fully served, there can be no legitimate reason to disrupt a confidential relationship between a reporter and his source. To do so would not aid the administration of justice and would only impair the flow of information to the public. Thus, it is to avoid deterrence of such sources that I think the government must show that there are no alternative means for the grand jury to obtain the information sought.

Both the "probable cause" and "alternative means" requirements would thus serve the vital function of mediating between the public interest in the administration of justice and the constitutional protection of the full flow of information. These requirements would avoid a direct conflict between these competing concerns, and they would generally provide adequate protection for newsmen. . . . No doubt the courts would be required to make some delicate judgments in working out this accommodation. But that, after all, is the function of courts of law. Better such judgments, however difficult, than the simplistic and stultifying absolutism adopted by the Court in denying any force to the First Amendment in these cases.

■

Alone in this case, Justice William O. Douglas argued for total and unqualified reporters' privilege. He even scolded the *New York Times* for conceding, in a separate friend-of-the-court brief, that the protections of the First Amendment must be balanced against other public needs. (Implicitly he also seemed to be scolding his fellow dissenters, Justices Stewart, Marshall, and Brennan, for supporting only a qualified form of reporters' privilege.) Douglas dismissed this as the product of a "timid, watered-down, emasculated" interpretation of an amendment which the Framers had cast "in absolute terms."

NEWSPAPERS NEED BLANKET PROTECTION
Justice Douglas's Dissent

. . . The District Court had found that Caldwell's knowledge of the activities of the Black Panthers "derived in substantial part" from information obtained "within the scope of a relationship of trust and confidence." It also found that confidential relationships of this sort are commonly developed and maintained by professional journalist[s], and are indispensable to their work of gathering, analyzing, and publishing the news.

The District Court further had found that compelled disclosure of information received by a journalist within the scope of such confidential relationships jeopardized those relationships and thereby impaired the journalist's ability to gather, analyze, and publish the news.

The District Court finally had found that, without a protective order delimiting the scope of interrogation of Earl Caldwell by the grand jury, his appearance and examination before the jury would severely impair and damage his confidential relationships with members of the Black Panther Party and other militants, and thereby severely impair and damage his ability to gather, analyze, and publish news concerning them.

The Court of Appeals agreed with the findings of the District Court but held that Caldwell need not appear at all before the grand jury absent a "compelling need" shown by the Government. . . .

It is my view that there is no "compelling need" that can be shown which qualifies the reporter's immunity from appearing or testifying before a grand jury, unless the reporter himself is implicated in a crime. His immunity in my view is therefore quite complete, for absent his involvement in a crime, the First Amendment protects him against an appearance before a grand jury and if he is involved in a crime, the Fifth Amendment stands as a barrier. Since in my view there is no area of inquiry not protected by a privilege, the reporter need not appear for the futile purpose of invoking one to each question. And, since in my view a newsman has an absolute right not to appear before a grand jury it follows for me that a journalist who voluntarily appears before that body may invoke his First Amendment privilege to specific questions. The basic issue is the extent to which the First Amendment . . . must yield to the Government's asserted need to know a reporter's unprinted information.

The starting point for decision pretty well marks the range within which the end result lies. *The New York Times,* whose reporting functions are at issue here, takes the amazing position that First Amendment rights are to be balanced against other needs or conveniences of government. My belief is that all of the "balancing" was done by those who wrote the Bill of Rights. By casting the First Amendment in absolute terms, they repudiated, the timid, watered-down, emasculated versions of the First Amendment which both the Government and the *New York Times* advances in the case.

. . . Today's decision will impede the wide open and robust dissemination of ideas and counterthought which a free press both fosters and protects and which is essential to the success of intelligent self-government. Forcing a reporter before a grand jury will have two retarding effects upon the ear and the pen of the press. Fear of exposure will cause dissidents to communicate less openly to trusted reporters. And, fear of accountability will cause editors and critics to write with more restrained pens.

I see no way of making mandatory the disclosure of a reporter's confidential source of the information on which he bases his news story.

The press has a preferred position in our constitutional scheme not to enable it to make money, not to set newsmen apart as a favored class, but to bring fulfillment to the public's right to know. The right to know is crucial to the governing powers of the people. . . . Knowledge is essential to informed decisions.

As Mr. Justice Black said in *New York Times Co. v. United States,* 403 U.S. 713, 717 (concurring opinion), "The press was to serve the governed, not the governors. . . . The press was protected so that it could bare the secrets of government and inform the people."

Government has an interest in law and order; and history shows that the trend of rulers—the bureaucracy and the police—is to suppress the radical and his ideas and to arrest him rather than the hostile audience. . . . Yet as held in *Terminiello v. Chicago,* 337 U.S. 1, 4, one "function of free speech under our system of government is to invite dispute." We went on to say, "It may indeed best serve its high purpose when it induces a condition of unrest, creates dissatisfaction with conditions as they are, or even stirs people to anger. Speech is often provocative and challenging. It may strike at prejudices and preconceptions and have profound unsettling effects as it presses for acceptance of an idea."

The people who govern are often far removed from the cabals that threaten the regime; the people are often remote from the sources of truth even though they live in the city where the forces that would undermine society operate. The function of the press is to explore and investigate events, inform the people what is going on, and to expose the harmful as well as the good influences at work. There is no higher function performed under our constitutional regime. Its performance means that the press is often engaged in projects that bring anxiety or even fear to the bureaucracies or departments or officials of government. The whole weight of government is therefore often brought to bear against a paper or a reporter.

A reporter is no better than his source of information. Unless he has a privilege to withhold the identity of his source, he will be the victim of governmental intrigue or aggression. If he can be summoned to testify in secret before a grand jury, his sources will dry up and the attempted exposure, the effort to enlighten the public, will be ended. If what the Court sanctions today becomes settled law, then the reporter's main function in American society will be to pass on to the public the press releases which the various departments of government issue. . . .

. . . Today's decision is more than a clog upon news gathering. It is a signal to publishers and editors that they should exercise caution in how they use whatever information they can obtain. Without immunity they may be summoned to account for their criticism. Entrenched officers have been quick to crash their powers down upon unfriendly commentators. . . .

The intrusion of government into this domain is symptomatic of the disease of this society. As the years pass the power of government becomes more and more pervasive. It is a power to suffocate both people and causes. Those in power, whatever their politics, want only to perpetuate it. Now that the fences of the law and the tradition that has protected the press are broken down, the people are the victims. The First Amendment, as I read it, was designed precisely to prevent that tragedy.

As is so often the case with Supreme Court decisions, *Branzburg v Hayes* served to ignite several related controversies. One of the more prominent cases involved *New York Times* reporter, Myron Farber. Farber was jailed for contempt of court when he refused to divulge the source of his information concerning a doctor who was charged with murder. This set the stage for a classic confrontation between the freedom of the press and the right to a fair trial.

Epilogue One: "Doctor X" and Myron Farber

Four years after the *Branzburg* decision, a series of articles appeared in the *New York Times* which developed evidence which suggested that a New Jersey physician, identified in the articles only as "Dr. X," deliberately killed a number of hospital patients by injecting them with lethal doses of a drug. The articles led authorities to charge Dr. Mario E. Jascalevich, the "Dr. X" of the articles, with murder. The *Times* reporter who wrote the articles, Myron A. Farber, testified at the trial but refused to reveal any information which, in his opinion, might compromise his sources. Jascalevich's lawyer then subpoenaed Farber's notes, saying that some of the unreported information in them might be essential to the case. Farber refused to produce them, citing both the First Amendment and New Jersey's "shield" law as protection against having to disclose information obtained by a reporter under promise of confidentiality. The trial judge demanded that Farber turn over the notes to him for *in camera* (private) inspection. When Farber refused, the judge fined him $2,000, sentenced him to jail until he complied, plus an additional six-months punitive sentence. The *Times* was fined $100,000 plus $5,000 per day until the material was handed over.

The Farber case differed from *Branzburg, Caldwell,* and *Pappas* in that a reporter's notes were being sought not by the state but by a defendant's attorney. Jascalevich was being tried for the most serious of crimes, first-degree murder, carrying a maximum penalty of life imprisonment. His attorney claimed that Farber's refusal to yield the notes deprived the court of information which might prove his client's innocence. The case did not have quite the same David-Goliath quality—the courageous reporter standing up to the investigative arm of the state—inherent in previous cases involving reporters' claims of immunity. In this case, it was a reporter asserting statutory and First Amendment claims against a defendant relying upon his Sixth Amendment right to a fair trial. Media critic (and former CBS producer) Fred Friendly even hinted that the David-Goliath scenario might be reversed in this case. "Usually, it has been the free press against the almighty power of the government. But here, it is the press against one man, if you will, 'fighting for his life'." The fundamental issue in this case turned upon balancing one provision of the Bill of Rights against another.

There were other, more personal, issues in the case. Raymond A. Brown, the 63-year old black attorney representing Jascalevich, was sometimes depicted as hostile to civil liberties. An article in *Esquire* magazine began by acknowledging that Brown often defended poor people without charging fees, but then it went on: "This month Brown is engaged in a new pursuit: putting a reporter in jail and threatening the First Amendment." An anonymous defense attorney was quoted as accusing Brown of demanding Farber's notes not because he thought there was anything relevant in them but simply to get the case thrown out of court. "Ray's demand for Farber's notes is a trick. He knows Farber won't give them up. Then he can argue that he doesn't have the information he needs to give the doctor a fair trial. He's counting on that to give Jascalevich an acquittal or even just a mistrial."

If Brown's motives were questioned, so were Farber's. In an attempt to win Farber's freedom the *Times* appealed to a federal court in Newark, New Jersey, seeking a writ of *habeas corpus* for unlawful imprisonment. During the course of the appeal it was disclosed that Farber had accepted a $75,000 advance from Doubleday and Company for a book he was writing about the trial. Charging that Farber had a financial stake in seeing Jascalevich convicted, the federal judge said: "This is a sorry spectacle of a reporter who purported to stand on his reporter's privilege when in fact he was standing on an altar of greed." The judge considered it indefensible for Farber to refuse to turn over his notes to a court while showing no hesitation in turning over a manuscript bearing on the same case to a publisher.

Eventually Farber did turn over his manuscript to the judge presiding at Jascalevich's trial, but he remained steadfast in his refusal to submit his notes. He served a total of forty days in jail (the six months' punitive sentence was lifted), and his newspaper paid $285,000 in fines, before the Jascalevich trial ended—in acquittal. The trial's end brought cessation of further fines and punishments, but Farber and the *Times* sought review of the issue by the United States Supreme Court. (The New Jersey Supreme Court had upheld the contempt citations by a 5 to 2 vote.) On November 27, 1978 the Court served notice that it would not hear the case, thus ending this particular instance of colliding claims under the Bill of Rights.

Yet the issues underlying the Farber case are not likely to lose their bite any time soon. In an interview, Farber looked back over his case, brought out some of the background facts which may not have been clear to those who followed it in the press, and reflected on some of its implications.

A CONVERSATION WITH MYRON FARBER

From an Interview with George McKenna, 1981

What did he think of the argument that the defendant's Sixth Amendment right to a fair trial was at least as important as a reporter's rights under the First Amendment? "It has never been my position that under no circumstances must a reporter ever give up any of his notes. I could see being asked for selected materials. But the defense simply asked for *all* of my notes, and the judge upheld the motion without even granting us a hearing. The judge was then locked into upholding his own order—his authority was on the line—and each higher level of court saw fit to uphold him." Would he have yielded materials if they were asked for piecemeal? "Possibly. We could at least have discussed the relevance and materiality of each requested piece of information had we been given a hearing. But the blanket request for everything, all at once, left us with no recourse. I am disturbed at being described as 'recalcitrant'. The real recalcitrant individuals were those refusing us a hearing on the defense motion to turn over all my notes."

Did he think that his case had a crippling effect on investigative reporting? "I'm almost entirely sure it's the opposite. Even the New Jersey Supreme Court decision that went against me acknowledged that a court normally should hold a hearing before ordering a reporter to yield his notes." Farber contended that reporter's "privilege" ("a word I'm not enamored of") has been upheld in a recent decision of the New Jersey Supreme Court, in part because of the result of his own case. "We may have advanced the freedom of reporters to gather news."

How would he reply to the argument that, if one grants special privileges to reporters, why not to professors doing research, and why not to the lonely pamphleteer operating with a mimeograph? "I'm not an authority on that. I do know that I am associated with an institution which is clearly performing a function specifically recognized by the First Amendment. The institutional press is performing a vital information function. It should be protected in going about its task. Whether others—professors, pamphleteers, and so on—should also be protected, I don't know. I am not certain where you draw the line. But it doesn't make sense to say that, because not everybody can be protected by the press clause of the First Amendment, therefore nobody should. That's silly. I do not know all the publications that can be called 'press'. I do know that the *New York Times* fits the description. I happen to be a 'true believer,' if you will, in this paper. I happen to think it is superbly run and edited. It is an institution which aspires to excellence, and I like being part of it. This is my life."

Would he go to jail again if necessary? "If my work entailed it, yes. It was not pleasant going to jail, and not just. There was a specific statutory protection in my case, to say nothing of the First Amendment. One should not be jailed for invoking these rights, certainly not before one has exhausted his appeals. But if, in the end, you can't work as a reporter without facing the possibility of going to jail, then so be it. Still, it's an appalling state of affairs."

With particular ardor, Farber extolled what he called "the institutional role of the press." "There is value in having *some* readily recognized institution outside of government—some institution in society with offices—that people can go to with their troubles and complaints. I'm thinking of Frederick Jackson Turner's description of the frontier as a 'safety valve.' Newspapers serve as a safety valve. Look, I truly believe in the functions I perform and that the Founders of the Constitution intended that there should be this climate for newsgathering. The corollary to that is that I must have the freedom to perform my functions. In the end, the public is being served."

What about the charge of "greed" leveled at him by the federal judge? "For writing a book? A lot of people write books, including judges. I had no idea of writing one on this or any other topic at the time I wrote the articles. I was persuaded to do it only after the articles appeared. As for the draft manuscript, as soon as the judge made an issue of it, I submitted it. And it was never opened in court. It makes me wonder whether they really wanted it."

Epilogue Two: Police Raids on Newsrooms

Late in the day on Friday, April 9, 1971, nine police officers from Palo Alto, California and the surrounding county responded to a call from the director of the Stanford University Hospital requesting the removal of a large group of demonstrators who had seized the hospital's administrative offices. As the police tried to evict the demonstrators they were attacked with sticks and clubs. All nine were injured.

Two days later a special edition of the *Stanford Daily,* the university's student newspaper, carried a series of articles on the clash. More important, it carried photographs of it. Figuring that the newspaper staff probably had further negatives and prints which might help to identify the assailants—though nobody alleged that the newspaper staff was in cahoots with them—the police obtained a search warrant and entered the offices of the newspaper. They searched the paper's photo labs, wastepaper baskets, filing cabinets, and desks. A month later the newspaper brought suit, charging that its rights under the First, Fourth, and Fourteenth Amendments had been abridged by the police raid. Though the newspaper won in the lower courts, the Supreme Court ruled 5 to 3 that the police had not acted unconstitutionally.

The majority opinion in *Zurcher v. Stanford Daily,* (1978), by Justice Byron White, held that pressrooms were not entitled to any greater immunity from police searches than other places—banks, stores, doctor's offices, or whatever. This case was not a case of a warrantless search. The police had first gone to a judge, listed the materials being sought and the reasons for conducting the search. The warrant had been duly issued by a municipal court judge. The Framers of the Constitution, Justice White said, did not forbid newsroom searches. They did not require that the police show that they could not get the material any other way, nor did they make the police prove that the press was implicated in the crime before newsrooms could be searched.

Justice White did concede however, that warrant requirements should be applied "with particular exactitude when First Amendment interests would be endangered by the search."

Among the three dissenters in the case was Justice Potter Stewart. Speaking for himself and Justice Thurgood Marshall, Stewart's dissent was notable for its underlying philosophy that the press occupies a unique position because it is *explicitly* protected by the First Amendment.

> Perhaps as a matter of abstract policy a newspaper office should receive no more protection from unannounced police searches than, say, the office of a doctor or the office of a bank. But we are here to uphold a Constitution. And our Constitution does not explicitly protect the practice of medicine or the business of banking from all abridgment by government. It does explicitly protect the freedom of the press.

The problem comes in trying to define the word "press." Does it include, as Justice White asserted in the *Branzburg* decision, "the lonely pamphleteer who uses carbon paper or a mimeograph"? If so, then press means virtually anyone who can come up with some medium of communication. Justice White has already noted (see p. 161) that this might open up the danger that some criminal group could start putting out a periodic newletter and thus claim "press" immunity! Professor Robert Bork will discuss the problem of press "specialness" at greater length beginning on page 178.

The problems which result from giving special status to the press are also difficult to resolve. The danger should be obvious: it may have a chilling effect on freedom of the press. It seems to allow law enforcement authorities to go storming into newspaper and broadcasting offices any time they can get a subpoena. By the summer of 1980 that danger seemed to be more than hypothetical. In May of that year police searched the offices of *The Flint* (Michigan) *Voice,* trying to discover who leaked a report to that paper confirming allegations that some city workers were being forced to donate to the mayor's campaign. In July, police demanded entrance to KBCI-TV in Boise, Idaho. After being admitted, they spent ninety minutes rummaging through desks and file cabinets looking for unedited copies of videotapes showing prisoners rioting inside the Idaho State Penitentiary. Three days after the KBCI search, officers of the Georgia Bureau of Investigation ransacked the home files of an *Albany* (Georgia) *Herald* reporter, seeking material relating to the recent escape of four murderers from a state prison.

These incidents, and the coverage they received in the press, generated enough pressure on Congress to pass the Privacy Protection Bill, which, in effect, reversed the *Stanford Daily* decision. The bill enjoyed wide support, including that of arch-conservative Senator Strom Thurmond and super-liberal Senator Edward Kennedy. In signing the bill on October 14, 1980, President Carter explained its purpose and content:

"The Supreme Court's 1978 decision in Zurcher v. *Stanford Daily* raised the concern that law enforcement authorities could conduct unannounced searches of reporters' notes and files to seek evidence. Such a practice could have a chilling effect on the ability of reporters to develop sources and pursue stories. Ever since the court's decision, my administration has been working with Congress to prevent this result by enacting legislation.

"This bill requires federal, state and local authorities either to request voluntary compliance or to use subpoenas—with advance notice and the opportunity for a court hearing—instead of search warrants when they seek reporters' materials as evidence. The bill also covers others engaged in First Amendment activities such as authors and scholars. Searches are allowed only in very limited situations.

"The bill also directs the Attorney General to issue guidelines for federal law enforcement officers to minimize intrusion when documentary evidence of a crime is sought from innocent third parties who are not members of the press. Those guidelines are already being written, and the Attorney General expects to issue them in the near future. I am pleased that the federal government is taking the lead in providing these privacy protections. I urge the states to follow suit.

Epilogue Three: The Lie That Won the Pulitzer Prize

"Jimmy is 8 years old and a third generation heroin addict, a precocious little boy with sandy hair, velvety brown eyes and needle marks freckling the baby-smooth skin of his thin brown arms."

In September of 1980 a *Washington Post* reporter named Janet Cooke wrote this moving tale about the plight of a boy turned into a heroin addict by his mother's boyfriend. It described the needle being pushed into "the boy's soft skin like a straw pushed into the center of a freshly baked cake."

The story won the 26-year-old reporter a Pulitzer Prize for news reporting. It should have been for fiction. The story was fabricated.

How did it happen that a 26-year-old cub reporter, later characterized by the *Post's* Executive Editor, Ben Bradlee as a "pathological liar," was able to bamboozle Bradlee and other seasoned newspaper staff members? Without even attempting to answer that question fully, we can look at one factor relating to the issue being examined here. When she submitted the story she told her editor that she could not reveal the identity of "Jimmy" and those who were administering heroin to him, for she had promised them confidentiality. She even said that her life would be endangered if she revealed identities. Her editors believed her and did not question her further before running the story.

New York Times columnist Anthony Lewis sees the resulting scandal as the ultimate fruit of press "hubris"—the name the ancient Greeks used to describe the tendency of prideful people to overreach themselves.

FIRST AMENDMENT HUBRIS

Anthony Lewis, from the *New York Times*, April 18, 1981

BOSTON, April 18—The fabricated story that won a Pulitzer Prize has made newspaper people think about their business as nothing else has for years—and not just on the paper that printed it, The Washington Post. There is a sharpened concern about the responsibility of reporters and editors: the standards we impose on ourselves.

But the episode points to a deeper problem, and I wonder how many in the press will face it. That is the danger of hubris, the overweening pride that leads to a fall. In our case it is a constitutional hubris, a belief that the First Amendment gives journalism an exalted status. It is in particular a belief that the Constitution gives us a right to use anonymous sources without being called to account.

The prize-winning story, about a supposed 8-year-old heroin addict in the Washington slums, did not name the child or the drug dealer who pushed a needle into "the boy's soft skin like a straw pushed into the center of a freshly baked cake." The reporter told her editors that she had promised to keep the names secret and could not tell even them.

When the hoax was finally uncovered, The Post said in an editorial that "warning bells of some kind should have sounded" at the paper. A good many bells were rung, in fact, but they were not heard. The Mayor of

Washington and the police chief, among others, said from the beginning that they did not believe the story.

The question is why those warnings did not provoke a critical re-examination by the paper before the prize unraveled the story. A major reason was evidently the mystique of confidential sources. When officials questioned the tale, the paper was concerned significantly—perhaps primarily—with repelling a challenge to the claim that it had a constitutional right to keep its sources secret.

The idea that the Constitution gives journalists a privilege not to testify about their sources is a recent one. The claim was made for the first time in a 1958 case. But it is now a part of journalistic litany. The Post editorial on the hoax warned against using the episode "to discredit the various First Amendment protections that were activated . . . when the conflict sharpened between the paper and the authorities on the question of identification of sources."

But there is no First Amendment privilege for journalists when the law demands their testimony in an appropriate case. So the Supreme Court held in a 1972 case, Branzburg v. Hayes. It rejected a reporter's claim of a First Amendment right to ignore a subpoena to tell a grand jury about drug traffickers he had described, without using their names, in a story.

"We are asked," Justice Byron White said for the majority, "to . . . interpret the First Amendment to grant newsmen a testimonial privilege that other citizens do not enjoy. This we declined to do."

Notwithstanding that defeat, the press has continued to talk about a "First Amendment privilege" as if it existed. It does not, and in my strong opinion it should not.

The press has always used confidential sources, and it must. But necessity is a long way from exalting the practice into a constitutional right. That can bring—it has brought—unhealthy consequences.

In recent years the confidential source has become a mythic figure in American journalism. In Watergate he got a provocative name and a shrouded appearance in the movies. Every young reporter and journalism student dreams of finding his own Deep Throat.

The danger in that development is that nameless sources will be used too loosely. They should be the last resort, not the first. They should be confined to the necessity that alone can justify them.

Abuse of power is an even greater danger. A column by Jack Anderson last October attributed to unnamed "intelligence sources" the claim that a high U.S. official had disclosed a major intelligence secret. If that official sued for libel, should Anderson be able to escape responsibility—or should the papers that published the column—by relying on confidential sources? I think such a doctrine of irresponsible power would be unwise, and harmful to the press.

When confidential sources are used as incidental elements in a story, there is no great risk. Nor is there when their point of view is made clear:

"White House sources" or "Western diplomats." It is another matter when the unnamed source is the heart of the story, especially one making charges of crime or other misconduct. Then the bells should sound.

Reporters who promise confidentiality to get a vital story must keep that promise. Not many judges will push them to disclose, in the end. But if a few brave journalists go to prison for their promise, it is no disrespect to them to say that the battle is better fought that way—in the balance of courtroom interests and public opinion—than under the distorting guise of constitutional privilege for journalists.

Floyd Abrams is the chief legal counsel to the *New York Times*. As one who submitted a friend-of-the-court brief supporting press immunity in the *Branzburg* case, it is appropriate for him to reply to Anthony Lewis. And so he did, in a letter to the *Times*.

PROTECTING SOURCES IS NO SPECIAL PRIVILEGE

Floyd Abrams, from *The New York Times*, April 20, 1981

Anthony Lewis's transformation of The Washington Post Pulitzer Prize disaster into a vehicle for denouncing claims by the press for legal protection for their confidential sources (column April 19) is hardly sustainable. Such sources "must" be used by the press, Mr. Lewis concedes, and reporters who promise confidentiality "must keep their promise." Yet there should be no legal protection for the press in this area, Mr. Lewis says: there is no "First Amendment privilege" and there should not be.

Well. One may leave to the courts the question of whether such a privilege already exists: it has, in fact, been recognized in a wide range of cases decided by courts that do not interpret the none-too-scrutable Branzburg decision of the Supreme Court as does Mr. Lewis. Just last week, for example, the U.S. Court of Appeals for the District of Columbia summarized the law as establishing a qualified First Amendment privilege "in some circumstances even when a reporter is called before a grand jury to testify" and as being "readily available in civil cases."

Case law aside, it is Mr. Lewis's view of the interrelationship of law and journalism which is so troublesome. Why are journalists alone to be characterized as asserting a right to some "exalted status" when they seek legal protection for their confidential communications? Do we so disparagingly dismiss claims of, say, doctors (exalted as they may be) for legal protection for their confidential communications with their patients? In fact, as between doctors and journalists, who needs legal protection more?

More troubling still is Mr. Lewis's view on the legal process itself. What kind of legal system is it which would totally deny legal protection to promises which "must" be made and "must" be kept? The law is not usually so foolish as to require a "few brave" individuals to be jailed to give effect to promises which are essential to the functioning of our society. Why must it behave in so irrational a fashion because these individuals are journalists?

■

One of the key issues underlying the *Branzburg* case and the three above "epilogues" is the question of whether press representatives deserve special immunities normally denied to other people. If an ordinary citizen were to witness a crime he could be compelled, under pain of imprisonment and fines, to testify about it. The citizen also must comply with subpoenas for notes, documents, or other materials. Finally, the police can search our homes and offices provided they obtain a proper warrant. Why, then, should the press enjoy a special status?

The question is not only a legal but a moral one. If reporter Janet Cooke were indeed telling the truth about watching an eight-year-old being injected with heroin, was it sufficient to write a story about it without giving names and addresses to the police so that they could rescue the child? And what of Cooke's editors? Did they not have some responsibility to extract the full story from her to help save a child? The Executive Editor of the *Post*, Ben Bradlee, replied, "we're not cops."

In the following selection Yale law professor Robert Bork explores both the legal and moral dimension of the press immunity issue. The occasion was a symposium in honor of the late Justice William Douglas, conducted by the Center for Democratic Institutions in California. Bork's published remarks retain the flavor of what must have been a good oral presentation.

THE FIRST AMENDMENT DOES NOT GIVE GREATER FREEDOM TO THE PRESS THAN TO SPEECH

Robert H. Bork, from *The Center Magazine*, March/April, 1979

Under the general topic of "Freedom, the Courts, and the Media," we have been given for consideration this passage from Mr. Justice Douglas' impassioned dissent in *Branzburg v. Hayes:*

"I see no way of making mandatory the disclosure of a reporter's confidential sources of the information on which he bases his news story. The press has a preferred position in our constitutional scheme, not to enable it to make money, not to set newsmen apart as a favored class, but to bring fulfillment to the public's right to know."

Here, as always, Justice Douglas is lucid, articulate, and thought-provoking. The passage moves, as I am sure we will, from the immediate and fairly narrow question then before the Court to the more general question of the position of the press in our constitutional regime, which is to say, in a democratic society where the powers of the majority are hedged about with the protections for freedom, including the freedom of speech.

The issue of a reporter's right to protect the confidentiality of his sources is interesting in itself. It is more interesting in its bearing upon the role of the press in our society. But that bearing and that relationship are particularly interesting now because of the rhetoric with which it is debated, the tactics employed by the contenders, and the mood in which the press and its allies enter the debate. . . .

The conflict may be posed as one between the historic [sic] right of the grand jury to every man's testimony and the still-developing right of the press to gather and disseminate news effectively. Neither of those rights has ever been absolute. On the one hand, for example, the grand jury cannot compel a lawyer to disclose his client's confidences and, on the other, the press has no automatic right of access to information the government wants withheld.

If we stayed at that level of abstraction, the case would be a difficult one for me. Since neither the rights of law enforcement nor those of the press are or can be absolute, and since both are of constitutional dimension, a decision between them ought to be made with knowledge of the respective costs imposed upon law enforcement and news gathering. We really have very little idea of what those costs are. I would suspect that if journalists told their sources they would keep their confidences unless the information became directly relevant to a criminal investigation, they would still get most of the information they get now. But I cannot prove that. Certainly, the opinions in *Branzburg* do not attempt to measure the costs to law enforcement, probably because that information does not exist. The Department of Justice has virtually given up subpoenaing reporters, but that fact does not tell us a great deal. We do not know at what cost that has been done.

One dissent in *Branzburg* made it appear that the cost of news gathering would be enormous, and a footnote refers the reader to affidavits submitted by such eminent journalists as Walter Cronkite, Eric Sevareid, Mike Wallace, Dan Rather, and others. Those affidavits are undoubtedly correct in asserting that the general inability to keep sources confidential would severely hamper the press in the performance of its function, but a general inability to protect sources are not at issue in *Branzburg*.

This, I think, is the problem inherent, for example, in Mr. Justice Potter Stewart's dissent in *Branzburg*. He spoke movingly of the need for the press to perform its constitutional function, of the consequent need to protect sources, and he said: "An officeholder may fear his superior; a member of the bureaucracy, his associates; a dissident, the scorn of majority opinion. All may have information valuable to the public discourse, yet each may be willing to relate that information only in confidence to a reporter whom he trusts, either because of excessive caution or because of a reasonable fear of reprisals or censure for unorthodox views."

But hardly any of that which Justice Stewart spoke about was at stake in the Branzburg case. Nobody that I know of contends for a general power in government to force disclosure of sources. I think that certainly would be unconstitutional. The Court was faced with a much narrower issue, that is, the amenability of a reporter to the compulsion of a subpoena in the course of investigation to determine whether a crime has been committed, when there is cause to think that a crime has been committed. That is a much narrower category of cases than those cited by Justice Stewart, and the public interest in disclosure is much greater.

The Branzburg decision's impact upon news gathering is further lessened by a fact mentioned by Mr. Justice Byron White, who wrote for the majority. A conditional privilege of the sort the press asked for is itself likely to inhibit sources from talking because they must risk the not inconsiderable possibility that a judge will later determine that the reporter must testify. Only an absolute privilege would give the press what it wants and that nobody on the Court, except Mr. Justice Douglas, was willing to grant.

For me, at least, the fatal difficulty with the press's position in *Branzburg*—and perhaps in *Farber* and in *Lando* as well—lies in another point Justice White made. He said if a privilege were attached to "the press" in the manner sought, it would become necessary to know who "the press" is. "Sooner or later," Justice White said, "it would become necessary to define those categories of newsmen who qualified for the privilege, a questionable procedure in the light of the traditional doctrine that liberty of the press is the right of the lonely pamphleteer who uses carbon paper or a mimeograph just as much as of the large metropolitan publisher who utilizes the latest photocomposition methods."

There is more wrong with identifying and giving special privileges to a group defined as "the press" than that. It is a subject I want to come back to in a moment because I think the difficulty of defining who is "the press" lies at the core of many of the positions being taken today by the press and one, perhaps, that it should recognize and accept in its own self-defense.

I am not talking simply about the related point made by Justice White that a press privilege might be claimed by groups that set up newspapers in order to engage in criminal activity and to insulate themselves from grand jury inquiry under the First Amendment rather than the Fifth Amendment, which the grand jury can defeat by a grant of immunity. That raises the interesting possibility of papers with names like the *Costa Nostra Ledger and Reporter,* manned by groups who really know how to get information out of sources.

One of the more interesting aspects of *Branzburg,* however, is not the outcome nor the merits of the arguments, but the nature of the rhetoric, and it may be significant that the two dissents—one by Mr. Justice Douglas and one by Mr. Justice Stewart—were rhetorically much more highly pitched than the majority opinion by Mr. Justice White and the concurring opinion by Mr. Justice Lewis Powell.

The dissents did not really discuss the mundane problems of the case—how much press freedom should be purchased at how much cost of effectiveness of law enforcement, or how to deal with the reluctant witness who falsely claims he is planning to write an article or book. Instead, the dissents swept at once to the broadest principles and indeed, if I may say so, the most apocalyptic statements, suggesting that to require reporters to go before grand juries was virtually to reduce the press to printing government press releases. With respect, that is a considerable overstatement.

I am not sure that the significance is in the contrast between the tone of the majority and minority opinions, but it tends, although it need not, to make many people think that the position of the press has now been pushed to extremes, so that it cannot be argued in detail but must consist of doomsday rhetoric and breathtaking overstatement of the consequences of deciding against the press's claims.

The matter ought to be put in perspective. The issues in *Branzburg,* and *Farber,* and *Lando* do not strike to the heart of either the sanctity of the law or the freedom of the press. Those cases could go either way without endangering either of those profound values. What the courts are engaged in doing is making adjustments at the margins of competing values. If the press does not win all of these border disputes, that does not presage the coming of the totalitarian night.

Perhaps a change in the composition of the Supreme Court may result in temporary victories for the press position, but those victories are unlikely to be permanent. Those who take comfort in ringing statements like the quotation we have read from Mr. Justice Douglas in his Branzburg dissent, should reflect that equally stirring words were spoken in majority opinions celebrating the constitutional freedom of corporations from regulation. No such opinion is to be found after the mid-nineteen-thirties.

I very much hope that what has happened to other corporations in our society does not happen to the press. Our economy is badly overregulated, and it would be an even greater disaster if speech and press freedoms came under similar controls. I agree with Justice Douglas that the press has a preferred position in our constitutional scheme, though I would add that it is speech and press. And in fact, the burden of my remarks here is that it is impossible to read the press clause of the First Amendment as giving greater freedom than the speech clause gives. This means that the press should never gain rights superior to those of other citizens, under the First Amendment. If the press does gain those rights, for reasons I will give in a moment I think it will rue the day. Speech and press have preferred positions because of their intimate relationship to the ways in which we govern ourselves. This is a point Justice Douglas makes, and it is an entirely sound point.

That preferred position rests upon grounds so strong that they could properly have been inferred by judges from the structure of the entire Constitution, even if no First Amendment had ever been adopted. The Constitution prescribes in great detail a representative democracy, which is to say government resting upon the choice of the electorate. That form of government makes no sense, even without a First Amendment, unless speech and writing critical of government are freely permitted, and unless the electorate is able to make itself informed. That theory requires great freedom for both speech and press; it does not require absolute freedom in all circumstances. To insist that it does is to lose the intellectual argument before it has begun.

If they would preserve their freedoms, the members of the press might do well to realize that freedom is not merely a right, it is also a problem. Increasingly the press is perceived by many people as being a center of irresponsible power. I do not perceive it that way, and I do not regard the press as monolithic. Nevertheless, it has great power and in some cases it is irresponsible. It can and does do enormous damage to individuals and to institutions by inaccurate and sometimes biased reporting, and there is very little in the way of mechanisms to call it to account. . . .

I recall attending a seminar on "Law and the Press," at which some very prestigious journalists, lawyers, and judges were present. At the end, the lawyers and judges were aghast at the adversarial spirit that seemed to grip the journalists. One judge summed it up by saying that the conference ought to be retitled "Law *or* the Press." During the course of it, I asked a prominent journalist why, if the government was entitled, for example, to keep grand jury deliberations secret, he thought the press was entitled to induce grand jurors to violate their oaths and tell the press what went on in the grand jury room for publication. He answered that that was all right, because if the press could get the grand jurors to talk, that showed the system was breaking down. Apparently the press, in his view, was entitled to attack the system and use the system's success as justification for attacking it.

There was much more of this kind of talk than I can repeat here, but one instance was particularly worrisome. My wife, who was present, was unable fully to credit all that she was hearing, and she asked a group of journalists a hypothetical. She said, suppose they were looking into allegations that there was a pusher of heroin at the local high school, they found pretty good evidence of who the pusher was, but, for one reason or the other, they decided not to run the story. Would they give the police the evidence they had gathered? An amazing number of the reporters there said that they would not, that it was their business to criticize government, not to assist it. I can hardly believe I heard that answer, but I did; by no means from all the journalists present, I stress, but from a very sizable number.

Something of this same attitude, that it is the press's sole function to get the information and publish it regardless, must underlie the publishing practices of some investigative journalists no matter what harm may be done to the nation. I have never understood yet—perhaps some day I will hear an explanation—the decision to run a front-page story disclosing that an American submarine had managed to tap into an underwater Soviet military communications cable. The result of the story, of course, was that the tap had to be discontinued.

I once met with a group of editors, one of whom roundly criticized Alexander Bickel for conceding in the Pentagon Papers case that there might be some case where courts could enjoin publication—as, for example, when in wartime a paper proposes to publish the location of a troopship in mid-ocean. When I raised that problem, which Bickel had discussed, one editor said, "Why do you blame us for publishing? Blame the man who sent the troopship out."

The position seems to be, with some segments of the press—and it doesn't take more than a sizable segment of the press, a sizable minority, to begin to worry people very much—that the public's right to know is the press's right to publish anything, even things the public most definitely thinks ought not to be known.

I stress this attitude, not because it enrages me; it doesn't. I have heard it so many times now. I stress it because it seems to me dangerous to the press's freedom in several respects.

First, the public generally is simply not willing to put press freedom above all other values in the society; and if one day the irresponsible publication of secret information does direct and palpable damage to national interests, the backlash may lead to greater restrictions than there ought to be.

Second, the press may eventually succeed in convincing the other institutions of the society that it really is, in the full sense, the adversary. . . .

It seems to me particularly dangerous for the press to attack the judiciary as the government, and therefore inherently an adversary, when the press depends upon the judiciary for the protections of the First Amendment. You cannot expect Olympian detachment of that sort. . . .

It is arguable that danger more insidious than the press's failure to get additional privileges is the danger that it may get them—immunity from discovery, from grand jury subpoenas, from compulsion to testify at trials—privileges which are accorded to no one else. The reason I say that may be insidious is that if they get those privileges, they will get them because shield laws, or other laws, have been passed, and agreed to by the courts; and those laws will necessarily have to define who is the press. Not everybody can say he intends to write and therefore is the press, because that would break down the judicial process.

Laws that define who is the press in order to grant privileges are, in effect, legislative and judicial licenses. They enlist the First Amendment to support a kind of licensing it was supposed to prevent. More than that, a license is a special privilege, and the grant of special privileges is almost always accompanied by regulation of the licensee. That has been true historically and the broadcast media ought to know it now. The rhetoric that special privilege carries with it special responsibility will not be long in coming, and it is a rhetoric which the enemies of press freedom can use with telling effect. The price for special privilege may be disastrously high, perhaps something like the fairness doctrine, spread over the press at large. . . .

The press may properly claim great freedom; it may not claim—or at least it is not likely to do so successfully—the exclusive or the special possession of it. ∎

Bork's critics have been known to remark that he dismisses too easily the idea of resistance to governmental authority—indeed, dismisses too easily those who resist governmental authority. To some of them he is still remembered as "the man who fired Archibald Cox." Bork served as Solicitor General during the Nixon administration, and when Harvard Professor Archibald Cox, serving as Special Prosecutor during the Watergate investigations, insisted that Nixon turn over to him some tapes of Oval Office conversations, Nixon ordered him fired. The one who would have normally carried out the order, Attorney General Elliot Richardson, refused to do so and resigned. The next in line to carry out the order was the Deputy Attorney General; he also refused and was himself fired. Bork ended up doing the firing.

None of this may be relevant to the present issue, though there may be some irony in the fact that Bork was then serving as an instrument of Nixon's confidentiality (by dismissing the man who demanded to hear the so-called Watergate tapes) but is today unwilling to protect the confidentiality of news sources. At any rate, Floyd Abrams, who appeared on the same podium with Bork, gallantly refused to make use of these *ad hominum* notes, which is perhaps just as well.

Abrams, the chief legal counsel to the *New York Times* and the attorney who argued the case for the producers of "60 Minutes" in *Herbert v. Lando*, did not directly reply to Bork's argument that the press is no more special than anyone else who exercises free speech. He rested his argument on the contention that there is simply no alternative to granting some sort of "shield" to reporters.

PROTECTION FOR CONFIDENTIAL SOURCES IS ESSENTIAL FOR GOOD JOURNALISM

Floyd Abrams, from *The Center Magazine*, March/April, 1979

I am pleased to appear today with my friend and sometime colleague, Robert Bork—"sometime" because my own teaching visits to Yale are on a once-a-week basis. Some years ago, Professor Bork wrote a most provocative article on the First Amendment in which he attacked very sharply the Holmes-Brandeis view set forth in a variety of post-World War I cases. His article supported the views of those of the all-but-forgotten majority in those cases. Professor Bork's argument had, as he himself observed in his article, "at least the charm of complete novelty." So taken was Justice Douglas by the charm of Professor Bork's submission that he devoted a rather lengthy footnote to it, describing it as a "regressive view of free speech" which had "surfaced but had thus far gained no judicial acceptance."

I, myself, was, as Professor Bork observed, to a far more limited extent, perhaps, the subject of stern commentary by Justice Douglas in a somewhat different context. I was one of the authors of an *amici* brief submitted on behalf of *The New York Times*, the National Broadcasting Company, the Columbia Broadcasting System, and others in the case of *Branzburg v. Hayes*. The chief author of that brief was the late Alexander Bickel, Professor Bork's colleague and friend and my law school teacher and friend. That brief sought a qualified First Amendment protection for journalists not to disclose their confidential sources, a protection which could rarely be overcome, but was nonetheless qualified. The test would, if adopted, have avoided many, but surely not all of the conflicts that we have had since the Branzburg ruling. But it *was* qualified; and it led Justice Douglas to comment in his opinion about the "timid, watered-down, emasculated version of the First Amendment, which *New York Times* advance[s] in this case." . . .

I bear witness—and my clients bear wounds—to the proposition that courts too often do not contemplate what they are as well as what they do. But what does all this mean in practice? Surely judges must decide cases. Surely there are hard cases that they must decide. And, to be sure, it is, is it not, a knee-jerk response to conclude that the First Amendment must always prevail when it is contrasted with some other right, sometimes even constitutional in nature? All this is, I submit, somewhat true but also false. It is reminiscent to me of the observation attributed to Lloyd George to the effect that "I am a man of principle, and my first principle is that of expediency."

The difficulty is that many judges seem to view every exception to the First Amendment as an invitation to the next one; and every limitation on the First Amendment as a signal that, in the language of a high Central Intelligence Agency official, "the First Amendment, is, after all, just an amendment." And they view, alas, every Farber case as an imprimatur for the next one. . . .

In opposing any balancing test, in urging that journalists should be held privileged not to disclose their confidential sources and materials, Justice Douglas observed that "[t]he function of the press is to explore and investigate events, inform the people what is going on, and to expose the harmful as well as the good influences at work." It is the ability of the press to fulfill that function which, I believe, is and ought to be at the heart of the question as to whether, and to what extent, journalists should be exempt from the obligation of any other people to testify as to such matters. To the extent the question is one of *fact*, will the obligation to testify in fact substantially limit the flow of news to the public? And with respect to that significant question of fact, I share Professor Bork's view that one must, as best one can, try to divine what articles might have been written that were not; what articles were written that could not have been written otherwise; and what truly would have happened had we not had some kind of protection for confidential sources. We must consider whether, to allude to the obvious example, Carl Bernstein and Bob Woodward could have done their work if they had been ordered, midstream or perhaps afterward, to disclose their confidential source or sources.

Some will disagree on the facts. One of the panelists, Anthony Lewis, writing about the shutdown in England of the *Times* of London and the *Sunday Times*, expressed the view earlier this week that it is merely "the current press mystique" in the United States which holds that a newspaper cannot "get vital information from confidential sources without any special legal protection." I think Mr. Lewis is wrong in his formulation of the issue: no one, to my knowledge, has urged that the press cannot gain *any* information without legal protection. I think he is wrong in citing the English press—which has been described by the editor of the *Sunday Times* as the "half-free press"—as an example to American journalism. And I think he is wrong as a matter of fact: virtually all journalists whom I know make use of confidential sources *need* confidential sources to write their stories.

But what I find more troublesome than any disagreement Mr. Lewis and I may have about this issue is the nature of the judicial reaction to it all. For example, the Branzburg decision is based, in part, on the notion that it is speculative to say that journalists will, in fact, be deterred from gathering information if they are not protected from being obliged to testify about their confidential sources. But when, two years later, the question arose as to whether the President needed confidentiality in his discussions with his advisers, we were instructed by the Court, unanimously, that "[t]he importance of . . .confidentiality is too plain to require further discussion."

Similarly, although *Branzburg* was based upon the proposition that states may adopt "qualified or absolute" shield laws, I think I do the judiciary no disservice if I observe that virtually every shield law has, after judicial scrutiny, not shielded what was sought to be shielded. In the language of Justice Morris Pashman, dissenting from the ruling of the New Jersey Supreme Court in the Farber case, "There is no reason to accord this statute an unfriendly reception in any court of this state. There should be no eagerness to narrow it, or to circumvent it. The shield law is not an irritation. It is an act of the legislature." But shield laws, in the Farber case and in other cases, have too often been treated as little more than irritations.

And so I find myself returning to the dissenting opinions in *Branzburg* and asking myself whether any balancing test can serve, or whether Justice Douglas' language is indeed prophetic in stating that "[s]ooner or later, any test which provides less than blanket protection . . . will be twisted and relaxed so as to provide virtually no protection at all."

It is a difficult choice, even for me, as an advocate. For one thing, to put it crassly, there are no votes on the Supreme Court for Justice Douglas' position. For another, some states, such as Wisconsin, have adopted a First Amendment balancing test much like that set forth in Justice Stewart's eloquent dissenting opinion in *Branzburg,* and have done so in a way which will provide much, if not total, protection for the press. And I am cheered to hear Professor Bork's comments today about his own views, which it seems to me are, whatever else I may have to say in disagreement with him, far more supportive of the press than I detect from the United States Supreme Court, and surely than I detect in a variety of courts around the country as they handle press issues.

Yet, there remains much to be said for Justice Douglas' formulation. If it is, after all, as I believe it is, the function of journalists at their best, unlike the rest of us, to expose public officials—judges included—at their worst, do we not ask too much of those same public officials to make a series of *ad-hoc* balancing decisions as to the circumstances under which journalists will be permitted to protect their sources? Do we not need some firm rules—rules at least as firm as those that exist for other testimonial privileges that are *not* at all constitutionally rooted? Can we, in short, look to the judiciary for judicious treatment of the press when conflict appears to pit the press against the judiciary itself?

I have, alas, no answers to these questions. And, on any pragmatic short-term basis, they may even be the wrong questions. In the courts today the question is hardly whether the press should receive qualified or absolute protection; it is whether it should receive qualified or no protection. And to say the least, in setting forth, at least inferentially, some views of my own about the rights of the press in this area, it does not mean that I would oppose extremely broad free speech rights in a variety of circumstances and in many instances precisely the same as those involving the press. The situations do, it seems to me, become distinguishable in the area, for example, of confidential sources of information.

But as these issues continue to surface in the courts, I leave you with two thoughts for your consideration—one relating to the press, the other to the courts. As regards the press, I offer you this telling observation of Alexis de Tocqueville: "I admit that I do not feel toward freedom of the press the complete and instantaneous love which one affords to things by their nature supremely good. I love it more from considering the evils it prevents than on account of the good it does."

The question, I suggest to you, is thus whether the press can prevent the evils that only it is able to prevent, if journalists cannot promise (and in a meaningful fashion) confidentiality to their sources. . . .

I believe the facts, based on my knowledge, at least, would show that without protection for confidential sources, much of what we would all agree is journalism at its best would simply disappear. If that is apocalyptic-sounding, I do not mean it to be. I have no choice other than to say that I do not understand how the press could persist in covering certain types of stories without being able to afford just those promises. . . . ■

A book of interest to serious students of media rights and responsibilities is THE POLITICS OF BROADCAST REGULATION by Erwin G. Krasnow and Lawrence D. Longley (2nd edition, St. Martin's, 1978). The authors warn that "the book you hold in your hands represents our best shot at a moving target."

That the "target" is indeed hard to hit was apparent to anyone watching the developments in broadcast regulation in 1981. At the beginning of July the Supreme Court decided the case of *CBS v. Federal Communications Commission*. In it the Court said that the FCC was right in forcing the TV networks to sell a half-hour of air time to the Carter-Mondale campaign committee in January of 1980. In its 6-to-3 decision the Court said that the Communications Act as amended in 1972 creates an "affirmative right of access to the broadcast media." Access advocates rejoiced—until the following September, when the FCC, under its new, Reagan-appointed chairman, Mark S. Fowler, voted 4-2 to urge congressional repeal of both the Fairness Doctrine and the "equal time" laws. "My position on these laws," Fowler told a broadcasters' convention, "is simple and clear—get rid of them."

Fowler's position is similar to that of William S. Paley, Chairman of CBS, whose argument is presented in the next chapter along with two other arguments which attempt to answer the question: "What is to be done about the mass media in America?"

CHAPTER 7

The Media and Public Policy: What Should Be Done?

It is fun to speculate about the future of the mass media. One can talk about video disks, back yard microwave dishes, and all sorts of futuristic hardware. A more difficult topic is the question of what *should* be the future of the media. What sort of policies should America adopt in regard to the media?

Here is one response: America should not adopt *any* media policies; it should leave the mass media alone. That answer, however, is based on a misconception. It is no longer possible to do nothing about the media. Even the most ardent advocate of *laissez-faire* would not be likely to want to repeal the Communications Act of 1934 and put nothing in its place. If that were to happen there would be chaos as stations kept cutting into one another's signals. The existence of electronic media means that government is necessary as a traffic cop. Whether government should go further: whether it should require that the electronic media operate in the "public interest, convenience, and necessity," whether it should require "equal time" and "balance," whether it should break up media concentrations, whether it should subsidize radio and TV—these are the kinds of questions that must be debated. They cannot be dodged, and whatever emerges from the debate will be national policy. It may be a policy of minimal government interference, but it is still a policy. It is policy, moreover, that should be the result of widespread debate. It will have to be something more than the product of quiet negotiation between the lords of the press and the power brokers in Washington. In a democracy, the government is supposed to be responsible to the people. The future of the media, therefore, is our business.

We can reach the same conclusion by a different route if we recall the words of Justice Black in the Pentagon Papers case and of Justice White in the *Red Lion* case. Justice Black said, "The press was meant to serve the governed, not the governors." He was defending the right of the press to publish classified documents because of its role as public servant. The press was meant to serve *us*—not the politicians, but also not just itself. Its freedom derives from its duty to serve the public. In the *Red Lion* case, Justice White made much the same point when he said, "It is the right of viewers and listeners, not the right of the broadcasters, which is paramount."

Policy of some sort, therefore, has to be made, and all of us should be thinking about what sort of policy we need for an industry which plays such an influential role in contemporary America. What follows, and concludes this book, are three different perspectives on what is to be done.

The first, by columnist and author Kevin Phillips, attempts to lay the intellectual groundwork for more government regulation of the media. Phillips thinks that the media have become a "new class," a "mediacracy" which has displaced the industrial class which once dominated American political life. Though often characterized as a "conservative" (he once served as an advisor to Richard Nixon), Phillips sees himself as a kind of populist. He claims to articulate the point of view of ordinary working people, who, he thinks, now regard the East Coast, intellectual establishment with the same aversion with which they used to view the East Coast moneyed class.

THE CASE FOR MORE REGULATION

Kevin Phillips, from "Controlling Media Output," *Society*, November/December 1977

There are a few people in the national media who will deny the great power they wield, but only a few. More argument comes over whether this so-called "new" role is indeed really new. After all, talk about the press being a fourth branch of government began in the French Revolutionary era. All of our great presidents—from Washington through Jefferson, Jackson, Lincoln, and Roosevelt—tangled with the press, and their supporters made frequent reference to its power and ability to set the agenda of the national debate. Which brings us to the central question: if today's argument about the media power is to be differentiated from those of the 1790s, 1860s, or 1930s, what new factors make it so?

COMMUNICATIONS REVOLUTIONS

America has undergone a postindustrial or communications revolution elevating the major media to an economic size, technological sophistication, and cultural (political socialization) importance totally unmatched in the day of Edmund Burke or even Robert A. Taft. Increasingly, we live in a polity and society that can be described as a "mediacracy"—where communications mechanisms and the "knowledge industry" elite play the dominant role that (1) land ownership, landed elites, and their values played in aristocratic societies and (2) manufacturing, capitalist elites, and the rising middle-class values played in the Western democracies of the industrial era.

If one accepts this notion of media power having reached a new critical mass because of postindustrialism, a lot of other things follow. So let us back up and look at some reasonably solid data.

In 1790, when Edmund Burke and others were talking about the press as a fourth branch of government, what was it—newspapers alone with a circulation of a couple of hundred thousand in countries with populations of five or ten million; no more than that. The communications industry—the production, consumption, and dissemination of knowledge—might have accounted for a few percentage points of the Gross National Product. Even a century later, when manufacturing had displaced agriculture as the mainstay of economic life in both Britain and the United States, the knowledge and communications industries were small potatoes, totaling no more than several percentage points of the GNP.

All of this began to change with the rise of electronic communications in the 1920s and 1930s. And the other economic segments of the knowledge industry grew, too—vast research, swelling bureaucracy, massive education, mushrooming skilled professional ranks, proliferating service workers. As a result, the percentage of the GNP accounted for by the production, consumption, and dissemination of knowledge soared. In 1920 it had been about 12 percent; by 1950 perhaps 20 percent; by 1960 about 25 percent. By the early 1970s Peter Drucker and others put it at between 30-40 percent of the GNP. The knowledge industry, broadly construed, had replaced manufacturing as the critical element of the U.S. economy.

THE "NEW CLASS"

Quite a few scholars have already painted this upheaval with a richness of statistics and theoretical amplification. Daniel Bell has called it the Postindustrial Revolution. John Kenneth Galbraith, in his book *The New Industrial State,* observed that "one should expect, from past experience, to find a new shift of power in the industrial enterprise, this one from capital to organized intelligence." Organized intelligence is a short description for the knowledge industry—an admittedly overgeneralized but nevertheless useful term.

Irving Kristol has provided elaboration of another useful point—the notion of a "New Class." To Kristol the rising knowledge industry elite is anticapitalist, and anxious to flex its new muscle. In bygone days the press used to reflect competing segments of aristocratic or industrial society. Now—at least in the national media—that is less and less true. The major national media represent the interests of the emerging New Class—their *own* class. This is unique. It has not happened before. Until the postindustrial revolution, the New Class of the knowledge industry was too small to be a power elite in its own right.

Needless to say, the process is not complete. In New York, Boston, Washington, Chicago, and Los Angeles, the national media *do* strongly interact with the larger knowledge industry—with its scholars, bureaucrats, foundation executives, interest groups, and friendly politicians. Thus the major national media—the television networks, *Time, Newsweek,* the *New York Times,* the *Washington Post*—typically mirror New Class values. But not so the television affiliates or local newspapers in many, other, smaller cities. Irving Kristol, who believes that "the media *are* the New Class," and that educators *are* the New Class, ignores these regional differences. But it was equally true that in William Jennings Bryan's day, small town Nebraska bankers did not share the politics of culture of the Wall Street titans.

For our purposes, though, the major national media set the pace. Thus their articulation of New Class attitudes is enormously influential. And this new role is a far cry from the old one (which still prevails in many small towns and cities) of being a spokesman for local agricultural or industrial interests. The national media are the linchpin of knowledge industry interests and values, and this new role has lured many of the most talented members of the New Class.

None of this would be possible except for the new technological impact of the media. But the same postindustrial revolution that has elevated the knowledge industry to 35 percent of the GNP has given the media—especially the electronic media, but they all interact—an unprecedented ability to reach people and mold national opinion. As the *Columbia Journalism Review* proclaims, new heroes and villains can be introduced to the American people overnight.

POLITICAL IMPACT

At this point, it is useful to switch focus and consider just how the new political impact of the media is different from the old. Let us begin by setting aside superficial remarks about bias and loaded coverage of liberals versus conservatives. The real problem is a good bit more complex.

First, if we are going to think about the idea of a mediacracy, it is necessary to think in terms that go beyond CBS, *Time,* and the *Washington Post.* Use of computerized voter registration lists is reliance upon a communications medium. So use of direct mail for fundraising. So are telephone banks. So is a presidential press conference or a presidential nationwide hook-up. And it would be foolish to forget the increasing importance of rock concerts. This, too, is media politics: music is a medium. Most of what is important in U.S. politics is now media based—using this larger view of the words "media" and "medium."

Has this changed politics? Sure it has. The old politics used to depend on local machines, on individuals with a lot of money, on powerful industrial era institutions. Today's politics is changing styles. For example, most of the 1976 Democratic presidential candidates came out for marijuana decriminalization. Otherwise, few rock stars would have helped their campaigns raise money.

Television, of course, has also changed the style of politics. It puts a premium on mediagenic candidates rather than on the machine loyalists of yesterday—and the national media in general put a premium on people who embrace the general progressivism and value structure of the New Class. (An example of this can be found in the derogations by Lyndon Johnson of media politicians in David Halberstam's *CBS: The Power and the Profits.*) Celebrityhood is shifting. The old type of celebrity was a general, a local landholder, a big businessman. Now the celebrities increasingly come from the world of knowledge, artistic performance, and media (broadly construed). The difference is quite real.

The media are also increasingly the source of new fortunes. Agriculture and land yielded to manufacturing in this capacity a century ago, and now the knowledge industry and media are taking over. To paraphrase Marshall McLuhan, the medium is also the money. Books and movies have become a major source of wealth. And even in the field of business and industry, many of the new fortunes come from the knowledge industry—computer technology (both hardware and software), communications, various processes and patents. A growing percentage of America's rich have made their money in—and are interested in—the flow of change, ideas, information, systems. A media-based politics resting on this kind of establishment simply cannot be conservative in the traditional sense.

Moreover, a number of scholars have begun to argue that the rise of the media is directly related to the emerging alienation and instability of U.S. society. A media culture wallows in the exciting, weird, negative, and different. That is the nature of the beast. Think of the institutions that have suffered: business, the military, the neighborhood, and the family. As pre-communications revolution institutions, these are arguably less important to the New Class than to the average citizen. Considering all of these issues together, the impact of the major media arguably has been to increase instability and alienation.

This level of media analysis—looking at the impact of the communications revolution on the parties, the political process, ideology, society, and political socialization—is more productive than elaborate computations of minutes (or lineage) devoted to different candidates in different elections. On the national level, the real, critical power of the media does not lie in the hypothetical ability to tip an election to presidential candidate X rather than candidate Y. Instead, it lies in the ability to trumpet an issue, cripple a power center, fan a mood, create a villain (topple two presidents?), or scuttle a war.

POWER CENTER

Which brings us to the question of the media as a power center ranking with the executive, legislative, and judicial branches. This is the key. Back in 1974, when the Watergate fire storm was raging most fiercely, a survey of national opinion leaders by *U.S. News* and *World Report* found that television was ranked ahead of the White House as the country's number one power center. By 1975, with Richard Nixon out of office, the presidency was ahead again, and television was in second place.

By way of background, the big loser in the postindustrial power struggle of the last fifteen years has been Congress. During the 1960s the power centers gaining were clearly the executive, the judiciary, and the media. The legislative branch was losing ground. Superficially, to be sure, the toppling of Richard Nixon changed all of that. The presidency lost ground, the Congress gained. But in many ways the seeming rise of Congress has been a mirror image of the real rise of media power. Putting things another way, could it be that the new visibility—and "power"—of Congress comes from the fact that the legislative branch is the branch increasingly willing to voice what the national media want voiced?

Congress now reflects the will and interest of the press, and the American people are supposed to think and act accordingly. The major media exercise a form of censorship. To gain a place in the media sun, senators and congressmen must stay out of the shade of liberal establishment disapproval. Part of the power shift also flows from media monitoring increasingly technical political decision making and selection processes. Whatever the dynamics, a growing band of conservative theorists see the power of the media as having dwarfed, displaced, and even captured that of Congress. Thus the national media—linchpin of the New Class—are seen as *the* principal foe. The media are a bigger obstacle to conservatives than the Democratic party; only a powerful presidency can turn the tide.

I substantially agree with these analyses. However, if it is difficult to see any "conservative" politics succeeding unless it challenges the media, it is also difficult to see any politics that succeeds in challenging the media as being very "conservative." In this postindustrial era of ours, the national media and knowledge industry are too central a part of the U.S. power structure. Any politics that challenges that position will have to face up to its very real neopopulist nature. Any any such challenge will profoundly divide those who presently wear the conservative label.

It is becoming very difficult for the national media and their New Class allies to deny power elite status. They dislike my "mediacracy" thesis and its implications. Yet American history suggests that major emerging socioeconomic elites have generated strong political oppositions, and this one is no exception. Indeed, partly as a result of post-1960 negative reaction to the liberal politics of the New Class, "conservatism" finds itself strongest in areas like the South and West that were the strongholds of previous *populist* movements. Elite areas are the *least* conservative.

This is not the digression it might appear. We are talking about power centers. To do this, one has to think in terms of classic issues, tactics, and constituencies—less traditionally "conservative" than the populist. The arguments to which the major media are vulnerable are not piddling analyses of bias but the age-old themes of privilege, concentrated power, secrecy, oligopoly, wealth, and arrogance toward the values and institutions of ordinary Americans.

INTELLECTUAL MARKETPLACE

Raising these issues is not easy. At the first sound of tough criticism, many in the media pull the First Amendment out of their pockets and charge us with trying to extinguish freedom of the press. And anyone who is cowed by this simply becomes an easier target. The best argument is the most direct and legitimate: that the rise of major communications interests in the last fifty years has inflated the First Amendment into a protective device in much the same way that the Fourteenth Amendment was perverted in the late nineteenth century to serve as a bulwark for emerging corporations asserting the amendment's "due process" clause to block public economic regulation.

Wait a minute, you will say. Does not the First Amendment and all it implies go back to the 1790s? Yes and no. There was very little interpretation of the First Amendment until after World War I. Only in the years since the rise of the communications industry has the First Amendment become what it now so clearly is—a legal umbrella of industrial protection. Publishing stolen classified documents, listing the names of CIA agents (who can then be assassinated), printing the names of rape victims, merchandising prejudicial pretrial publicity, showing pornography, or staging bottomless dances and nude ballets are or may be protected forms of communication. Fifty years ago they would not have been—or had yet to become—key questions. Law follows power, and the expansion of the First Amendment is no exception: it has followed the expanding power of the communications industry.

Critical mass will come when the major media are perceived as enormously powerful commercial operations—indeed, as among the newest and most highly developed forms of U.S. economic activity—that bear no socioeconomic relationship to the struggling backroom press of the 1790s. Gone are the days when anyone could start up the only existing communications vehicle—a newspaper or periodical—with a minimal outlay. Today it is still possible to start up a local newspaper or a specialized periodical, but who can start up a television network, a *Newsweek*, or a *Washington Post?* Nobody can. We are dealing with economic mass and concentration that would have been beyond the imagination of a Thomas Jefferson or James Madison. To hear their names invoked on behalf of, say, CBS is tawdry and specious.

Perhaps increasing realization of this commercial magnitude and concentration will lead to more acceptance of the ideas of Ronald Coase, who argues that the normal treatment of governmental regulation of markets makes a unique distinction between the market for goods and services and the market for First Amendment-related commodities like speech and writing. Regulation of the goods market is applauded, regulation of the other condemned. As Coase notes, the ideas market is the only one where laissez faire is still respectable.

Conservatives may applaud, but more careful analysis is likely to be discouraging. Bear in mind that as manufacturing and industry had its laissez-faire period one hundred years ago, its elite used that freedom to triumph over agriculture and aristocracy. Laissez faire policies were a tool and expression of that triumph; a hundred years later, with business on the run, there is no more chance of restoring laissez faire in industry than there is of selling Manhattan back to the Indians. What is more, today's laissez faire license for the media oligopolies and their New Class viewpoints identified by Irving Kristol can generally be said to further threaten American manufacturing, agriculture, and natural resource producers. Indeed, laissez faire for the media under the banner of the First Amendment represents a threat to non-knowledge industry private business and a force for the expansion of the knowledge industry-favored public sector, just as laissez faire for mid-nineteenth century industry was a force for aggrandizement of the industrial segment of the economy at the expense of the agricultural sector.

To be sure, the emergence of the knowledge sector is a force that will not be denied. But it seems just as certain historically that more and more regulation will be imposed. Coase suggests that although intellectuals "exalt the market for ideas and deprecate the market for goods," the market for ideas is equally commercial—the place where the intellectual does his trading—and worthy of regulation in the public interest. As the media gain importance, this will happen. Would it not be a fair turnabout if media products advocating busing, forgiveness for criminals, and the like could be removed from circulation by an Intellectual Product Safety Commission?

REGULATING THE MEDIA

If, as I have argued, the media have emerged as a massive national power center, and if the answer is (as I believe it to be) active and innovative regulation, the last question is "What kind of active and innovative regulation?"

In the case of the television networks, it seems high time to more fully assert public control of and authority over the airwaves. Increased competition from cable has by and large proven to be a pipe dream; that uncertain hope should no longer distract us from strong measures. If a reformer could work in a political vacuum, the following would seem desirable: (l) strengthening the fairness doctrine; (2) applying tough antitrust measures to break the three networks into eight or nine, and forcing all networks to divest themselves of their owned-and-operated stations in opinion-molding national markets like New York, Washington, and Los Angeles; and (3) establishing a national commission (like Ontario's much applauded Royal Commission on Violence and the Communications Industry) to consider the impact of television in promoting crime, violence, social disintegration, and alienation, and then propose the necessary legislation and controls.

As for the print media, the leading cartels and concentrations deserve careful attention. We should begin by thinking of companies and marketplaces and narrowing the expanded industrywide First Amendment protections of the last forty or fifty years. For example, the *Washington Post* has a dominant or substantial share of the market on four levels—newspaper, newsweekly, television, and AM-FM radio—in Washington, D.C., a market which differs from others in the country in that it serves as a national news dissemination center. Concentration in this market—or in New York—should be treated differently regarding a national information product than a similar concentration in Boise. New antitrust legislation ought to differentiate media products and markets.

There is another aspect to considering media conglomerates as commercial entities rather than sacred First Amendment cows: should an editorial or other favorable media accolade be considered as a corporate contribution? Take the example of two corporations in the drug business: one also owns a newspaper, one does not. The one without a newspaper may not be able to use corporate funds to run advertisements in support of industry political goals. But the one with a newspaper can (1) run all the editorials it wants in support of drug industry political goals; (2) endorse any candidate it wants without giving space to an opponent; and (3) run all the editorials (or advertisements) it wants in support of the First Amendment and other items of political and commercial importance to the media industry. In the future this paradox will become clear, with more attention being paid to the public or shareholder interest in restraining the self-serving acts of media as well as other corporations.

PUBLIC'S "RIGHT TO KNOW"

At this point it may be appropriate to discuss that other great protest cry of the major media—"the public's right to know." Whenever a media corporation is seeking a privilege, like the right to boost its sales and peer group reputation by printing stolen classified information or other secrets, we hear about "the public's right to know." What they are doing is not really for themselves, but for the *people*. However, in the privacy of court or legislative deliberation, there is none of that. The major media, when other privileges are involved, dismiss any public "right to know."

The major media have become so important that they exercise some quasi-public functions in which the public clearly has a regulatory interest. This could prove to be a critical tool and approach. Using the Fourteenth Amendment, which prohibits states from denying anyone equal protection or due process, courts have held that this prohibition on state action can be extended to private corporations where corporations are working for the government or performing a public function. In this connection, bear in mind that thirty-odd years ago, the then whites-only primaries of the Democratic party in the South were deemed to be private affairs beyond the reach of federal law. But in 1944 the U.S. Supreme Court found that the Texas Democratic primary was, in essence, serving so critical a political function that it amounted to governmental action, and (Fifteenth Amendment) regulatory jurisdiction was thus established.

If the whites-only Democratic primary of Texas in 1944 represented so much of the political process that it could no longer be called "private," how long will it be until the major media fall afoul of a kindred standard? Richard Reeves, Edward Hunter, Jeffrey Hart, Pat Buchanan, and others have all bluntly described the relentless flow of political and quasi-governmental power in these private hands. And even *New York Times* reporter Les Brown, urging greater TV coverage, has characterized the networks as a "government of leisure" because of the average 6—7 hours the average American family views TV each day.

Which brings us back to the question of "the media" as "a power center." Speaking of the national media, of course, they are—one that will get bigger and bigger and bigger without effective countermeasures. And the politics of the next few decades will in no small measure be determined by what people are courageous enough to do about it. ∎

Phillips sees little difference between regulating the businesses of industrialists (which, unlike most Republicans, he supports) and regulating what is said by the mass media.

What about the First Amendment? Does it not explicitly protect speech against interference by government? Phillips' reply seems to be that it is being abused by the "mediacracy" so that it serves as an "umbrella" to cover all sorts of activities that the Framers would have never dreamed of protecting—pornography, publishing stolen government documents, and so on. Phillips thus refuses to make any distinction between "regulation of the goods market" and regulation of speech and writing. Both are justified. The only difference is that "the ideas market is the only one where laissez faire is still respectable."

But is that really the only difference? Is there not an intrinsic difference between the production of goods and the production of words, thoughts, and ideas? Is it not far more dangerous to regulate speech than to regulate property? These are of course rhetorical questions, and they are intended to introduce the next selection by William Paley. As Chairman of CBS, Paley is the very personification of the Eastern-based "mediacracy" that Phillips has attacked, but that is no reason not to listen carefully to his argument that the electronic media need less regulation, not more, and that newspapers and broadcasters should work together to resist government incursion.

WE MUST FIGHT GOVERNMENT INCURSION

William Paley, from "Press Freedom: A Continuing Struggle," address before Associated Press Broadcasters, June 6, 1980

This is a lively and impressive gathering. Your agenda is timely. The subjects are vital. All of it bodes well for the profession of journalism.

To be in this setting would be stimulating to me in any case. But to be here to receive this singular award from you has its own special impact. I am very proud of this honor. And I also appreciate this opportunity to speak on a subject which has been close to my heart for the major portion of my adult life.

As historians have often observed, history is replete with ironies. To take an example very much on our own doorstep, the growing adversary relationship in America between two of our most important institutions, the courts and the press, is an irony of the choicest kind. We have a constitution which guarantees freedom of the press in a way unique among nations. Yet the Supreme Court, which has long been considered among the staunchest defenders of press freedoms, has in recent years, handed down a series of decisions which seriously weaken press rights which many of us believe the Constitution clearly intended to confer. The time has come when we need to ask ourselves what this new trend may mean to our future as a democracy.

My purpose today is not only to discuss what I see as the gradual erosion of press freedoms in general; I also want to focus on a new and rapidly developing situation—namely, that communications technology is creating for the print media some potential new First Amendment problems which are similar to those that we have faced in broadcasting for many years.

I don't believe anyone would argue seriously against the proposition that if a democracy is to function efficiently the public must be informed of the actions of all its governing institutions—including those of the judicial system. Jefferson's familiar words on this subject are even *more* valid today. He said:

> "The basis of our government being the opinion of the people, the very first object should be to keep that right; and were it left to me to decide whether we should have a government without newspapers, or newspapers without a government, I should not hesitate a moment to prefer the latter."

Modern technology has made not only newspapers, but magazines and books available to everyone, while radio and television have brought the world into the homes of nearly all Americans.

In the midst of this abundance, however, there have been a number of recent Supreme Court decisions which have limited the First Amendment rights of the press. We've been complacent in the belief that no matter what the shifting ideological complexion of the Court might be, the First Amendment's meaning would, on balance, be preserved. But the trend of recent decisions gives us ample reason to believe that our complacency may not have been justified.

These decisions are remarkable for the range of their implications and deserve our thoughtful examination. In *Zurcher v. Stanford Daily,* the Court, in 1978, held that government agents could obtain a warrant to search a newsroom for photographs, notes and research files if they were seeking criminal evidence. It has since been argued that the press overreacted to this decision, and that no newsrooms have yet been searched. Nevertheless, the power to do so exists. And that fact represents an ever-potential danger and inhibits press freedoms. As this case reflects, a majority of the Supreme Court has refused to recognize the need of the press for protection of its right to gather news.

In another series of cases the Court ruled that the press had no special right of access to a prison to report on prison conditions, despite the strong public interest in access to that information. The effect of that decision, quite simply, is to prevent the public from learning first-hand of the conditions of their own public institutions—and this may come as a result of decisions by public officials who may have their own strong interest in preventing disclosure of such conditions.

In 1979, the Supreme Court stunned the press with its decision in *Gannett Co. v. DePasquale.* There the Court ruled that a criminal court judge had the right to exclude the press and the public entirely from pre-trial proceedings. As a result, pre-trial proceedings have been closed with alarming frequency. Indeed, some courts have used this decision as the basis for conducting actual trials behind closed doors. It was only four decades ago that the Supreme Court said that the business of the courts is public business. I suggest that in a democracy it is intolerable for the judicial process to be put beyond public scrutiny.

In the last few years, other decisions have further amplified these negative First Amendment trends. What it comes down to is this: Our long-standing concept that the media represent the public interest—that they are the buffer state between the governors and the governed—is now threatened by judicial decisions as never before in modern times.

As we reflect on this growing threat to our ability to inform the public fully, it is just as important to remind ourselves of our own primary obligation. We must report the news fairly and accurately. Objectivity may be an impossible ideal. But it is an ideal toward which we must strive constantly, maintaining standards so high that the public will be convinced of what we are trying to do. If we make errors—as inevitably we will—it is our duty to correct them and without delay. We must regard objectivity and accuracy as basic to our responsibility as custodians of a free press.

It is worth remembering that the First Amendment was enacted at a time when there was no concept of responsibility in the press and no inclination to create one. The ideals of objectivity and responsibility, voluntarily assumed by the press, are a product of *this* century, and it is an odd paradox that now, when the press has attained by far the greatest degree of responsibility and objectivity in its long history, is precisely the time when press freedoms have been given such adverse treatment by the Supreme Court and others.

Too many of us in print and broadcasting have imagined that we had separate destinies and separate problems, but the destinies and the problems of each are becoming the same.

The print media have a long tradition of freedom in this country, dating from the time in the early eighteenth century when they broke away at last from the control of British press licensing, then later from restrictions by provincial legislators.

The history of the broadcast media is quite different. In the early Twenties, the sudden, uncontrolled proliferation of radio stations filled the air with confusion. As a result, the broadcasters themselves appealed for government control to bring about technical order. But the government did more than that. It acted on the theory that the government, on behalf of the people, had a right to control the airwaves—which meant controlling the means of transmission. And so the Congress produced the Radio Act of 1927, with a Federal Radio Commission to enforce its terms, and then the Communications Act of 1934, enforced by a Federal Communications Commission.

It is certainly true that the framers of the First Amendment did not foresee the technology of broadcasting. But neither did the legislators who drew up the various communications acts foresee the pervasiveness of that technology: that very soon news broadcasting would become a most important part of the press especially in terms of numbers of people reached. Whatever the merits of the competing media may be, it is a fact that more people watch television news than read newspapers, and the polls show that more people believe what they see and hear on television and radio than what they read. It's strange, to say the least, that the medium on which the public places most reliance for news is the medium with the least First Amendment protection. Yet the Congress has resolutely refused to confront that fact, never seriously considering that broadcast journalism should have the same First Amendment protections enjoyed by the print media.

The fact is that today the print and electronic media are still running on separate legal and regulatory tracks. On the one hand, the print media are increasingly restrained by the actions of the courts; on the other, broadcast journalism is restrained, not only by the same courts, but even more by such obsolete legislative and regulatory restrictions as the "equal time" and fairness doctrine provisions, the inhibiting effects of which are clearly inconsistent with the spirit of the First Amendment.

I believe broadcasting has, in fact, earned its claim to freedom. It has generally adhered to the principles of fairness in dealing with news and public affairs, and has followed its own voluntary guidelines to assure responsibility. Under the First Amendment, it seems to me, there can be no doubt that broadcasters—and not the government—must have the responsibility to define and resolve problems of fairness. They are answerable to their audiences. They are vulnerable to their competitors. They are exposed to constant public criticism. And they are conscientious, professional journalists. Is any government agency better qualified, even assuming it had the right?

Yet the FCC chose to enunciate the policy known as the fairness doctrine. The doctrine so contradicts the basic premise of the First Amendment that the FCC has often exhibited moderation (and at times confusion) in implementing it, but the doctrine unquestionably gave a government agency the right to judge a news organization's performance. If it had been applied to newspapers instead, it is hard to believe that any court would have been able to construe it any other way than as a violation of the First Amendment.

Critics of broadcasting have long charged that the basic reason for regulating the medium through such measures as the fairness doctrine is that there is only room for a certain number of stations on the broadcast spectrum, but that there is no technical limitation on the number of newspapers that could be printed.

To anyone still arguing that this "scarcity principle" has any meaning as a grounds for enforced fairness, I can only point to the fact that a scarcity of broadcast outlets, as compared with daily newspapers, simply no longer exists. Indeed, it's the other way around. In 1927, there were 677 broadcasting stations in the United States and 1,949 daily newspapers. Today there are 1,756 daily newspapers and 9,774 broadcasting stations. The number of voices these stations produce far exceeds that provided by any other mass medium at any time in our history. It is also important to be aware that for every half hour spent with network news, viewers spend more than twice as much time with locally produced newscasts.

I believe we must remove the "equal time" and fairness doctrine provisions from the books. They were wrong when promulgated, and they are wholly unreal today.

There is another First Amendment development we should focus on, a relatively new phenomenon involving print and broadcasting. Broadcasters and print people have been so busy improving and defending their own turf that it has escaped some of us how much we are being drawn together by the vast revolution in "electronification" that is changing the face of the media today, and thereby bringing the issue of government control for both of us into even sharper focus.

What we've done is to create a vast complex of information machines, which are being fed by a storehouse of knowledge and entertainment of every conceivable kind. This endless mass of material is fed from diverse sources into the process, and it comes out the other end in a variety of ways. Technology is greatly increasing that variety every day. Even now, sitting at home, the consumer is able to tap not only the conventional radio and television broadcasts, comprehensive as they are—the phonograph records which stock his shelves—but a vast and growing array of audio and video cassettes, tape and film. What isn't packaged can come into the house by cable. With the aid of new computerized equipment, people will be able to select a remarkable range of what they want to see and hear, and have it brought to them aurally and visually, whether by pictures or printout. It is already technically possible to bring newspapers and magazines into the home, both on the television screen and by printout. Before long all this will be delivered as easily as the television pictures which now come to you. And all of this refers to technology which already exists. Just think of the next wave of revolutionary communications technology which is in planning or will soon be off the drawing boards. The possibilities border on the incredible.

This new era of information plenty, with its convergence of delivery mechanisms for news and information, raises anew some critical First Amendment questions about our freedom which merit comprehensive rethinking. Once the print media comes into the home through the television set, or an attachment, with an impact and basic content similar to that which the broadcasters now deliver, then the question of government regulation becomes paramount for print as well.

Already the FCC has the same "equal time" and fairness doctrine powers over cable originations as it does over conventional broadcasts. And print may well find its way into the home through cable. It would be foolish indeed for the print media not to be concerned that their output in this form may be drawn into the regulatory web whether through cable or other technology.

Before such a foothold is established, the print and broadcast media will have to unite and fight against the imposition of governmental controls on them, beginning with the removal of the present regulatory restraints on broadcasting. Let us recognize that our interests no longer run on separate tracks. It is imperative, in my view, that print and broadcasting people understand they have a common cause, and that cause is the removal of governmental intrusion in the editorial process. We must make our case not only to the courts and to the legislators, but most important, to the public itself.

Alexander Hamilton well understood that point. In 1788, Jefferson had argued that the press could be kept free merely by placing guarantees to that effect in the Constitution. But Hamilton was more prophetic. He observed that no matter what guarantee was inserted in any constitution, press freedom would never be secure without the support of public opinion. It depended, as he put it, "on the general spirit of the people and of the government."

I am fully convinced that one of our most urgent goals must be to help create that general spirit in the people and in the government—a spirit that will preserve the freedom of the press that is so essential to our democratic society.

Gaining freedom never comes easily. Remaining free calls for a matching measure of conviction and diligence. ■

Columnist Joseph Kraft seems to agree with Phillips that the media have become elitist in culture and arrogant in behavior, but he also agrees with Paley and other media spokesmen that any more government regulation could lead to disaster. On the surface, this seems to be a case of fuzzy thought resulting from an effort to take both sides of an issue at the same time.

For Kraft, however, the juxtaposition of these two views leads to a conclusion which is clear and inescapable: the time has come for the media to start putting their own house in order—before the government does it for them.

THE NEED FOR SELF-CRITICISM

Joseph Kraft, from "The Imperial Media," *Commentary*, May, 1981

You can tell Superman is Superman in lots of ways. He can fly. He has X-ray vision. He can stop a bullet in mid-flight. But perhaps the most singular of his qualities is the ability to do the transformation trick. He can change identities without paying a price. One minute he's Clark Kent, a reporter mild as Perry Como. The next he's Woody Hayes, slugging all the bad guys on the field. But he moves smoothly between the two roles. He doesn't get found out. He doesn't make people mad at him for being duplicitous. And, above all, he isn't schizophrenic; he isn't full of unavowed self-doubt.

Those things don't happen in the real world, and that fact says perhaps the most interesting thing there is to say about the imperial media. In the past two decades, those of us in the press and television have undergone a startling transformation. We have been among the principal beneficiaries of American life. We have enjoyed a huge rise in income, in status, and in power. In the process we have edged away from roles and standards hallowed by tradition. We no longer represent a wide diversity of views. We have ceased to be neutral in reporting events. We have moved from the sidelines to a place at the center of the action. Inevitably we have become subjects of hot controversy among ordinary people, political leaders, and even in the courts. Inevitably also we have experienced a tension between what we are supposed to do and what we actually do—between myth and reality. This inner tension finds relief in a self-serving creed or ideology—the ideology of the First Amendment. And that ideology implicitly stakes the imperial claim—the claim that what is good for the media is good for America.

Before going any further, a word of definition is in order. By the term media I mean something fairly precise. I am not talking about local papers or radio stations. I am talking about the relative handful of national news enterprises—the three networks; the news magazines; and the one or two leading regional papers which most of us read.

I also want to say a word about my own relation to journalism. It is a profession—and I use that word advisedly and in contrast to such other possibilities as craft, trade, or calling—which I cherish. It has been generous to me and given me cause for gratitude. I admire and like most of the people in the business. In the next few pages I am going to be fingering the weaknesses, pretensions, follies, biases, and insensitivities of my profession. I will dwell extensively on its occupational deformations. Sometimes I will cite myself as an example, sometimes other people. But I should say at the outset that when it comes to apportioning blame, I have no illusions of immunity. To the charges I am going to be leveling, I want to enter a plea of guilty.

Now to the recent change in our status. Let me first point to the scene of a play about the newspaper business, *The Front Page*, written almost exactly fifty years ago. The setting is the press room in the Criminal Courts Building in Chicago. Here are a couple of the details:

> It is a bare, disordered room, peopled by newspapermen in need of shaves, pants pressing, and small change. Hither reporters are drawn by an irresistible lure, the privilege of telephoning free. . . . An equally important lure is the continuous poker game that has been going on for a generation, presumably with the same pack of cards. Here is the rendezvous of some of the most able and amiable bums in the newspaper business; here they meet to gossip, play cards, sleep off jags, and date up waitresses between such murders, fires, riots, and other public events that concern them. It is little wonder that Hildy Johnson [the hero of *The Front Page*] refers to his fellow journalists as a cross between a bootlegger and a whore.

In contrast, let me cite the lines from the final broadcast given by Eric Sevareid after nearly forty years as a radio and television commentator for CBS. Sevareid said:

> We are not the worst people in the land, we who work as journalists. Our product in print or over the air is a lot better, more educated, more responsible than it was when I began some forty-five years ago

as a cub reporter. This has been the best generation of all in which to have lived as a journalist in this country. We are no longer starvelings and we sit above the salt. We have affected our times.

Those two citations express to me a neglected, but I think centrally important feature coloring the lives of those of us who work in the media. We have not merely been upwardly mobile, as the cant phrase goes. We have been shot from cannons. We have advanced almost overnight from the bottom to the top; from the scum of the earth described by Hildy Johnson to the seats of the high and mighty. We have become a kind of *lumpen* aristocracy in American society, affiliated, as priests at least, with the celebrity culture.

The rise in the status of journalists finds many, many causes. Probably the most important is the change in the character of the news. The reporters in *The Front Page* were preoccupied by local events which they could feel and smell and see—fires, murders, riots. The real, live journalists of that day— the H.L. Menckens and Ben Hechts—could walk into police headquarters and sniff around and get a feel for what was actually happening in Baltimore or Chicago. But that is clearly not the kind of event which preoccupies the national media today. Whatever else we do, we rarely deal with village affairs. We write and speak of far-off places—Iran, Poland, Namibia. We deal with huge aggregates—budgets in the billions; work forces in the millions. Finally, we deal with intrinsically difficult matters— the calculus of deterrence and the anti ballistic missile for example; or the full-employment budget, or parity prices in agriculture; or monetary aggregates and their impact on mortage rates.

Given this kind of work, journalists these days have to be well-educated. And so, increasingly, they are. Probably the most striking evidence of the change lies with the specialists. At the Supreme Court on any decision day, among the best-informed people in the place are the reporters who regularly cover the court. The last time I checked, twelve of the fifteen were lawyers. The same pattern applies in virtually every other distinctive area of reportorial work. In foreign policy, there are specialists in Africa, Europe, China, the Soviet Union, defense—even India. Every major newspaper, and each network, has specially trained people who cover the economy. Among the political reporters there are White House watchers, and congressional experts, and even people who follow—as though it were the stock of IBM—the ups and downs of the Senate Finance Committee.

Moreover, the specialists are only refined versions of the generalists. Managing editors, with a certain gruffness that hangs over from the Hildy Johnson era, like to say that they want good, solid reporters, trained in police work, whom they can assign to any beat. Maybe so. But it turns out that the general-assignment reporter covering the Department of Housing and Urban Development has to learn about inner cities and red-lining and mortgage rates. The general-assignment reporter covering the Department of Interior has to learn about wilderness policies, and the bureaucratic rivalry between the Corps of Engineers and the Council of Environmental Quality, and the interplay with Congress and private interests. The general-assignment reporter covering the Department of Health and Human Services has to learn about drugs and doctors and the containment of hospital costs—every one of them a complicated subject. No doubt it helps in trying to understand such matters to be savvy and shrewd. But you have to be more than that. You have to learn to think in abstractions; you ought, if you're going to be any good, to learn to think in terms of trade-offs—to see things not only now but whole; to look at not just parts but at systems. You have to be, in an apprentice way at least, a kind of intellectual.

The condition is now well-recognized. The publisher of the Los Angeles *Times*, Otis Chandler, made the point in a lecture series at the University of Maryland not long ago. "It was not too many years ago," he said,

> that most reporters came from ordinary, working-class homes, and reflected pretty much the values and prejudices of the mass market. Today, because of the increasing sophistication of the average newspaper reader, because of the trend toward specialized reporting, we are hiring, as many other newspapers are, many reporters from the upper and middle classes, men and women who in general are better educated, are more sophisticated, and are certainly paid more than most of our general citizens.

The same note has been struck, in a slightly more apprehensive way, by Lou Cannon of the Washington *Post*. In his recent book, REPORTING, Cannon writes:

> As reporters climb up the income scale, their social values also change. Reporters who a few years ago were preoccupied by the basic economic issues of life are now more likely to be aroused by energy or environmental issues, or, for a long decade, the Vietnam war. . . The gulf is growing between reporters and working-class Americans. . . .This is particularly likely to be true on the big national newspapers and television networks where reporters, correspondents, and editors are apt to be in the upper 10 percent of national-income levels.

Cannon quotes a colleague on the *Post*, David Broder, to this effect: "Reporters are by no means any kind of a cross-section. We are over-educated, we are overpaid in terms of the median, and we have a higher socioeconomic stratification than the people for whom we are writing."

It is a mark of how far the upgrading process has proceeded that the change in status and outlook can now be described almost as a matter of course. That was not the case when the point was made by one of the most perceptive of our social critics, Daniel P. Moynihan, back in 1971. Bombs of controversy exploded all around him when Moynihan, writing in *Commentary* ("The Presidency and the Press," March 1971), observed:

> One's impression is that twenty years and more ago the preponderance of the working press, as it liked to call itself, was surprisingly close in origins and attitudes to working people generally. They were not Ivy Leaguers. They are now, or soon will be. Journalism has become, if not an elite profession, a profession attractive to elites. This is noticeably so in Washington, where the upper reaches of journalism constitute one of the most important and enduring social elites of the city, with all the accoutrements one associates with the leisured class. . . .

A relative decline in competing professions makes the surge in journalistic status look all the more pronounced. During the past twenty years most of the intermediate groupings in American society—groups which interpose themselves between government, on the one hand, and the unorganized people, on the other, have lost status. Churchmen may be important on specialized issues, but they have ceased to give general tone to American opinion. Labor, which gave the country so much of the New Deal, is no longer a source of light on intellectual problems and has even, witness the rise of George McGovern and Jimmy Carter, lost the power of veto within the Democratic party. Business, which used to buy up parts of government, was made to pay through the nose in the Watergate scandal. Instead of well-known tycoons, today's business leaders are, in David Riesman's phrase, "a bunch of people who went to Purdue."

Within government itself, there has taken place the same falling off. Everybody knows that the political parties aren't what they used to be— even in Cook County. Lyndon Johnson, Richard Nixon, Gerald Ford, and Jimmy Carter all testify to the declining power and prestige of the Presidency. Nor can it be said that the Congress has taken up the slack. Giants do not stalk the hallways of the House and Senate.

If most of the best-known ingredients of the national power structure have been losing authority, there is one element—one much-imagined component—which I think has never acquired strength, never indeed come into being. For most of American history there has existed the quaint conceit that this country has an establishment or elite. But that view resists serious analysis.

Social power may still reside, in the older cities, in a group of Protestant families who came on the scene early, and developed certain tony schools and clubs. But economic power is dispersed, and intellectual power even more so. We have no *grandes ecoles,* as in France, where persons of high talent are amalgamated with the aristocracy. There is no House of Lords, as in Britain, where persons who have made it can take their ease while deliberating about the nation and enjoying a sure measure of respect.

The absence of an absorptive national establishment explains something that is almost unique to this country—the celebrity class. Celebrities are in our country the functional equivalent of dukes and earls in Europe. They bring glamor and excitement, and gossip and some hope even, into otherwise drab lives. But if celebrities play an important part in American culture, it is not an assured part. The cast keeps changing all the time. Today's star is tomorrow's has-been. So the atmosphere is full of furious rivalries. Moreover, the plight of the castoffs is cruel. To go from the glare of publicity to the edge of oblivion is a harsh fate. Those on the edge not only cling to their positions with furious tenacity, they harbor a deep and obscure resentment—a pervasive hostility toward a system that does not have a capacity for putting those who succeed at ease, that makes life so jumpy and edgy.

That last point brings me full circle. I have tried to show that those of us in the media enjoyed an enormous surge in status and power in recent years. That surge coincided with the decline of various other groups, to the point where we could almost perceive ourselves as the only institutional force left on a well-nigh devastated plain. But while we have acquired confidence and self-assertiveness, there is no security. We are driven to keep moving forward, and in an adversary way. We are thus highly prone to that disease of the times—narcissism. The narcissism of the journalist, of course, is not mere conceit. It consists in the belief that because we describe events, we make them happen. . . .

The general assumption of most of my colleagues, and I do not suppose I am much of an exception, is that behind every story there is a secret, and that every secret is a dirty secret. As an example, let me cite the treatment given by the three networks to what should have been one of the straightest of news events—the national budget for fiscal 1980. All three networks cited President Carter's description of the budget—"lean and austere." But all three presented that view in terms which suggested it was so much malarkey. Here is the NBC account:

> Good evening. . . .
> The President sent Congress the first federal budget since Proposition 13 . . . the first since the public outcry against taxing and spending rattled the windows in government offices across the country.
> Well, this new budget calls for more spending and higher taxes than the last one.
> The President nevertheless calls it lean and austere—meaning that while the spending is higher it is not as much higher as it might have been.

Here is the ABC account:

In a maze of figures inside this book is the projected level of federal spending for the next year—$531.6 billion. That would leave the government $29 billion in the red, and would represent the nineteenth deficit in the last twenty years. Despite the fact money will be pouring out of the federal till at a record rate, the budget is austere. Spending will be a smaller percentage of the gross national product than in recent years.

Here is the CBS account:

It sounded more like a cut of meat than the biggest federal budget in history—$531.6 billion. President Carter called it lean and austere, tough and fair. But Republican Senator Roth of Delaware said calling it lean is like looking at a package of bacon in the supermarket: you don't see the fat until you open the package.

In the follow-ups, in opening the package, the networks merely presented the various complaints *seriatim*. Thus NBC featured a ticking clock which kept count of the billions of dollars spent by the government. The commentator pointed out that if you paid $10,000 in taxes that year, the government would spend it in two-thirds of a second. He noted that many Americans were paying as much in social-security taxes as in income taxes. He added that while individuals had to balance their books, the government could spend more than it took in by printing money which, of course, fed inflation.

NBC also included a special section on HEW. The special section pointed out that the new budget included a cut in the social-security benefits which had the effect of:

Ending benefits to college students who could qualify for student loans.
Ending the $255 lump-sum death benefit.
Ending social-security benefits to widows when their children reach age sixteen.
Reforming the disability-insurance program so that disabled workers have incentives to return to work.
And ending the minimum monthly benefit of $122 to workers who also draw government pensions.

All of those cuts were represented as scandals, without any mention of the fact that there were other programs—outside social security—which paid many of the same benefits.

The NBC presentation also included an account of the increased monies paid out for defense. It set up, in the fashion dear to television, a clean-cut, good guy vs. bad guy fight—social-welfare cuts vs. defense increases. One of the commentators said: "Although the administration won't admit it, many of the nation's social programs are being cut so that more money can be spent on defense."

ABC set up the same conflict. A reporter on Capitol Hill asserted that "some Democrats were concerned about the proposed increase in defense spending, especially on the MX missile. They feel budget cuts should not be saddled on just the old, the poor, and the minorities." Then two Democratic Senators—Kennedy and Cranston—were interviewed complaining about the unfair distribution. Senator Cranston said: "There's no reason for national defense to be expanded while we contract aid to people who desperately need help from our government."

The distinguishing feature of the coverage was the listing of every single complaint without any effort at resolution. There was little or no emphasis on the obvious point that budgets are exercises in arranging competing priorities, and that conflict is a normal ingredient of the process—the name of the game, in fact. As a result, the stories missed two points that in retrospect stand out as the most significant of the entire episode: first, that Carter did his budget trimming, not by asserting priorities, but by cutting tiny bits and pieces across the board; second, that making decisions at the margin, in the fashion dear to incrementalists, yielded the worst of both worlds—cuts inadequate to restrain inflation, and defense spending inadequate to close gaps and give adversaries second thoughts. Not only was the coverage slanted, but the bias was uniform. It did not reflect the diversity of viewpoint normally evoked by a complicated state paper dealing with many controversial matters. It thus went beyond what I used to think of as the last best defense of media objectivity—the pluralistic defense.

The pluralistic defense starts from the premise that no person, no paper, no magazine, no network can possibly be objective and unbiased. It assumes that our knowledge of events is bound to be highly imperfect. It also assumes that there will be intense rivalry among competing media, between one network and another, and even among the reporters working on a single news show or paper. From those factors there springs the conclusion that the biases roughly cancel each other out. The theory is that the complexity of events blends with the ignorance of the beholders and the rivalry of the news media to present a pluralistic version of what took place. No one account is exactly right. Neither, however, does the sum total produce a distinct tilt. The truth is not established by any single journalist or paper or network. It is surrounded.

But the pluralistic model of an unbiased system depended upon the person in the news media being broadly representative. The theory was that every view would find some expression, some sympathetic presentation across the broad spectrum of bias making up the media diet. We have seen, however, that increasingly the media are staffed by an unrepresentative group—a group that is better-educated, more highly-paid, more sure of itself, and more hostile to the system than the average. Indeed, far from reflecting the population as a whole, those of us in the media replicate the set of deep splits that make up the American class system.

As I see it—and this I must emphasize is a highly personal view without any serious support in systematic research—the basic line of cleavage in American society separates upper-income, highly educated America from what I have called Middle America—persons with family incomes of $20,000 or less who have not been educated beyond high school or junior college. The outlook of upper-income Americans tends to be "enlightened." We are skeptical about established authority, particularly in the field of national security and matters of law and order. We are sympathetic to the claims of those with grievances—whether black or brown or Indian or senior citizens. We tend to favor helping them, even though the benefits—integrated neighborhoods, school busing, affirmative action—tend to be paid for by Middle America. As for Middle America's complaints—about gun control, anti-abortion rulings, abolishing the death penalty, yielding Panama—we tend to write them off as disconnected single issues.

Not only are we not representative, we are aligned on one side in the hottest class contention now dividing America. The TV programs I have cited at such length seem to me a case in point. They implicitly knock the whole government system, and make it seem that the President and the Defense Department, in particular, are offering bogus arrangements. They side with the dependent classes—the castes of American society. They put a finger in the eye of Middle America.

The bias reflected in the single case of the budget becomes more apparent when the historical record is unfurled. The media, as we have seen, were out front in assailing Vietnam and the national-security state; similarly in exposing Watergate and the "imperial Presidency." Before that we sided openly with the protesting minority groups. We not only gave them publicity which they believed, we caused them to overplay their hands. And when their time of troubles came, when the Middle American majority turned against the exaggerated claims, we blamed the Defense Department and the President.

Insofar as we in the media caused the minority groups to overplay their hands, we bear some responsibility for the setbacks they have suffered during the past few years. We helped to foster the overreaction of the Middle American majority. To me, at least, it seems plain that Middle America feels it commands little sympathy and next to no attention in the media. Middle Americans are convinced they don't get a square deal on television and in the newspapers. That is one of the reasons so many people rallied to the crude attacks made by Spiro Agnew on the press and television in 1970. It is also one of the reasons so many Americans lined up against the media and for Mayor Daley at the time of the police riots during the Chicago convention of the Democratic party in 1968. More importantly, lack of confidence in the press and television is what caused Middle America to announce its views through other media. In 1968, it sent a message through George Wallace at least in part because it didn't trust the networks. In 1978, it sent a message through Proposition 13 in part because it didn't trust the press. In 1980, to a degree at least, it masked intentions to vote for Ronald Reagan because it didn't trust those handmaidens of the media—the pollsters. In the eyes of most Americans, in other words, we have not been neutral.

Not only have we traded objectivity for bias, but we have also abandoned a place on the sidelines for a piece of the action. We have ceased to be referees and drama critics and become players in the game and actors on the stage. The more candid of my colleagues have admitted as much for a long time. The Alsop brothers back in 1958 acknowledged that reporting "offered the sense of being engaged in the political process of one's time." Douglass Cater expressed the same view when he called his book on the press, THE FOURTH BRANCH OF GOVERNMENT. In it he wrote that "the reporter is the recorder of government but he is also a participant. He operates in a system in which power is divided. He, as much as anyone, and more than a great many, helps shape the course of events."

Examples of helping to shape the course of events are legion—so commonplace indeed that they go almost unnoticed. Thus Tom Wicker, in his recent book, ON PRESS, describes with admiration the detachment of the Saigon press corps during the Vietnam war—an attitude which made them skeptical of the information regularly handed out by government spokesmen at the regular briefings. Wicker noticed that quality while he was on a tour of Southeast Asia with Vice President Hubert Humphrey. After Saigon, the party went on to Bangkok in Thailand. Here is Wicker's account of what happened: "That night in Bangkok, some of us tried for hours to persuade Humphrey staff men to take the word to the Vice President that he'd been given an over-optimistic report." In other words, even as he was praising his colleagues in Saigon for being detached, one of the most thoughtful and honest of American journalists was himself getting into the swim—trying to put in a fix of sorts with no less a person than the Vice President.

Far more explicit examples are well known. Tom Wicker himself played a highly public role in the negotiations which led up to the massacre at Attica prison in New York. James Reston of the *Times* was part of the conversation which caused Senator Arthur Vandenberg to abandon isolationism for internationalism on the morrow of World War II. Walter Lippmann, who was often thought of as "Olympian" in his insistence on standing above the petty play of events and men, agreed to see advance texts of speeches prepared for both Presidents Kennedy and Johnson. Not only that, he made comments upon them, and found that the comments were acted upon in the final drafts. Nor, I think, would anybody else have done it differently. . . .

Perhaps the most vivid expression of the changed role of press and television emerges from comments by public figures. Political leaders, of course, have always been sensitive to criticism. Jefferson, well known for the remark that if forced to choose he would rather have a press without a government than a government without a press, also asserted that what he mainly found in the press was lies. Teddy Roosevelt did not popularize the term "muckrakers" in any laudatory spirit, but rather to point up the proclivity of certain journalists for dirt. Harry Truman once observed to a friend that "I really look with commiseration over the great body of my fellow citizens who, reading newspapers, live and die in the belief that they have known something of what has been passing in the world in their time." But there is a difference between those generalized assaults and the invidious attacks that have recently become prominent. It wasn't just good clean fun when President Eisenhower warned the delegates to the 1964 Republican convention that they should not let themselves be divided by "those outside our family, including sensation-seeking columnists and commentators." Agnew's shots at the "nabobs of negativism" and the "effete Eastern establishment" were dark with hostility. So was President Nixon's injunction to Ron Ziegler to treat the press "with contempt."

During the Nixon administration not a few newsmen were deliberately cut up in ways calculated to hurt them. The Washington *Post* had a television license called into question. A blatant attempt was made to get Dan Rather transferred from the White House beat. All kinds of personal investigations were opened into the lives of the reporters who worked with the Pentagon Papers—especially Neil Sheehan of the New York *Times.* Half a dozen of us were made the subject of wiretaps.

Other far more damaging and punitive measures were taken against press and television at lower levels of government and in local settings. Congress tried to punish CBS for its program, *The Selling of the Pentagon.* A House committee tried to get Daniel Schorr for releasing a document that it classified after most of the release had been accomplished. Finally, local law-enforcement officials, whether from the North or South, have not been exactly sympathetic to the free play of information in civil-rights matters.

Moreover, it is not as though the end of Vietnam, and the outcome of Watergate, vindicated the press and television (as some of us fondly believe). On the contrary, our stock with the general public continues to sink. The Harris Poll reports public confidence in television news fell from 34 percent in 1975 to 29 percent in 1980. Confidence in the press fell from 24 percent in 1975 to 19 percent in 1980. A survey by the University of Texas found that 84.4 percent of the sample believed that journalists slanted the news.

If the disparity between our actual role and our mythic claims for ourselves has caused others to hit out at the press and television, it has also generated inner doubts and uncertainties, a defensiveness within the media. A subject that was once singularly barren has now become a major topic of interest. No self-respecting foundation has failed to commission some study on the press and television. Virtually all newspapers and magazines of note have appointed inside ombudsmen to be sure that they are behaving in a fair way. The television networks, in what I would call a transparent effort to ingratiate themselves with Middle America, have moved away from reporters and correspondents with a strong working knowledge of their subject. The typical up-and-coming man in network news has been described by one television critic as Mr. Al Average. He has no point of view, he has no regional marks—especially no accent—and he can change at a moment's notice into the costume and habits of a farmer, a tycoon, a hardhat, or you name it. Finally, a defensive tone has crept into the work of even the most self-confident journalists. Dan Rather's book, THE CAMERA NEVER BLINKS, starts with a confrontation between himself and President Nixon in a press conference in Houston. Rather then spends about nine pages telling how he happened to challenge the President. He puts the blame on an effort by the White House to manipulate the news. He says of the President and his men: "They had seen the enemy and it was us."

The sense of being under attack expresses the feelings of the profession as a whole. We have become painfully aware that much of the outside world is hostile, and regards as bogus our claims to fairness and objectivity. We have responded the way people under that kind of pressure generally respond—by coming up with a defensive rationale, an ideology.

I want to use ideology here in a neutral tone—after the fashion of Karl Mannheim, as developed especially in the book THE AMERICAN BUSINESS CREED, by Francis Sutton, Seymour Harris, Carl Kaysen, and James Tobin. That book points out that American businessmen have been subjected to a tension between the myth of free enterprise and the realities of a commercial and industrial world largely dependent upon government and influence in high places. The response of the businessmen to this strain has been to create a creed, or ideology, a way of thought, which stresses all the old-time values of free enterprise and thrift and self-reliance. The creed causes businessmen to advance with special force precisely the claims that in their bones they know are least applicable. Sutton and company give this definition of ideology: "Where a role involves patterns of conflicting demands, then occupants of that role . . . respond by elaborating a system of ideas and symbols, which in part may serve as a guide to action, but chiefly has broader and more direct functions as a response to strain."

My contention is that those of us in the media have developed a journalistic creed, an ideology of the First Amendment. The essence of our claim is that what we do is central to the health and survival of American society. We strongly imply that our claims come ahead of those of everybody else. We are better than other citizens; we have rights that are higher than those of the Congress, the executive branch, and even the courts. Thus we are saying that what's good for the media is good for the United States.

A series of celebrated court cases chart the development of First Amendment ideology. The starting point in each case was a broadening of constitutional rights and protection afforded the press. Thereafter circumstance called into question the expanded grant of protection. The Supreme Court tried to adjust accordingly. Each adjustment was denounced as a mortal blow to the freedom of the press. But in fact, nobody could seriously argue today that the suppression of information by tyrannical authority—the peril envisioned in the Constitution—represents a serious problem for modern American society.

The law of libel lies at the center of the first set of cases. In 1964, the Supreme Court upheld a claim by the New York *Times* that printing falsehoods about public officials was not, in view of the First Amendment privilege, automatic grounds for libel. The Court said that when public officials were involved, libel occurred only when the untruth was "published with knowledge that it was false or with reckless disregard of whether it was false or not." In 1967, that definition was broadened so that it applied not merely to "public officials" but also to "public figures"—namely, the football coach Wally Butts. In 1970, the privilege was broadened still further so that it applied to private individuals, innocent bystanders, so to speak, who might be "involved in an issue of public or general concern."

In 1973, Lieutenant Colonel Anthony Herbert filed a libel suit against the CBS show, *60 Minutes,* its star, Mike Wallace, and one of its producers, Barry Lando. Colonel Herbert claimed he was libeled when the show asserted that he did not, as he had claimed, report to his superior officers various atrocities committed in the Vietnam war. Herbert acknowledged that he was a "public figure," and that he would, under the *Sullivan* case ruling, have to prove malice. The CBS producer, Lando, balked at answering questions about conversations with Wallace and about his judgment of the truthfulness of persons interviewed for the show. In 1979, the Supreme Court ruled that the First Amendment did not protect Lando against the questions put by Colonel Herbert. In the majority opinion, Justice Byron White argued that it would be difficult to prove malice without some "focus on the defendant's state of mind." Indeed, it is hard to see, if Lando had won, how any libel case could ever be brought. Still Bill Leonard, the president of CBS News, said the Lando decision was "another dangerous invasion of the nation's news rooms" and that it reduced "constitutional protection to the journalists' most precious possession—his mind, his thought, and his editorial judgment."

A second example of the same pattern—but with a different outcome—arose in the Stanford *Daily News* case. In 1971, local police were assaulted as they tried to quell a demonstration at the Stanford University hospital. Pictures of the demonstration were published by the Stanford *Daily News*. The county prosecutor, under a search warrant from the local judge, authorized a surprise search of the newsroom. The *Daily* sued on the ground that it was an innocent party in no way connected with the demonstration; therefore, it argued, issuance of a search warrant without prior notice was a violation of the First Amendment. The Court, in 1978, ruled that the First Amendment did not shield the paper against the higher claims of the "public need" for information pertinent to law enforcement. Not only was the decision limited, but the court indicated that the law was fuzzy and could usefully be changed. Nevertheless, the decision was denounced in the most virulent terms. For example, Howard K. Smith, then of ABC News, harked back to the days of Hitler:

> When I was a young reporter at the United Press in Nazi Berlin there was a kick at the door . . . and five Gestapo men barged past me, began opening every desk and studying every piece of paper they could find. Six hours later they left. . . . I remember thanking God this could not happen in America. Well, now it can. It is the worst, most dangerous ruling the Court has made in memory.

Of course it did not happen in this country, nor was there ever the slightest danger it would. On the contrary, two years later, Congress passed, and President Carter signed, a bill prohibiting federal, state, and local authorities from conducting surprise warrant searches on newsrooms, except in the most limited cases. . . .

Probably the most egregious examples of . . . insensitivity emerge from the series of cases involving the right of those of us in the media to keep sources confidential. Here the master case is the *Branzberg* decision rendered by the Supreme Court in 1972. The Court ruled that reporters, like most people, had to testify at a "grand jury or a trial and give what information" they possess. At the same time, the Court acknowledged that in certain specified cases, journalists, under the First Amendment, did have certain rights to maintain confidentiality of sources. Judge Lewis Powell in the swing opinion wrote that "the Court does not hold that newsmen . . . are without constitutional rights with respect to the gathering of news or in safeguarding their sources. The courts will be available to newsmen under circumstances where legitimate First Amendment interests require protection."

Just such a case came up in the matter of the New York *Times* reporter Myron Farber, who did some fine investigative reporting which resulted in the indictment of a New Jersey doctor on charges of first-degree murder. The doctor's lawyer requested access to Farber's notes for the purpose of preparing his defense. Farber and the *Times* refused on grounds that giving up confidential material would violate their First Amendment rights. At that point the judge made what seems to me to have been a distinctly unwise ruling. Instead of asking the defense to specify what materials it needed and for what purpose, he asked Farber and the *Times* to turn over their notes for his inspection *in camera.* He would then decide what material was relevant or not. The *Times* and Farber refused, and were found in contempt.

Though I think the judge made a foolish decision, I believe he made a decision that lay well within his prerogatives. The case did involve a conflict between a reporter's rights under the First Amendment, and a defendant's rights under the Sixth Amendment. In our system, judges—bad judges as well as good judges—are quintessentially responsible for deciding such conflicting constitutional claims. Nobody in the media I have ever heard of—certainly not the New York *Times*—denied that quintessential responsibility when the Supreme Court decided that President Nixon was obliged to turn over *his* tapes to the special prosecutor. But in the *Farber* case the *Times* protested at every level of the judicial system that the original ruling was a violation of the First Amendment. It lost each appeal, and rightly so, because the courts do have the special prerogative of deciding about conflicts of constitutional rights.

Eventually the case became moot when the alleged murderer was acquitted, but not before Farber had spent six weeks in jail for contempt of court, and the *Times* had shelled out thousands of dollars in fines. Yet, far from ending at that point, the case became the subject of a long and painful howl from the media. I do not have the space—or the stomach—to summarize all the complaints. But a good example is the article Theodore H. White wrote about the *Farber* case in the New York *Times Magazine.*

In that article, White argues that protection of sources is not an aspect of journalistic enterprise (as I would maintain), but the very essence of the free press. He says that without such protection Watergate would never have been uncovered. He also asserts that the "conduct of American public affairs was rooted in the right of the American press and its reporters" to protect their sources. He warns that "now the courts, in a new departure, seem bent on erasing a protection built into the very foundation of the American system":

> Every veteran reporter knows that not all judges are spiritual descendants of Holmes, Brandeis, and Warren. All too many judges wrapped in the black robes of court, are graduate politicians, neither scholars nor solons, and as one descends the hierarchy from the federal to state to local levels one finds more and more of them are hacks.

White stigmatizes the hacks as agents of ethnic groups, political cabals, and even the Mafia. He sees them, in the *Farber* case, eroding the soul of our liberty and greatness, the First Amendment. He concludes: "The First Amendment, in the final analysis, was not devised to protect any reporter or publisher from the law or to give us special entitlements. The First Amendment is listed as First to protect the people. . . ."

There you have the full-blown ideology. The interest of the press is the interest of the people. What's good for the media is good for the United States. The courts have to yield their prerogatives to the media. So do defendants in murder trials. Why? Because journalistic enterprise—the right of papers to investigate cover-ups—is the heart of the First Amendment. In my judgment that is clearly not the case. In fact, it is a long, long way from what the framers of the Constitution had in mind. And we in this country are a long, long way from even coming close to killing the First Amendment protection. Indeed, I submit that the freedom of the press has not abated one whit since the *Farber* case came up and went down.

I do not mean to say that the First Amendment is not precious. I think the privilege is exceedingly precious—too precious to be the plaything of journalistic self-righteousness. I think the courts, far from being bad guys as White implies, have, over the years, been the most powerful guardians of First Amendment rights. I think that in a conflict between us and the courts, the right of the courts to decide—even though some judges are not Brandeis—is paramount. So I take the furor over the First Amendment and the *Farber* case in particular to be an exaggerated claim—a piece of ideology.

No doubt there is something to the ideology. A free system of information-gathering and distribution is important to the United States. So is a free-enterprise system. But neither one is transcendent in value. For those in the media, especially, self-interest dictates a little modesty in staking claims for our importance. Rather than adopting a self-righteous ideology, we ought to acknowledge our weak spots—not only by printing corrections, not through a press council, and certainly not through control by government, but by being more sensitive to what we have become. I think we need to acknowledge—to ourselves at least—that we are shapers and movers; that we are biased; that we are not representative. Most important of all, it seems to me we need to see that in our new roles we have a new set of responsibilities. It is no longer good enough to say that we mirror the world, or merely report things as they are. If things go wrong, we bear some blame. And it seems to me vital that we admit—to ourselves at least, and in public as much as possible—when we do go wrong. And I don't just mean misspelling the name of the Vice-Premier of China. I mean seeing that at times, anyway, we went overboard on the Great Society and on civil rights, and the imperial Presidency. I mean admitting that some of the consequences of our noblest efforts have turned sour.

That kind of responsibility, it seems to me, is required, because it is only by admitting our larger mistakes that we can deserve public support. Public support, given the dangerous role we play, is absolutely essential in a populist country such as ours. As Alexander Hamilton once put it: "What is the liberty of the press? Who can give it any definition which would not leave the utmost latitude for evasion? I hold it to be impracticable, and from this I infer that its security, whatever fine declarations may be inserted in any constitution respecting it, must altogether depend on public opinion, and on the general spirit of the people and of the government." ∎

Afterword

Two themes are wound together throughout this book.

The first theme is an article of faith; we must believe in the ability of people, after hearing a number of points of view, to decide which is the soundest. In the words of Oliver Wendell Holmes, "the competition of the market" provides the best means of reaching truth. Some would question that proposition, but we have staked everything on it. For if the majority cannot finally be trusted to know the difference between truth and error, how can the majority be trusted with the reins of government? But the necessary precondition is that there must be a fair, free, and open exchange of ideas.

The second theme running through this book is the concentrated power of the press. In the eighteenth century, when the First Amendment was written, the word "press" referred to a long-handled contraption for pressing inked type on paper. Today the term is rarely used to describe apparatus. Now it is used to encompass a society or class of people who operate the nation's mass media.

The Media

We are often innundated by the media; we find it almost impossible to go through the day without hearing their voices. The most influential media voices come from what are sometimes called "the big seven": ABC, NBC, CBS, *Time, Newsweek, The Washington Post,* and *The New York Times.* These are the leaders of what Kevin Phillips, in Chapter 7, calls "the mediacracy." Reporter and author David Halberstam calls them "the powers that be."

It is the friction between these two themes; the ideal of "free trade in ideas" and the reality of "big media," which generates a good deal of heat today. Spiro Agnew's complaint about "bias" in Chapter 4 would have lost its point if Agnew had not accompanied it with the charge of "a handful of men" running the media. The arguments for "access" in Chapter 6 also proceed from the premise that the media wield monopolistic, or at any rate "oligopolistic," power.

Some defenders of the media deny that the media are controlled by the few. Chapter 2 presented Lee Loevinger's argument that there is "a plethora of media voices." Others insist that the media objectively "mirror" reality. That seems to be the view of William Small in his debate with Ernest Lefever (Chapter

4). But the most intriguing position may be that taken by Tom Wicker, in Chapter 3. He seems ready to concede that media voices like those of the *New York Times* and the *Washington Post* are major institutions, and ones that have not been detached from political battles. But, Wicker argues, this is as it should be, given the dangerous power of government today. Indeed, the press needs more power if it is to serve as check on runaway government.

The argument, then, is that the media collectively serve as a kind of adversary institution in America, a state within the state. In the final chapter CBS Chairman William Paley characterizes the press as "a buffer state" between the people and the government. In chapter 6 *New York Times* reporter Myron Farber says that "there is value in having *some* readily recognized institution outside of government. . . that people can go to with their troubles and complaints." But if the press is indeed an "institution and a "buffer state," then whom does it represent and to whom is it responsible? Patrick Buchanan's question in the introduction to Chapter 3 still rings in the ears: "Who elected these guys, anyway?"

In one sense Buchanan's question is terribly unfair. But if we put it in a less antagonistic tone, as an honest inquiry about the responsibilities of the media, it does not seem entirely out of order. Other private institutions in America have had to submit to government regulation. Why should the press be exempt? American citizens must provide evidence to courts and grand juries. Should reporters be given special privileges? American homes can be searched provided the police obtain warrants. Press rooms are now exempt from such searches. Why? The reply that the First Amendment specifically protects the "press" may win over legal fundamentalists, but it is less convincing to the public at large.

It is precisely among the public at large that the media have become the most vulnerable. The least persuasive part of William Paley's argument against the Fairness Doctrine is his statement that "the media represent the public interest." The people who run the "big seven" bear little resemblance—in terms of income, education, ideaglogy, religion, marital status, or ethnic background—to the majority of Americans. What the historian Jacob Burkhardt said of "great men" most Americans might say of the glamourous men and women of the big media: "They are all that we are not." This can be pronounced in reverential tones. It can also be shouted in anger.

It has been well over a decade since Nixon and Agnew launched their attacks on the media. Most of the criticism today comes from *ad hoc* private groups. The present occupant of the White House is a genial man thoroughly imbued with the philosophy of *laissez-faire*. But the time may come when a populist or pseudo-populist comes into office with a different personality and fewer reservations about government intervention. At that point the security of the media may turn upon their support among the public at large. This is why the question of *hubris*, which Anthony Lewis touched upon in Chapter 6 and Joseph Kraft discussed at length in Chapter 7, becomes critical. Kraft invites the media to take stock of their own shortcomings with an eye to self-improvement. Perhaps we should turn to our friends in the media and whisper: this is an offer that can't be refused.

Index

Abrams, Floyd: on *Miami Herald v. Tornillo* decision, 117; on press immunity regarding confidential sources, 177-178, 185-188
"actual malice:" editorial privilege vs. proving in libel suits against media, 139-152.
advertising, power over newspaper's conduct, 58
"advocacy journalism," 114
affirmative action, 65
Agnew, Spiro: 50, 66; campaign against the press, 12; on liberal bias of news media, 67-74
"alternative means," requirement for grand jury inquiries of newsmen, 164-166
American Civil Liberties Union, on freedom of press vs. public access, 119
Associated Press v. NLRB, 156
Associated Press v. United States, 156
audience flows, 85

Bagdikian, Ben: 33, 34, 39-41; on mass media monopolies, 22-31
Bailey v. Alabama, 138
Beauharnais v. Illinois, 136
Bell, Daniel, 191
Bethell, Tom, and power of media, 49-53, 60
Black, Justice: 168; in Pentagon Papers case, 189
Black Panthers, Earl Caldwell's articles on, 153, 154, 167
Blair v. United States, 157
Boorstein, Daniel, 90, 91
Bork, Robert H., on legal and moral implications of press immunity, 178-185
Bradlee, Ben, 175, 178
Branzburg v. Hayes: 176; controversies resulting from, 169-188; Justice Douglas's dissent on, 167-169, 178-179; Justice Stewart's dissent on, 163-167, 180; Justice White on, 154-163, 176, 180

Brennan, Justice William: 163; on libel suit in *New York Times v. Sullivan*, 133-140
Bridges v. California, 137
Brinkley, David, 14, 15, 70
broadcasting: alternatives to government regulation of, 125-126, 129; concentration of control in, 23; lack of First Amendment protection for, 201-203; myths of, 123-124; vs. publishing in cost and story updates, 32, 33; vs. publishing and right of reply, 120-132
Brown, Raymond A., 170
Buckley, William, 34
Burger, Chief Justice Warren: dissenting opinion on Pentagon Papers decision, 47, 48; on right of reply in *Miami Herald v. Tornillo*, 114-116, 118, 119
Burnett, Carol, suit against *The National Enquirer*, 132, 133

cable television, 125
Caldwell, Earl, 153, 154, 167
Carter, Jimmy, 13, 43, 174
CBS Evening News, debate on bias of, 76-79
chain ownership, of newspapers and effect on quality, 57, 58
civil rights movement, and press media, 13
coercion, as way of tampering with free trade, 21
Commoner, Barry, 131
Communications Act of 1934, 121, 189
confidential sources: consequences of disclosing, 179-180; dangers of granting journalists' privilege in, 180-181; as essential to good journalism, 185-188; newsmen's immunity regarding disclosure of, 152-188
Cook, Fred, suit against Red Lion Broadcasting Co., 120-130
Cooke, Janet, 175, 178

Index

corporations, and control of information organizations, 23, 24, 25
Cronkite, Walter: 12, 13, 14; study on bias of news reporting by, 76-79
culture, influence of mass media in shaping popular, 16, 17, 26, 27
Curtis Publishing Co. v. Butts, 141, 143

debate, Supreme Court decision on uninhibited, robust, and wide-open, 134-140
DeGregory v. Attorney General of New Hampshire, 160
Diamond, Edwin, on fairness of Fairness Doctrine regarding broadcasting, 123-126
Doctor X, 169
Douglas, Justice William O.: dissent on *Branzburg v. Hayes* decision, 167-169; 178-179; on grand jury inquiries of newsmen, 166-167; on Red Lion case, 189
Dry Salvages, The, (Eliot), 11
Due Process Clause, of Fourteenth Amendment, 139

"Eastern press conspiracy," 56, 57; and accused liberal bias of, 65, 66, 67
"editorial advertisements," 136
editorial privilege: as Constitutional right, 152; Michael Kinsley on, 147-152; of immunity to questions regarding "state of mind" in libel suits, 142-145, 147; *see also*, reporters' privilege
Eisenhower, Dwight D., use of mass media in campaigns, 12
Eliot, T.S., 11
Elliot, Osborn, 56
Ellsberg, Daniel, and story behind the Pentagon Papers, 43, 44, 45, 50, 54, 55
Epstein, Edward Jay, on organizational theory of news media bias, 66, 67; 84-87
equal-time law, 130-131, 201, 202

Fairness Doctrine: 83, 121, 123, 202; definition of, 76, 85; Fred Friendly's 1975 study of, 125
Farber, Myron: interview with George McKenna, 171-172; refusal to reveal sources in Jascalevich trial, 169-172
Federal Trade Commission, 22
Federal Communications Commission (FCC), "Fairness Doctrine," 121
Federal Radio Commission, 123
Fifth Amendment, 152

First Amendment: 59, 60; and confidential sources of newsmen, 152-188; vs. grand jury subpoenas of newsmen, 154-169; implications of Supreme Court decisions involving press, 199-204; and industrial protection, 195-196; and journalists' privilege vs. proof of actual malice, 148-152; regarding libel suits of public figures against media, 141; and Pentagon Papers controversy, 45-49, 52; and right of reply in broadcasting, 120-132; and right of reply in press, 114-120
First Amendment Clarification Act of 1977, 125
First Amendment ideology, and journalism, 215-220
Ford, Gerald, 13
Fourteenth Amendment: Due Process clause of, 139; and libel suits of public figures against media, 135-141
freedom of press: and First Amendment, 46; and grand jury testimony, 154-169; vs. public access, 113-120
freedom of speech: and right of reply in broadcasting, 120-132; and right of reply in press, 113-120
Friendly, Fred: 170; recommendations on Fairness Doctrine for Federal Communications Commission, 125

Galbraith, John Kenneth, 191
Gannett Co. v. DePasquale, and Supreme Court decisions limiting First Amendment rights of press, 200
Garland v. Torrel, 156
Gertz v. Robert Welch, Inc., 140, 141, 143
Gibson v. Florida Legislative Investigation Committee, 164, 165
government regulations: alternatives to in broadcasting, 125-126, 129; by Federal Communications Commission, 120-132; of public access to press, 116, 119
Graham, Katherine, 13, 56
grand jury: power of, 161, 166; "probable cause" and "alternative means" requirements of, 164-166; recommended conditions for obligating newsmen to appear before, 164-166; role of, 157; subpoenas of newsmen, 154-163

Harlan, Justice John: 51; dissenting opinion concerning Pentagon Papers decision, 48, 49

Harriman, Averell, 68
Hearst, William Randolph, 23, 24
Heiskell, Andrew, 56
Herbert, Anthony, 141, 142, 148, 150
Herbert v. Lando: consequences of to journalism, 145-152; Justice White on, 140-145
Hidden Persuaders, The (Packard), 88
Holmes, Justice Oliver Wendell, 21, 119
Humphrey, Hubert, 54, 72, 97

"image" advertising, and political candidates, 89-98
"image" campaigning: 97; and McGovern campaign, 99, 100; as not working, 98-104
"imperial press," 43
informants, effect of grand jury subpoena of newsmen on, 158-160
In re Pappas, 153, 154
Institute of American Strategy, and study concerning bias of TV news reporting, 79-87
"interpretive reporting," 114

Jascalevich, Dr. Mario E., and Myron Farber, 169-170
Johnson, Lyndon, 38, 92
journalists: narcissism of, 210; power of, 62; rise in status of, 205-208
journalists' privilege, *see* editorial privilege; reporter's privilege

Kennedy, Senator Edward, 174
Kilpatrick, J.J., 34
Kinsley, Michael, on fairness of journalists' privilege, 147-152
Kraft, Joseph, on the imperial media, 204-220
Kristol, Irving, on mass media as "New Class" of knowledge industry, 191-192

Landau, Jack, 147
Lando, Barry, 141, 142, 148, 150
Lefever, Ernest: as example of news media power, 74, 75; on liberal bias of T.V. news, 75-87
Lewis, Anthony, on fabricated story that won a Pulitzer Prize, 175-177
libel suits: proving actual malice in, 139-152; as threat to press freedom, 132-152; *see also,* specific cases
Liebling, A.J., 130
Lincoln, Abraham, 11
Lippmann, Walter: 71; and power of media in creating stereotypes, 17
localism, and daily newspapers, 28, 29
Loevinger, Lee, statement concerning the lack of media concentration, 31-38

Madison, James, 46
Making of the President (White), 93
malice, *see* "actual malice"
Marshall, Justice Thurgood: 163; dissent on *Zurcher v. Stanford Daily,* 173-174; on journalistic self-censorship, 146-147
mass media: as power center, 53-65; 193-195; power of T.V. news media, 67-74; use of by Presidents, 12, 113; and public access to broadcasting, 120-132; and public access to newspapers, 113-120; and public policy, 189-220; regulation of, 196-197; rights and responsibilities of, 113-188; and public's right to know, 52, 197-198; schools of thought on bias of, 66, 67; importance of during the sixties, 153; influence of on society, 15-20, 26, 27; controversy on bias of, 65-87; as big business, 190-198; and concentration of control of, 22-31, 31-38, 38-42, 118-119, 127, 128; as knowledge industry, 191-192; limited-access, 129; manipulation of public by, 89-111; problems brought by diverse media voices, 34, 35; example of as monopoly, 37, 38; influence of news reporters on viewers, 14, 15; objectivity and pluralistic defense, 211, 212; political impact of 10-15; 192-193; use of by politicians, 11-15; and creating stereotypes 17; treatment toward Middle America, 212-213; lack of unity among, 60; and value formation, 16; *see also,* specific media forms
McClure, Robert, 97
McGinnis, Joe, on selling of the President, 89-97
McGovern, George, 99, 100
McKenna, George: interview with Myron Farber, 171-172; interview with Susan Veatch, 128-132; on right of reply, 127-128
McLuhan, Marshall, 92
McNamara, Robert, 43
media, *see* mass media
media concentration, and mass media as a monopoly, 22-42
"mediacracy," 190
media-government alliance, 49-53
media image, and Presidents, 12
media operators, and influence on human behavior, 26, 27
media voices, problems and confusion with diverse, 34, 35
Miami Herald Publishing Co. v. Tornillo, 114-120

Index

Middle America, media treatment of, 212, 213
mirror analogy: and bias of news media, 66; example of 79-87
monopoly, media as, 21-38, 118-119, 127, 128
Moynihan, Daniel P., 43
Murdoch, Rupert, 59

N.A.A.C.P. V. Button, 137, 164
Nader, Ralph, 34
National Enquirer, The, Carol Burnett's suit against, 132-133
national security, restrictions on press, 62-64
New Class, of knowledge industry, 191-192
New York Times: 11, 12, 28, 56, 59, 60, 65, 84, 86; and Pentagon Papers, 44-46, 49-51
New York Times v. Sullivan, 115, 133-143
New York Times Co. v. United States, 168
News From Nowhere (Epstein), 66
news media: debate on bias of, 75-84; and Fairness Doctrine of Federal Communications Commission, 76; liberal bias of, 65-74; manipulation of American voter, 89-104; objectivity of, 211-213; organizational restraints on, 84-87; schools of thought on bias of, 66, 67
newspapers: advertisers power over, 58; vs. broadcasting media in cost and story updates, 32, 33; chain ownership of, 57, 58; circulation competition among, 59; concentration of control of, 23, 28-30, 39, 40; monopoly ownership of, 118-119, 124, 127, 128; obligation to print replies, 114-120; public unhappiness with, 117-120; quality of, 58; responsibilities vs. broadcasting, 120-126, 129; and "selling papers," 58, 59
news reporters: influence on viewers, 14, 15, 85, 86; "journalistic" power of, 62
newsroom cabinet meeting, and Pentagon Papers, 51
Nixon, Richard M.: 43, 68, 70; use of mass media in campaign, 12; and Pentagon Papers, 43, 44; use of television to manipulate voters, 89-97
Nixon Administration, 153

Oakes, John B., 56
Oklahoma Press Publishing Co. v. Walling, 156

organizational theory, and bias of news media, 66, 67, 84-87

Packard, Vance, 88
Paley, William S., 56; on adversary relationship between the courts and press, 199-204
Patterson, Thomas, 97
Pennekemp v. Florida, 136, 139
Pentagon Papers: 12, 59; and the First Amendment, 45; as example of "national security" restrictions on press, 62-64; story of, 43, 44, 50, 51, 53, 54, 55; Supreme Court opinions on controversy, 45-49, 117
Phillips, Kevin, on government regulation of mass media, 190-198
pluralistic defense, and media objectivity, 211, 212
politicians: and use of media, 11-15; use of T.V. to manipulate voters, 89-97
presidency: campaigning for and use of T.V., 89-97, 98-104; use of mass media, 12
press: adversary relationship with the courts, 199-204; compared to broadcasting, 32, 33, 120-127; characterlessness of, 41; and civil rights movement, 13; competition among, 57; confidentiality of sources, 152-188; concentration of control, 23, 28-30, 40; editorial privilege of, 142-145, 147-152; and government deception about Vietnam war, 54-56; grand jury testimony by, 154-188; as investigative arm of government, 11, 164; libel suits by public figures against, 132-152; and media-government alliance, 49-53; monopoly and power of, 43-65, 114, 118-119, 124, 127, 128; Pentagon Papers as example of government restrictions on, 62-64; politicians' attitudes about, 43; vs. presidency, 12, 13; and public right to know, 47; public unhappiness with, 117-120; right of reply and enforced public access to, 114-120, 152; safeguards recommended for grand jury inquiries of, 164-166; exemption from search warrants, 151, 173; self-censorship as result of Herbert ruling, 146-147; subpoenas of, 153-163; Supreme Court on determining "state of mind" of, 140-145; underground, 59, 60; unethical practices of, 58, 59; *see also,* newspapers, news media
Price, Raymond, 95

print media, vs broadcasting media and restrictions on, 201
Privacy Protection Bill, purpose and content of, 176
"probable cause:" requirement for grand jury inquiries of newsmen, 164-166; as requirement for issuing search warrants, 151
Proxmire, Senator William, 125
public: opinion and T.V. news bias, 67-74; unhappiness with newspapers, 117-120
public access: on broadcasting, 120-132; effect of on newspapers, 116; vs. freedom of press, 113-120; problems of enforcing mandated, 114-115
public broadcasting, see broadcasting
Pulitzer Prize, story by Janet Cooke, 175-177, 178

quiet diplomacy, 74
"quotas," 65

radio, see broadcasting
Radio Act of 1927, 121
Rand Corporation, 22, 44, 54
Red Lion Broadcasting Co. v. Federal Communications Commission, 120-130
Reedy, George, 38
Reporters Committee for Freedom of the Press, 147, 150
reporter's privilege: regarding confidentiality of sources of information, 169-172, 175-177; regarding grand jury testimony, 154-169
Reston, James, 35, 70
right of reply: in broadcasting, 120-132; vs. freedom of press, 152; in newspapers, 113-120; WCBS on, 126-127
right to know: vs. government secrecy and Pentagon Papers, 52; and the press, 47
Rosenbloom v. Metromedia, 140
Roth v. United States, 137
Rubin, Jerry, 13
Rubins, Ellis; questioning and summation in Zamora trial, 104-109

St. Amant v. Thompson, 141
"scarcity principle," 202
Schenectady Union Pub Co. v. Sweeney, 136
Schorr, Daniel, 12, 60, 62
search warrants: examples of in newsrooms, 172-174; and press, 151; and Privacy Protection Bill, 174; "probable cause" requirement for, 151

self-censorship, of media as consequence of *Herbert v. Lando* ruling, 146-147
Selling of the President, The (McGinnis), 89
Sheehan, Neil, 50, 54
Sherman Act, 156
Sixties, importance of the media during, 153
"60 Minutes" case, see *Herbert v. Lando*
slander suits, see libel suits
Small, William, debate on liberal bias of T.V. news media, 75-87
society, influence of mass media on, 15-20
"Son of Sam," as example of newspapers "selling papers," 58
spot ads, and image campaigning, 101
"squeaky-wheel" theory, 124
stereotypes, creation of by mass media, 17
Stewart, Justice Potter: dissent on *Branzburg v. Hayes* decision, 163-167, 180; dissent on *Zurcher v. Stanford Daily* decision, 173-174
Stromberg v. California, 137
subliminal seduction, 88
subpoenas, of newsmen to appear before grand jury, 154-163
Supreme Court: under Burger, 146-147; decisions weakening rights of press, 199-204; on libel action of public official against critics of official conduct, 134-140; on Pentagon Papers publishing, 45-49, 117; on determining press's state of mind in libel suits, 140-152; on reporters' privilege regarding grand jury testimony, 154-169; on right of reply in broadcasting, 120-126; and right of reply in newspapers, 114-116, 119; under Warren, 146
Sweezy v. New Hampshire, 164

television: and audience flows, 85; and bias of news reporting, 67-74; to sell a candidate, 90-104; pursuit of "controversy" by networks, 73; debate on bias of news reporting, 75-87; and Fairness Doctrine of Federal Communication Commission, 76, 83, 85; lack of First Amendment protection for, 201, 202; maintaining viewers interest, 85; manipulation of American voter, 89-97; news coverage and influence on public opinion, 67-69; and influence of news reporters on viewers, 14, 15, 85, 86; organizational restraints on news coverage, 84-87; political impact of, 192-193; power of news reporting, 67-74;

effect of sex and violence on, 88, 104-112; *see also,* broadcasting
TV and National Defense (Lefever), 75
Terminiello v. Chicago, 168
think tank, 22, 44, 54
Thurmond, Senator Strom, 174
Tornillo, Pat L., Jr., suit against *Miami Herald,* 114-120
Tornillo Case, *see Miami Herald Publishing Co. v. Tornillo*
Treleaven, Harry, 94
Truman, Harry S., use of mass media in campaigns, 12

underground press, 59, 60
Ungar, Sanford, 50, 51
United States v. Byron, 157
United States v. Caldwell, 153, 154
United States v. Nixon, 145

Veatch, Susan, interview with George McKenna, 128-132
violence, on T.V. and effect on viewers, 88, 104-111
von Hoffman, Nicholas, 126
voter, manipulation by media, 89

Washington Post: 11, 12, 28, 56, 60, 65; and Pentagon Papers, 45, 46, 49, 50
Watergate, 12, 13
Watkins v. United States, 160, 164, 165
WCBS, on right to reply laws, 126-127
White, Justice Byron: 72; in *Branzburg v. Hayes,* 176, 180; on grand jury subpoenas of newsmen, 154-163; on determining press's state of mind in *Herbert v. Lando,* 140-145, 147, 148; on search warrants and press, 151, 173
White Theodore, 93
Wicker, Tom: 13, 34, 213; on impact of *Herbert v. Lando,* 145-147; on power of the press, 53-64
wire services, 84
Wolfson, Lewis, on newspapers' responsibility to public, 117-120

Zamora, Yolanda, testimony concerning violence on television, 104-108
Zemel v. Rusk, 156
Zurcher v. Stanford Daily: 151, 173, 174; Justices Stewart and Marshall's dissent on, 173-174; and Supreme Court decisions limiting First Amendment rights of press, 200

About the Author

GEORGE MCKENNA was born in Chicago in 1937. He attended high school in the city and received his bachelor's degree from the University of Chicago in 1959, an M.A. from the University of Massachusetts in 1962, and a Ph.D. from Fordham University in 1967. He has been teaching political science at City College of New York since 1963. He edited, with his introduction and notes, AMERICAN POPULISM (Putnam, 1974), wrote a textbook, AMERICAN POLITICS: IDEALS AND REALITIES (McGraw-Hill, 1976), and has written articles in the fields of American government and political theory. He has edited volumes in the TAKING SIDES series, including social and political issues volumes, for the Dushkin Publishing Group. He teaches mass media courses at the City College of New York. His political science background gives him a special perspective on the interaction among the Government, society, and the voices of the media.